THIS *Complicated* FORM OF LIFE

THIS Complicated FORM OF LIFE

ESSAYS ON WITTGENSTEIN

NEWTON CARVER

Open ✻ Court

Chicago and La Salle, Illinois

First printing 1994

Printed and bound in the United States of America.

Library of Congress Cataloging-in-Publication Data

Garver, Newton, 1928–
  This complicated form of life : essays on Wittgenstein/Newton Garver.
    p.   cm.
  Includes bibliographical references and index.
  ISBN 0-8126-9252-7 (cloth).—ISBN 0-8126-9253-5 (paper)
  1. Wittgenstein, Ludwig, 1889–1951. I. Title.
B3376.W564G37   1994
192—dc20   94-15949
                                        CIP

In Memoriam
    Henry H. Price
    Max Black
    Alan Donagan
        Scholars, Teachers, Friends

Can only those hope who can talk? Only those who have mastered the use of a language. That is to say, the phenomena of hope are modes of this complicated form of life.

—Philosophical
Investigations

How could human behaviour be described? Surely only by sketching the actions of a variety of humans, as they are all mixed up together. What determines our judgment, our concepts and reactions, is not what one *man is doing* now, *an individual action, but the whole hurly-burly of human actions, the background against which we see any action.*

—Zettel

CONTENTS

PREFACE

In his marvelous essay, "Tradition and the Individual Talent," T. S. Eliot says that "no poet, no artist of any art, has his complete meaning alone." It is not meaning in any narrow linguistic sense that Eliot has in mind; he means that which makes an artifact into a work of art, that which gives it its significance and its artistic value. That is what no artist can determine alone. Eliot dodges the trap of too narrow a definition by avoiding any further specification. I take him to mean not merely that meaning and significance are determined in part by one's culture, but also that they depend in part on the long historical tradition of one's discipline, which itself undergoes changes through innovative work; so there can be no brilliant achievement that is unconnected to cultural and historical context.

Ludwig Wittgenstein has often been treated as an exception. The thrust of these essays is to insist—in the face of persistent neglect and denial—on the mutal relevance of Wittgenstein's work and the tradition of Western philosophy. Wittgenstein does not "overthrow" the tradition. He builds on it, draws from it, and contributes brilliantly to the fruition of certain elements in it. Particular attention is paid here to Kant, and to what Roy Finch calls Wittgenstein's completion of Kant's revolt against the Cartesian hegemony of epistemology in philosophy. Also very Kantian is the dualism that seems unavoidable in a perspective or *Weltanschauung* that contains both facts and meanings, since meanings always somehow transcend the plain facts that convey them and that they convey. With respect to the givenness of language-games and of "this complicated form of life," on the other hand, Wittgenstein seems closer to Aristotle than to Kant.

Seeing Wittgenstein within the tradition of Western philosophy requires a fresh look at Wittgenstein as well as at the tradition. Wittgenstein spent his philosophical career trying to make sense of philosophy and of human life, and of their relation to one another, and to do so without either presupposing or intruding on the domains of the special sciences. In doing so he made various significant contributions to philosophy. Since philosophy is a long-standing intellectual enterprise having many divergent traditions, one would be hard pressed to understand the significance of his work without first deciding with which traditions he is especially to be associated and giving the broad outlines of his affinities and contrasts within those traditions and others. These simple truths, which are perhaps not always as obvious as they first seem to be, form the working basis for the essays that follow.

Wittgenstein needs to be seen in the context of the critical philosophy of Kant. I shall put forward the doubtless-controversial claim that Wittgenstein's later work solves the Kantian problem that his early work stumbled over. The key to his later work is the substitution of grammar for logic as the basis of philosophy. This grammar is, however, not the grammar of the grammarians or linguists. It concerns uses of language, which he calls 'language-games,' rather than morphology and syntax. He spends the first part of the *Philosophical Investigations* saying and showing what he means by language-games and how he is going to make use of them. This is an extraordinary innovation because it simultaneously accomplishes five things crucial to his philosophical enterprise: (1) it latches philosophy onto an established and universal use of language, since teaching the language occurs everywhere; (2) it provides the basis for critical criteria, since grammar describes norms for language use; (3) it pulls the rug out from under foundationalism in philosophy, since grammar, which presupposes that there is already language in use, could not possibly be the first and original use of language; (4) it is as uncongenial to moralism as to foundationalism, since grammar can only instruct us how to say things, not what to say; and (5) it achieves self-reference without a hint of vicious circularity, since there is no problem about there being a grammar of grammar in the same sense as there is a grammar for avowals or for orders.

The first of these five points, which sounds completely innocent, has deep and far-reaching overtones that separate Wittgenstein sharply from most contemporary philosophers—just as my stress on it separates me from most Wittgenstein scholars. If philosophy is an aspect or a refinement of grammar, then its aim is not the search for knowledge. Philosophy may well still be a search for wisdom and understanding, but knowledge belongs to the province of science and its mundane everyday antecedents. Wittgenstein introduces this restriction to save philosophy rather then to cripple it. Whatever his intentions, however, the vast majority of philosophers, including many of those who have read and admired Wittgenstein, continue to think of their discipline as a search for knowledge. The sticking point for many is the radical dichotomy between natural history and natural science, which I explain and discuss in chapter nine and again in the final chapter.

The theme sketched in the preceding paragraphs differs from the usual pictures of Wittgenstein. It begins on a familiar-enough note, though one that Rorty expostulates against, namely that Wittgenstein falls squarely within a philosophical tradition inaugurated by Kant—a point made by Stenius, Kenny, Engel, early Hacker, Finch, Pears, and many others. I take Kant's central theme to be the development of a critical philosophy as an alternative to the dogmatisms that he found entangled in pointless and unresolvable metaphysical disputes. The *Tractatus*—too often misread as a kind of logical atomism, which could not be Kantian at all—was a first attempt to work out a twentieth-century version of the self-referential critical criteria that are at the heart of Kant's enterprise. It was a brilliant effort and still rewards close study; but it was an obvious failure, as Wittgenstein makes clear with the memorable invocation of silence in the final paragraph.

I make more of affinities between the *Tractatus* and the *Investigations* than most Wittgenstein scholars do, building on the scholarship of Hidé Ishiguro and Brian McGuinness. Ishiguro's identification of a thematic and conceptual continuity from the objects of the *Tractatus* to the language-games in the later work has been widely (though not universally) accepted as throwing useful light on the relation between the two periods of Wittgenstein's work. She cleared the way for others to identify other affinities. The next great step toward the picture of Wittgenstein's work presented in these essays was McGuinness's demonstration (still contested by David Pears and others) that there is no metaphysical realism in the *Tractatus,* since the objects that make up the substance of the world do not themselves belong to the world, and hence not to reality. Besides accepting Ishiguro and McGuinness on these points, I stress how much the opening installment of the *Tractatus*—the presentation of the world as the totality of facts—has in common with the natural history of the later work, a point on which there has been much less discussion. All these points, however, are subordinate to Wittgenstein's persistent effort to find a perspicuous articulation of critical philosophy, a problem inherited from Kant.

None of these essays was written with Richard Rorty in mind. He would, however, agree with much of what is said here, especially about limiting the domain of knowledge, and would of course be sympathetic to the attempt to situate Wittgenstein historically. But one of the sharp contrasts that emerges is our divergent assessments of Wittgenstein's place in Western philosophy. In *Philosophy and the Mirror of Nature* Rorty associates him with Dewey and Quine against Kant, while I associate him with Kant against Dewey and Quine. Since we are talking here about affinities and comparisons, there is perhaps room for both assessments. Nonetheless the contrast between the two pictures is stark, and noting it helps to indicate my theme. Chapters nine and sixteen make clear why, in my view, situating Wittgenstein with scientistic naturalists like Dewey and Quine does scant credit to the richness and depth of his work.

Some of the essays that follow involve close textual exegesis. Eliot did not mean to exclude such work. Understanding philosophy, like understanding any work of art, requires appreciation for the details as well as for the broader context that is emphasized in the quotation from Eliot with which I began.

All of the essays that follow have undergone editing or revision for the present publication. My main aims have been to reduce the number of footnotes, to harmonize the style and the manner of citations, to eliminate excessive duplication, to update references, and to give prominence to the unifying themes of the book. Such minimal revisions were made in chapters five, seven, eight, ten, eleven, and twelve. The first three sections of chapter three also remain substantially the same, the fourth section having been newly written to take account of Hubert Schwyzer's work. In the case of chapters two, thirteen, and fifteen, material has been restored to the text that was cut for reasons of space at the time of original publication. In the case of chapter one and chapter fourteen, and chapter six to a lesser extent, there were drastic revisions for the present publication. Chapters four, nine, and sixteen (the only chapter not previously published) have been completely rewritten; in their present form they bear little resemblance to any essays previously published.

There is an undeniable unity to the essays and the thoughts and themes of the essays collected in this volume. A collection of essays still leaves out a great deal. In these essays almost nothing is said about colors or mathematics; about intentions, feelings, and emotions; or about seeing and seeing as. A main advantage of such a collection is that the chapters are relatively self-contained so that each can be read on its own. In any case, what is incomplete is not therefore useless, and I am confident that the themes presented here have a considerable role to play, in one form or another, in subsequent discussions of Wittgenstein.

ACKNOWLEDGMENTS

A work such as this could never be put together without the support and encouragement of very many people over very many years. Some have been students, some colleagues, some friends, and some publishers and referees whom I barely know. Some are vividly in my memory, while others come to mind again only when I review notes from a distant time. As I write these paragraphs I am aware of my inability to do full justice to the debt I owe to so many.

For the immediate project of bringing together a selection of my essays on Wittgenstein, credit must go first to my friend and colleague Christoph Nyiri. Ten years ago he invited me to lecture on Kant and Wittgenstein in Budapest; his inquisitive and finely tuned mind led me to additional uses of 'form of life' in Wittgenstein's later work, and it was he who first suggested to Philosophia Verlag in Munich that a collection of my essays would be worth publishing. Details of the present collection were then worked out in correspondence with Frau Hilla Hueber of Philosophia Verlag, which was unable to proceed because of financial difficulties. Barry Smith, whom I had consulted and who had seconded Nyiri's proposal to Philosophia Verlag, then introduced me to Blouke Carus and David Ramsay Steele of Open Court, and I have no doubt that it was Smith's strong recommendation that persuaded Open Court to proceed with this book.

It was from 1952 to 1954 while at Oxford, where Henry Price was my B. Phil. advisor, that I made my first acquaintance with the work of Wittgenstein. At Ryle's seminar on the *Tractatus* in 1953 I learned a great deal from his trenchant scholarly criticism of the Ogden translation, as well as from discussion with and by other seminar members, who included Stephen Toulmin, David Pears, Brian McGuinness, and David Armstrong. In late fall of that year the *Philosophical Investigations* was published, and during the next term Elizabeth Anscombe lectured on that work, a memorable and formative occasion.

The earliest writing that is included here was done while I was at Cornell, more than thirty-five years ago. At Cornell I worked with Max Black, to whom I owe great debts not only for his guidance of my dissertation but also for his friendship and encouragement over the years and for the fine example of philosophical writing and commentary his work provided. His was by far the greatest influence on me at Cornell, even though I also profited there from work with Norman Malcolm, Georg von Wright, and (later) Jack Canfield. I continued for years to consult these scholars from time to time. A different kind of debt is owed to Richard Henson, Alan Donagan, Gene Mason, and Marjorie Clay. Henson, who taught at Cornell in the early fifties, has been a friend and supporter for forty-five years, and it was his suggestion and intercession that brought me to Cornell as a part-time instructor in 1956. Donagan, who chaired the Department of Philosophy at Minnesota in the late fifties, gave me my first job in philosophy and remained a mentor and friend for the rest of his life. Mason became a close friend when I was at Minnesota, and on many occasions I have profited from his wide knowledge and acute reading, most particularly with respect to the final two chapters. Clay was a student of mine at Buffalo and has read nearly everything I have written; the contribution of her comments and criticisms over the years is incalculable.

Europe has been as significant as the United States in providing a forum for my work on Wittgenstein. Twenty-five years ago I was introduced to German-language philosophers through Ulrich Steinvorth's translation and inclusion of the published version of chapter thirteen in a widely circulated four-essay volume published by Suhrkamp. In recent years one of my greatest debts has been to the annual International Wittgenstein Symposium at Kirchberg am Wechsel in Austria, organized by the Austrian Ludwig Wittgenstein Society. The society has invited me to several symposia, covering part of my expenses; more important has been the forum the symposia provided for my developing ideas and for making the acquaintance of European philosophers. Largely as a result of those contacts, early versions of chapter one were presented at the Universities of Budapest, Sofia, Moscow, and

Frankfurt, where I am particularly indebted to J. C. Nyiri, Nikolai Milkov, A. F. Griaznov, and Karl-Otto Apel, respectively. Chapter fifteen was presented even more extensively in Europe—at Vienna, Graz, Hamburg, Bielefeld, Göttingen, Heidelberg, and Cerisy-la-Salle, as well as at Kirchberg—and, thanks to Rudolf Haller, was published in German six years before it appeared in English (also in a European journal). Many people assisted my introduction to these European circles; in addition to Rudolf Haller in Graz I am particularly grateful to Fritz Wallner in Vienna, Hans-Rudi Fischer in Heidelberg, and Eike von Savigny in Bielefeld. I profited greatly from the discussions on these occasions, and I owe a debt of gratitude to my critics and other interveners as well as to my hosts.

After I began to say things about Wittgenstein, it was critics rather than expositors who were most useful. They have made me refine what I have had to say, as well as to withdraw tangential remarks whose contentiousness detracted from main themes. I am particularly conscious of having learned a great deal from several exchanges with Peter Winch and David Shwayder, both close students of Wittgenstein as well as thoughtful philosophers in their own right. Among the critics of chapter one I owe most to Elizabeth Wolgast and Rudolf Haller, though Nyiri, Smith, Apel, and Thiele also made me revise early versions. An anonymous referee saved me from making silly (or at least very dubious) remarks about Kant and Wittgenstein on mathematics in chapter two; comments by Lewis Beck (though they were, in his characteristic way, framed affirmatively rather than critically) were also helpful in working out this chapter. Chapter four owes much to John Corcoran, and I am indebted to Kurt Bergel for the invitation to the occasion for writing chapter five.

Chapter six benefited especially from comments by Ishiguro and McGuinness, though it was tempered by many other pressures as well. Chapter seven was stimulated by persistent questions from Ann Robertson about exactly how Frege influenced Wittgenstein, and then profited from input by Wolgast, Corcoran, Lars Svenonius, James Celarier, and Hartry Field.

Chapter nine endured fierce criticism from David Pears when first presented at Kirchberg, and I doubt he will think I have changed it enough; it later profited from the gentler comments and questions of Diane Gottlieb. Chapter fifteen owes more to Herbert Hrachovec than to any other person: he worked with me for some months over the language and the ideas in the original German version, and I discussed with him how to come to terms with questions and criticisms from Nyiri, Smith, Haller, and others. While working on this chapter I also had useful input from Clay, Fischer, and John Hunter. For the stimulus for chapter sixteen I am especially indebted to Souren Teghrarian.

While I have tried to give credit to significant influences in appropriate places, I am aware that certain works that I have studied with great profit have received scant mention in the text and notes. I have in mind the essays of David Keyt on the *Tractatus*; various works of David Shwayder, especially on the *Tractatus,* as well as conversations with him; Elizabeth Anscombe's wonderful introduction to the *Tractatus*; various essays by and discussions with Peter Winch; Anthony Kenny's two books on Wittgenstein; Joachim Schulte's learned and highly readable introduction to the whole of Wittgenstein (sadly marred in translation); David Stern's essay on Wittgenstein and Heraclitus; and Donna Summerfield's essays on Wittgenstein and Kripke. I cannot any more identify just what I have learned from each of these scholars, nor do I suppose that they will agree with what I have to say about the issues on which they have written; but I recognize their importance to the development of my thought and recommend their work to anyone trying to understand Wittgenstein.

The actual preparation of a manuscript from the published papers proved a far more arduous task than I had supposed. I could not possibly have managed it without the extensive assistance of Eileen McNamara, Joyce Soper, and Jane Bristol. Bristol is also responsible for most of the work in preparing the indices, for which I am exceedingly grateful. Although these three people are mentioned last, they are the ones to whom I owe the most in regard to the appearance of this volume.

Finally I need to thank the following editors and publishers who brought out earlier versions of my essays, on which for the most part they hold copyright: *Philosophy and Phenomenological Research* for "Wittgenstein on Private Language" and "The Variability of the Analytic"; E. D. Klemke and the University of Illinois Press for "Wittgenstein's Pantheism"; the Hegeler Institute as publisher of the *Monist* for "Analyticity and Grammar"; Hölder-Pichler-Tempsky Verlag for "The Metaphysics of the *Tractatus,*" "The Other Sort of Meaning," "Schemata and Criteria," and "Wittgenstein on Science"; Basil Blackwell as publisher of *Philosophical Investigations* for "Neither Knowing Nor Not Knowing"; John Corcoran and Reidel Publishers for "Notes for a Linguistic Reading of Aristotle's *Categories*"; *Modern Austrian Literature* for "Wittgenstein's Reception in America"; *Teoria* for "Wittgenstein's Dualism"; C. D. Rollins and the University of Pittsburgh Press for "Wittgenstein on Criteria"; *History of Philosophy Quarterly* for "Wittgenstein and the Critical Tradition"; *Dialectica* for "Form of Life in Wittgenstein's Later Work."

PART ONE

WITTGENSTEIN IN CONTEXT

1
Wittgenstein and the Critical Tradition

It is impossible to think clearly about the critical tradition in philosophy unless one distinguishes sharply between critical philosophy and Kantian philosophy. Kant was, of course, a great critical philosopher, and is responsible for there being such a thing as a critical tradition in philosophy today. But what this means, and what it entails for living contemporary philosophers, must be freed from the temptation to define critical philosophy just in terms of Kant's great works. It must become possible for us today to be critical philosophers without being tied to every point in the *Critique of Pure Reason*. I shall therefore begin in the first section with a rather elementary discussion of what critical philosophy is—of the main lines of its strategy by comparison with other philosophical strategies, and of the main obstacles or challenges which it must face along its chosen path. The remaining three sections discuss critical and problematic features to be found respectively in Kant, early Wittgenstein, and late Wittgenstein.

1. The Critical Road and Its Bumps

It is somewhat strange that there is, or needs to be, such a thing as a critical tradition in philosophy. To the extent that philosophy is the tradition founded or exemplified by Socrates, Plato, and Aristotle, it would seem that philosophy itself is bound to be inherently critical. Critical thinking—particularly critical examination of the positions stated by others—is a rich, deep component of their work and one of its enduring attractions. In the case of Socrates it may even be the case, as he himself seems to maintain, that his own thought consists entirely of negative criticisms, his "wisdom" being nothing other than realization of his ignorance. In the case of Plato and Aristotle there are certainly positive doctrines that go beyond the negative criticisms, but the dialectical method through which positive doctrines evolve out of critical considerations of previous views makes critical thinking an essential part of philosophy itself. Since the time of Plato and Aristotle there has never been a philosopher who did not base his or her thinking in part on a criticism of others. So criticism of some sort is always a part of any philosophical thought, and the critical tradition in philosophy has to be seen as a special refinement of what is common to philosophy in general.

Although critical thinking is common to philosophy in general, it has not been, and cannot ever be, the whole of philosophy. When one thinks of what has gone beyond critical thought, it is natural to think first of what has often been called "revisionary" or "speculative" metaphysics. I do not mean to suggest, however, that philosophy must always involve metaphysical speculation. The sceptical tradition has shown that we can imagine philosophy without its speculative component. When I say that criticism cannot be the whole of philosophy, I refer to the fact that there are different sorts of criticism, that there can be criticism of the basis of the different sorts of criticism, and that every critic needs some ground on which to stand. The contrast between Hume and Spinoza, or between Russell and Leibniz, or between Ayer and Bradley, exposes the vulnerability of criticism itself. Each member of the contrasting pair is critical—highly critical—of other philosophers, but there is a sharp contrast between the basis and method of their respective criticisms. Roughly speaking, Hume, Russell, and Ayer take as their ground that knowledge be based on direct empirical data; while Spinoza, Leibniz, and Bradley take rational coherence with an overall system to be the criterion of knowledge. Since 'coherence' and 'system' are not reducible to empirical data, and empirical data in turn need in no way be coherent or systematic, the rationalist party and the empiricist party each believes the other to be dealing with something other than knowledge. And each party can, of course, "prove" its negative point by using its own standards of criticism. The standards of criticism themselves, however, remain opposed and unjustified.

Criticism of criticism seems a hopeless affair. It threatens the bleak choice between endless regression and dogmatic stipulation, either of which seems to cast doubt on whether we can really know anything at all. The threat of endless regression cannot be ignored. If criticism can be criticized, then criticism of criticism can also be criticized, and so on indefinitely. If critical thinking requires that genuine knowledge satisfy a critical criterion, and also that any critical criterion must pass critical muster, it seems that we shall never be able to know anything. It is no wonder, then, that scepticism has eternally loomed as a plausible alternative. And dogmatism too, since stipulation of the standards of "genuine" criticism seems at first blush to be the only way to escape both the Scylla of infinite regress and the Charybdis of scepticism. The most famous example of the awesome marriage of dogmatism and stipulation is no doubt the well-known injunction with which Hume closes his *Enquiry Concerning Human Understanding:*

> If we take into our hand any volume; of divinity or school metaphysics, for instance; let us ask, Does it contain any abstract reasoning concerning quantity or number? No. Does it contain any experimental reasoning concerning matter of fact or existence? No. Commit it then to the flames: for it can contain nothing but sophistry and illusion.

Equally dogmatic stipulations with respect to the standards of critical thinking can be found in Descartes, Spinoza, Leibniz, Hegel, Bradley, Russell, and Ayer. It might at first seem that such a firm stance with respect to critical standards might forestall scepticism; but not for long. When such a stipulation is so obviously dogmatic, so obviously a preemptory exclusion of an articulated alternative, a thoughtful person will naturally become sceptical. Even a Humean might become sceptical of Hume's critical criteria, since they seem clearly to imply that the *Enquiry* itself should be cast into the flames.

The critical tradition in philosophy begins with Kant's recognition that empiricist and rationalist dogmatisms are equally unsatisfactory. It involves two crucial points. One is that the critical standards, however valuable they may be in their application to practical and to theoretical thinking, cannot themselves be immune from criticism. It may still be true—and indeed seems unavoidable—that *something* must be held immune from doubt, that there is some thought or idea or commitment which, as Wittgenstein puts it, "lies beyond being justified or unjustified" (*OC* 359). Whatever may have such a transcendental certainty, however, it cannot be critical standards themselves, if we are to avoid the dogmatism exhibited by empiricism and rationalism. The other crucial point is that certifying the critical standards must not lead to an endless regress. In practice this means that the critical standards must be certified by the critical standards themselves; that is to say, the very standards which show how empirical and logical and moral judgments are possible must also show, with no *ad hoc* emendations, that the critical judgments are themselves possible. So standards of criticism must be self-referential, as Rüdiger Bubner has usefully suggested (1974, 1975) —but self-referential in a way that avoids the obvious danger of vicious circularity.

At first glance this proposal seems as foolish as it is bold. The first of four dangers has already been mentioned, that self-referential criteria will have to assume what they claim to justify. In that case vicious circularity will prove to have been a hidden reef lying in the tempting channel between Scylla and Charybdis, and the attempt to steer a new course will have been blatantly fallacious. The second danger is that of unjustly impugning the critical standards of empiricism and of rationalism. Empirical testability remains an important criterion for critical judgment, as does logical consistency. Kant, or any other critical philosopher, must somehow make clear that insufficiency as a standard for the criticism of criticism does not entail insufficiency as a standard of criticism in general. The third danger is that what we have to take for granted, when we give up taking the standards of criticism for granted, will be something that we should not take for granted. What we take for granted in this way will have the standing, mentioned above, of transcendental certainty—transcendental because immune to examination in terms of the standards of criticism, and certain because taken for granted and not subject to doubt. It is not at all clear that there is anything which deserves such transcendental certainty. If there is not, the critical philosophy will be exposed as a new dogmatism. The fourth danger is that of dualism. One form of dualism threatens through a separation of knowledge into two domains, one governed by empirical criteria and one by rational or logical criteria; another form of dualism threatens through a dichotomy in experience between that which is taken for granted and that which is not. Perhaps dualism will prove unavoidable along the course Kant proposes to steer. Such an outcome would, however, be profoundly unsettling, since dualism precludes, or seems to preclude, just the sort of perspicuous overview which is the goal of philosophic search. A profound dualism can, therefore, never be altogether satisfactory.

These four dangers—of circularity, of critical arrogance, of disguised dogmatism, and of dualistic resignation—pose problems, and we ought not to prejudge how they can be handled, nor what will count as adequate solutions. They are dangers to be kept in mind not only when considering Kant, but also, and more importantly, when considering how to promote and strengthen in our own times the critical tradition in philosophy.

2. Kant's Awkward Achievement

In the prize essay that he submitted near the end of his life in response to the competition of the Prussian Academy regarding the progress in metaphysics since the time of Leibniz and Wolff, Kant (1804, 20:253–332) says that the progress he had achieved was due to his distinguishing the analytic/synthetic distinction from the pure/empirical distinction. He thereby calls attention to the ground covered in the expanded introduction to the second edition (1787) of the *Critique of Pure Reason*. Distinguishing between the two well-known dichotomies allowed Kant to acknowledge the rationalist criterion of logical consistency as the standard for all analytic judgments and the empiricist criterion of experiential testability as the standard for all empirical judgment, while at the same time maintaining that neither was a sufficient standard for certain other judgments, namely, those which are synthetic and pure (or apriori), among which are judgments about standards of criticism.

Kant's critical philosophy is designed to show how synthetic apriori judgment is possible, and thereby to present standards for such judgment. Such judgment is warranted by the fact that it is a prerequisite for something that is granted, namely, genuine knowledge. Kant regards the theorems of mathematics, and certain propositions of physics, as clear examples of synthetic apriori judgments. These propositions of mathematics and physics are taken by Kant to constitute genuine knowledge, and the critical philosophy must present the conditions and standards for such synthetic apriori propositions if it is to succeed in showing how knowledge in general is possible. Since genuine knowledge always relates somehow to experience, which is the only faculty that can *constitute* an object of knowledge, one of the standards for synthetic apriori judgment is that such judgment can have only a regulative and never a constitutive use. Philosophy also consists of synthetic apriori propositions, but much philosophical writing ignores the inherent limitations of such propositions. In the part of the *Critique* entitled "The Transcendental Dialectic," Kant distinguishes his own philosophy from other philosophical doctrines by arguing that they violate the canons for synthetic apriori judgment by making constitutive rather than merely regulative claims. In this way Kant uses the standards of criticism established within his philosophy—standards which he uses to rebut other philosophical claims—to validate that very philosophy.

It might be well to look at an example. Kant maintains that time is the form of inner intuition. This proposition is not one that can be certified by experimental means, since it is apriori. It cannot be certified by logical means, since it is synthetic. It does have a merely regulative use, since it presents a conception of time according to which time is not an independent objective entity but something through which we apprehend what our experience constitutes as the objects of our experience. It therefore meets the negative test of Kant's critical philosophy—as, for example, Newton's conception of time does not. If we then ask whether there is some positive test which this proposition has met, the answer is that positive proofs do not apply here, if you are thinking of such positive proofs as logical derivations (rationalism) or experimental tests (empiricism)—any more than they apply to the statement that $7 + 5 = 12$. Kant was an intuitionist in mathematics— that admittedly opens a large question about the nature of mathematical proofs—and he assimilates philosophical judgment to mathematical judgment. It is important to "see" how this conception of time contributes to an understanding of how knowledge is possible, but there is no explicit form of test or proof as there generally is in formal logic or experimental science.

Kant initially (in the first edition of *Critique of Pure Reason*) took a certain realism for granted. (I comment later on his foolhardy claim in the preface to the second edition that a proof is needed for this starting place.) The form of Kant's question, "How is knowledge (judgment) possible at all?" presupposes such realism. The question presupposes that knowledge and judgment are possible; that is to say, that some judgments are true, and that some true judgments are known to be true.

One of the consequences of this sort of Kantian project is that it pushes scepticism aside. To ask *how* something is possible, in the way that Kant and Wittgenstein ask that question, presupposes *that* it is possible. Of course, the presupposition differs for the two philosophers. In the case of Kant the assumption on the first page of "The Transcendental Aesthetic" is that we are affected by objects; that is to say, that there really are external objects which affect our senses. There is a notorious problem about whether these objects are phenomenal. If they are, then Kant reads, as Strawson has suggested (1966, 22, 35, 56, 193ff.), very much like Berkeley, and his vaunted empirical realism reduces to phenomenalism. If they are not, then since they cannot be noumena (because they affect us), there must be things which are neither phenomena nor noumena and whose status seems wholly indescribable within Kant's system. It is not my purpose here to settle this problem but simply to note Kant's rather plebeian assumption that there are external objects, in order to discuss his main question, how knowledge of them is possible. Everyone who has read Kant knows that he gives an imposing analysis of knowledge, but it is less frequently noted that he gives no analysis whatsoever of the objects of which he assumes we have such knowledge.

This realism parallels his realism in moral philosophy, where he similarly begins by assuming that some moral judgments are sound, and proceeds to investigate how it is possible that there should be moral (as distinct from prudential) judgments. Kant further fleshed out his realism by assuming the truth of Aristotelian logic, Euclidean geometry, and Newtonian physics; but it is not clear to me whether these further assumptions are central to the basic program in his critical philosophy. In any case there are so many difficulties with the subsidiary assumptions, including the assumption that mathematics and philosophy constitute genuine contributions to knowledge (science), as well as with the notion of synthetic apriori propositions,[1] that Kant's program cannot be carried unamended into the twentieth century. The problem for us is to see whether the critical tradition he founded can be strengthened and promoted in our day.

3. Wittgenstein's Early Effort: Self-reference Manqué

Let us begin examining the contribution Wittgenstein has made to the critical tradition by considering his early work, the *Tractatus Logico-Philosophicus*. The similarity of Wittgenstein's project with that of Kant has been pointed out by many scholars.[2] Though Wittgenstein scarcely

---

1. Witness Strawson (1966, 43): ". . . it must be concluded that Kant really has no clear and general conception of the synthetic apriori at all."

2. The first to give prominence to parallels between Kant and Wittgenstein was, I believe, Erik Stenius, in *Wittgenstein's "Tractatus"* (1960). Subsequent elaboration of such parallels are numerous, with those by Engel (1971), by Janik and Toulmin (1973), by Kenny (1973, 1984), and by Finch (1977) being especially useful. Recent persuasive discussions of profoundly Kantian features in Wittgenstein's thought occur in *The False Prison* by David Pears (1987) and in *Investigating Wittgenstein* by the Hintikkas (1986). As for opposing discussions, Apel (1973), Thiele (1983), and Haller (1988) all do a good job of articulating the differences between Kant and Wittgenstein that must be borne in mind.

mentions Kant, he must have had him in mind. Besides the acquaintance with Kant that is inevitable through Schopenhauer and Frege, it is known that Wittgenstein read and discussed Kant with Ludwig Hänsel while a prisoner in Monte Casino (McGuinness 1988, 270).

Perhaps the most striking way to begin is by noting, as does Stenius (1960, ch. 11), that Wittgenstein asks the same form of question as Kant: "How is X possible?" Kant asked how judgment is possible, and Wittgenstein asked in the *Tractatus* how *Sätze* are possible. It is important to see that this is the main project of the *Tractatus,* and that it results in what Stenius calls a "transcendental lingualism." Stenius deserves more credit than he usually gets for emphasizing these points.

Wittgenstein's assumption is that there is a world which is composed of facts. He differs from Kant in that he explicitly says that the world does not consist of "things." He differs further in that the facts are not ones that "affect" us but are ones we picture to ourselves:

We picture facts to ourselves. (*TLP* 2.1)

A third difference is that although Wittgenstein never gives any reason why we should believe that there are such facts, he does give an analysis of them. These differences provide ground for Hacker (1986) and others to insist that Wittgenstein is not really a Kantian.[3] Hacker and Haller are certainly correct in this, provided that we recognize a distinction between critical and Kantian philosophy; their points need to be taken into account by anyone trying to compare Kant and Wittgenstein. Nonetheless Kant and Wittgenstein have in common that they both assume the existence of an external world, and neither makes a plausible move toward justifying this assumption.

In the case of Kant there seems just an embarrassing uncertainty about what it is he is taking for granted, for the objects so crucial on the first page are never further identified, and Kant blocks the temptation to identify them with our everyday external world by later (B274–79) offering a proof of the external world. This point is made brilliantly by

---

3. Peter Hacker stressed rather strained parallels with Kant in the first edition of *Insight and Illusions* (1972), focusing on Wittgenstein's "metaphysics of experience" and on allegedly transcendental argumentation about private language. In the second edition (1986) he retracts these two points and devotes nine pages (206–14) to contrasts between the two, especially on matters having to do with synthetic apriori propositions and with proofs in philosophy. These contrasts, like those adumbrated by Thiele (1983), by Haller (1988), and in chapter four as well as elsewhere in this volume, cannot be denied. Neither do they cancel the affinities.

P. F. Strawson in his 1983 Woodbridge Lectures at Columbia, *Scepticism and Naturalism: Some Varieties,* by presenting three quotations (p. 24): (1) from the preface to the *Critique of Pure Reason* (*KdrV* B xi), where Kant proposes to remedy the "scandal" that philosophy has not yet given a satisfactory proof of the existence of things external to us; (2) Heidegger's riposte in *Being and Time* (1.6): "The 'scandal of philosophy' is not that this proof has yet to be given, but that *such proofs are expected and attempted again and again*"; (3) Wittgenstein's comment— clearly more in agreement with Heidegger than with Kant—in *OC* 471: "It is so difficult to find the *beginning*. Or better: it is difficult to begin at the beginning. And not to try to go further back." Strawson speaks of Wittgenstein's position as "social naturalism." This is certainly right, and one of the challenges is how to reconcile this naturalism with the "transcendental lingualism" which Stenius identified and which has not entirely disappeared from the later work.

Wittgenstein explicitly excludes the existence of the world from the realm of what is explicable or understandable:

> It is not *how* things are in the world that is mystical, but *that* it exists. (*TLP* 6.44)

Wittgenstein's position seems clearer than Kant's. Kant's program makes sense only on the assumption that we do have experience or knowledge, which would be impossible (B275) if there were no external objects. The very idea of critical philosophy requires such an assumption, for the strategy is to show that experience is possible only on the basis of certain limits and then to use the recognition of those limits to criticize other philosophies. By trying to prove what he has already assumed, Kant only muddies the waters. Wittgenstein puts his assumption of the world of facts right up front, in the very first sentences, where no reader can miss it, and there are no prior premises from which it might be supposed to follow.

Although Wittgenstein's world of facts has not been missed, it has been neglected. Pears (1987, vol. 1, ch. 5), for example, seems not to regard the world of facts as belonging to ontology, for he says that Wittgenstein starts off with an ontology of objects. Malcolm, similarly, in his book on the *Tractatus* (1986, chs. 1–3), neither discusses nor even cites either of the first two sentences of Wittgenstein's book, although Malcolm's aim is to expound its alleged metaphysical realism. This neglect leads to serious distortion of the *Tractatus,* which I discuss more fully in chapter six. Both Pears and Malcolm attribute to Wittgenstein a metaphysical monism, namely, the view that the world is ultimately composed of *Gegenstände*. Hence they convict him of an uncritical metaphysical realism, thus breaking the putative connection both with Kant and with Wittgenstein's own later philosophy, and thereby consigning the *Tractatus* to relative historical isolation as a sort of anomaly whose main role is to serve as a foil for the later work.

This reading of the *Tractatus* is neither natural nor necessary. The obvious alternative is to attribute to Wittgenstein a metaphysical dualism: the *world* consists of facts not objects, and the *substance* of the world—which determines possibility rather than fact and which therefore belongs to an entirely different category—consists of objects, not facts. Facts and possibilities are entirely different, and there is no reason to suppose that possibilities, which are transcendental rather than empirical, have or need have the same sort of reality as facts. Given this dualism, it is then natural to propose—as no one to my knowledge has—that Wittgenstein's metaphysics in this early period is dualistic: a combination of empirical realism and transcendental idealism.

This novel reading, based on the obvious dualism of the opening pages of the *Tractatus,* is elaborated in part two. It is necessary here, however, to say something about the implications of this reading for my main thesis, namely, that Wittgenstein made a substantial contribution to revitalizing critical philosophy. Some might argue that critical philosophy needs no metaphysics, but a strong case can be made—and has been by Ralph Walker (1978), for example—that a metaphysics combining empirical realism and transcendental idealism is essential to the project of critical philosophy. The argument is that critical philosophy needs a ground for the truth of ordinary factual and scientific knowledge, and another ground for the domain of concepts and rules which, all by themselves, have a beguiling appeal but cannot lead to genuine truth. That seems precisely the way Wittgenstein has used his metaphysical dualism: facts provide a grounding for ordinary factual truths, and objects provide a grounding for the human apparatus for stating (or misstating) those truths, an apparatus about which nothing can be said. The very end of the *Tractatus* counsels silence, but the counsel applies *only* to matters of semantics, logic, and philosophy:

> The correct method in philosophy would really be the following: to say nothing except what can be said, i.e. propositions of natural science—
> i.e. something that has nothing to do with philosophy—and then,

whenever someone else wanted to say something metaphysical, to demonstrate to him that he had failed to give a meaning to certain signs in his propositions. (*TLP* 6.53)

It is no accident that the dichotomy with respect to silence and speaking at the end of the *Tractatus* precisely parallels the metaphysical dichotomy at its beginning. In fact the dichotomy at the end motivates the metaphysical dualism at the beginning; the empirical reality of facts enables us to make factual statements, and the transcendental ideality of objects prevents us from making metaphysical or semantic statements.

It is important not to overrate the Kantianism of the *Tractatus*. Like Kant, Wittgenstein embarked on a project designed both to show how scientific claims are possible and at the same time why metaphysical claims are not. Both argue that factual claims are possible only on the basis of certain limits or restrictions which metaphysical claims fail to observe. But Kant's critical philosophy was self-referential in a way that the *Tractatus* is not. For Kant the very same criteria which showed the validity of science and the invalidity of speculative metaphysics also showed the legitimacy of Kant's critical philosophy, of his "metaphysics of experience." Kant saw this outcome as essential to his project; his critical philosophy must not only make sense in a way in which speculative metaphysics does not, but it must also constitute a genuine addition to human knowledge. On this central point Wittgenstein's early work is not Kantian.

It is not that Wittgenstein makes no attempt at self-reference in the *Tractatus*. He does. The self-reference, however, is a notorious failure. Wittgenstein's criterion for what sort of linguistic expression makes sense allows only for propositions that are "pictures" or models of facts, and for truth-functions of these propositions. Since none of the propositions of the *Tractatus* are of this character, Wittgenstein bravely concluded the work with the remark that anyone who has understood him will realize that those propositions are nonsense. It is true that Wittgenstein's remark in the preface about the "unassailable and definitive" truth of the thoughts expressed in the *Tractatus* seems incompatible with characterizing those thoughts as nonsense. One can sympathize with those who stress the preface, but a serious scholar must give priority to the body of the text. There the conclusion that the text itself is nonsense is a compelling inference from central points in the exposition. One cannot escape recognizing a catastrophic failure of that very test of self-referentiality which seems central to the project of critical philosophy. However promising its beginning and the nature of its project, the *Tractatus* is at the end poignantly deficient as critical philosophy.

4.   Critical Philosophy as Grammar

In the *Philosophical Investigations* Wittgenstein continues and refines the task, begun in the *Tractatus,* of characterizing uses of language that make sense, so as to show how meaningful speech is possible and thereby to enable us to identify nonsense. Again—or still—the parallel with Kant is striking. Wittgenstein still avoids the question *whether* the phenomenon in question is possible, thereby taking something for granted, and still derives a standard of criticism from the investigation. Just as Kant uses his standard of criticism to rebut cosmological speculation, so Wittgenstein uses his standard of criticism to rebut those who claim that sense data provide *knowledge;* for example, *PI* 246:

> It can't be said of me at all (except perhaps as a joke) that I *know* I am in pain. What is it supposed to mean—except perhaps that I *am* in pain?

In both cases the standards of criticism emerge from considering extremely familiar and altogether uncontroversial phenomena, and in both cases the derived standards prove inimical to familiar and popular philosophical views. In a broad sense there can be no doubt whatever that Wittgenstein is a critical rather than a speculative philosopher. Closer examination shows further that his later philosophy is self-referential, that he remains free of current doctrines in the special sciences, and that he deftly avoids the four dangers which challenge the critical tradition.

What Wittgenstein takes for granted is patterns of human behavior which he calls 'language-games'. As the name implies, these activities, which are "countless," are ones in which the use of language plays an important role. Wittgenstein makes no claim that language *must* play a central role in human life, since he is generally sceptical of necessities, but he notes that it does. Some of these language-games are simple or "primitive." Examples of primitive language-games are giving orders, asking questions, making reports, saying hello and goodbye, calling for help, and so on. Others are more complex in various ways. Particularly interesting is the complexity of those language-games that are neither primitive themselves nor combinations of primitive language-games, but which are possible only because they presuppose that certain primitive language-games already exist. This seems to be the case with hoping and with expressing intentions, for they seem to presuppose being able to *report* what is intended or hoped for. Such complex language-games are often as universal as the primitive ones, as Wittgenstein explicitly notes with respect to expressing intentions (*Z* 43). Making grammatical remarks, which could not possibly be the only use of language, is one of the complex language-games and is every bit as widespread as the teaching of language itself.

The recognition of making grammatical remarks—or of grammar, for short—is critical to the formulation and application of Wittgenstein's critical criteria. Wittgenstein's standard of criticism is this: linguistic expressions make sense only in the course of human activity, and an expression which makes sense as part of one activity may be nonsense in the course of another. For example, to say "I doubt it" in response to a reporter's saying "The court is adjourned" makes sense, because this is a context where expressing a doubt is a familiar pattern of behavior; but making the same comment after the presiding judge says "The court is adjourned" would be nonsense: the judge has adjourned the court, not reported that it is adjourned.

This comment is an example of what Wittgenstein calls a "grammatical remark," and he considers the proper business of philosophy to consist of such remarks. In this connection an important caveat is given by Hintikka and Hintikka (1986) in their repeated insistence on the primacy of language-games (practices) over rules in the appreciation of what grammar is. Perhaps the clearest evidence of the importance that Wittgenstein attaches to language-games as the touchstone of his work is the prominence he gives them in the *Philosophical Investigations*. The first part of this work is the only text other than the *Tractatus* that Wittgenstein seriously prepared for publication. It is clear from the history of his work on both books that a large part of the preparation consisted in selecting and arranging remarks he had already written. In particular it is important what comes first, at the beginning. In revising the *Blue Book* and the *Brown Book* and integrating them with other material from his notebooks, Wittgenstein chose to start with a study of language-games as a way to examine the picture of language suggested by the quotation from Augustine.

Lest this should all sound too simple, it would be well to note some of the deep problems that are embedded in the line of thought I have been presenting. One is the problem of the dualism (in part due to

Frege) which pervades the *Tractatus* and of which traces remain in the *Philosophical Investigations*. A second is the notion of "form of life," especially as that applies to human life, and its apparent conflict with Wittgenstein's attack on essences. A third is the very bold character of his conception of "grammar" and its relation to what the linguists study. A fourth is his notion of "natural history" as something distinct from natural science, in large part because doubts and explanations and theories are not part of it. A fifth is the puzzle about the status of mathematics and mathematical proofs. A sixth is the subtle conception of nonsense in the *Philosophical Investigations* and its relation to the one given in the *Tractatus*. All these issues are difficult and require sensitive consideration of both historical and contemporary texts.

Let me return to the four dangers mentioned above: the dangers of circularity, of critical arrogance, of disguised dogmatism, and of dualistic resignation. Wittgenstein did not succeed in overcoming the last three of these dangers in the *Tractatus,* but he avoids them all in the *Philosophical Investigations* by using grammar as the basis for his critical criteria. Grammatical remarks are clearly subject to grammatical criteria, but this seems no more circular than that the word 'spelling' has a correct spelling. Critical arrogance is out of the question, since Wittgenstein recognizes each language-game as having its own standards. Dogmatism is avoided by the fact that Wittgenstein says where the standards are to be found rather than what they are. The "dualism" that is left in the *Philosophical Investigations* is an opposition between grammar and experience, or between language and the world, and that hardly amounts to a dualism, since grammar is part of our experience and language is part of our world. Quite the contrary. In spite of his insistence on differences, in spite of his insistence on rules and limitations, in spite of his own sense that he could not quite get the whole picture in focus, Wittgenstein did manage to leave us with a sense of unity, that "light dawns gradually over the whole" (*OC* 141).

5.   A Summary of Further Parallels

I want to end by summarizing important parallels between Kant and Wittgenstein. I do so not to try to show that Wittgenstein was a Kantian or a neo-Kantian. In many important ways he was not. The point is rather that they adopt parallel or common stances which are powerful and which pertain to the very nature of philosophy:

1. Both develop a philosophy that is more critical than speculative. That is to say, both spend a good deal of time analyzing and condemning the incoherence and futility of much philosophy.
2. Both employ striking *reductio ad absurdum* arguments in refutations of contemporary philosophical viewpoints; Kant's chapter on the antinomy of pure reason and Wittgenstein's "private language argument" are among the most powerful passages in their respective works.
3. In both cases these refutations appear not as the starting point—much less as the be-all and end-all—but rather as a logical consequence of a constructive conception of proper philosophic activity, which is independently justified.
4. Both conceive that philosophy—at least as they themselves practice it—is explained and "justified" as a legitimate endeavor partly by itself (philosophy is self-referential) and partly by analogous endeavors (mathematics in the one case, grammar and grammatical explanation in the other) that are philosophically legitimate.
5. In neither case is the analogous activity empirical: both insist on a sharp distinction between philosophy and empirical science.
6. Both accept the world as real—it is presupposed, it turns out, by what is undeniable, if it is not itself undeniable. In both cases this leads to an explicit refutation of idealism.
7. Both hold that our genuine knowledge, our science, lacks a metaphysical foundation, without thereby being any shakier.
8. Both explicitly reject wholesale scepticism.
9. Both limit the scope of knowing (or rational justificational) and thereby make room for nonepistemic certainty (or faith).
10. Both insist that there are some unassailable propositions (tautological, grammatical, analytic) which do not constitute genuine knowledge.
11. Both embrace a kind of semantic or epistemic holism, taking judgments or propositions or "uses of language" as the basic units of significant discourse.

Mies van der Rohe once said, "God is in the details!" If this is at all right, then this essay, with its broad sweep, is undoubtedly a work of the devil. It is evident that details are lacking. All four sections of the essay are deficient in this regard. There is too cursory an examination of the principles and problems of critical philosophy; too little attention is given to the unity of Kant's philosophy and the consequent difficulty of retaining some bits of it while discarding others; a novel reading of the *Tractatus* is proposed with only perfunctory attention to existing literature; and the final section closes with a long list of alleged but unsubstantiated parallels between Kant and Wittgenstein (it is evident that many distinctions and qualifications will be needed to make that list stand up to close examination) and the brief dismissal in a single paragraph of four supposedly profound challenges to the very idea of a critical philosophy. Critical philosophy requires a more critical defense, and many of the necessary details and the required arguments are presented in the essays that follow. My aim here has been to sketch the continuing plausibility of critical philosophy, and the rich prospects of reading Wittgenstein as revitalizing the philosophical tradition that Kant inaugurated.

2
Analyticity and Grammar

> *Kant's theory is not so simple as it looks, and the nature of analytic judgments is not altogether clear.*
> —Paton (1936, 86)

Kant's distinction between analytic and synthetic judgments is best known through his metaphoric definition of an analytic judgment as one in which "the predicate *B* belongs to the subject *A*, as something which is (covertly) contained in this subject *A*" (B10). Although this is the most famous formulation of Kant's distinction, what strikes a student most forcefully about Kant's discussion of analyticity is the variety of different ways in which he explains the idea. One can identify passages which seem to make analyticity depend upon (1) containment, (2) identity, (3) contradiction, (4) our way of knowing the judgment in question, (5) our way of thinking the judgment in question, and (6) the function or role of the judgment in question. In addition to these six seemingly different conceptions of analyticity, there is also a question whether Kant intends his distinction to range over all judgments or only over subject-predicate judgments; if we apply these two alternatives to the six conceptions of analyticity, we have a total of twelve theories of analyticity contained in or suggested by Kant's discussion. This is a bewildering situation indeed, and it is no wonder that subsequent discussions of analyticity have often lacked the decisiveness that one might wish for in matters of logic.

I propose to give fresh consideration to what Kant said about the distinction between analytic and synthetic judgments. I shall first consider how widely we may presume Kant intended his distinction to apply, and then examine various formulations of the distinction in the *Critique*. These formulations lead to two broad lines of interpretation, in terms of logical form on the one hand and in terms of the phenomenology or function of the judgment on the other. I shall reject the first line, and offer an interpretation of Kant's notion based on the explicative function which he assigns to analytic judgments. This interpretation proves to be compatible with all that Kant has said about the analytic, and illuminating when applied to some of his puzzling remarks. It turns out that the explication achieved by an analytic judgment is very like the explication achieved by what Wittgenstein called a "grammatical" proposition, and hence that analyticity (in Kant's sense) is a part of grammar (in Wittgenstein's sense). It turns out, too, that Kant's distinction is more pragmatic than is generally realized, and that it therefore remains untouched by the main thrust of recent attacks on other distinctions between the analytic and the synthetic.

1. The Range of Kant's Distinction

The section of the *Critique* entitled "The Distinction between Analytic and Synthetic Judgments" begins with the words, "In all judgments in which the relations of a subject to the predicate is thought . . ." It appears that the remainder of this section is meant to be read with the condition of this opening phrase in mind, and this immediately suggests, as Richard Robinson (1958) and Konrad Marc-Wogau (1951) have pointed out, that Kant did not conceive of his distinction as applying to any but subject-predicate propositions. It may therefore be that theorems of logic, relational propositions, and simple existential propositions are not even to be considered in the light of the distinction which Kant sets for subject-predicate propositions.

In its broadest form such a suggestion has little to recommend it and is easily rebutted. A simple existential judgment, such as "God exists" or "There are aardvarks," can be regarded as having a logical predicate, even though (as Kant puts it) " 'Being' is obviously not a real predicate" (B626). Kant himself, for example, explicitly discusses existential judgments in regard to analytic-synthetic distinction, and argues that they are all synthetic (B625–26). Similarly a relational judgment can be looked upon as having a subject and a predicate, even though such an analysis of it is not final and may not be wholly satisfactory. Theorems of logic are perhaps more difficult to fit into the subject-predicate mold, but it is in any case implausible to regard them as judgments in the Kantian sense. It would seem, therefore, as Parkinson (1960) contends, that Kant may legitimately look upon his distinction as quite general and assimilate a variety of sorts of judgments to the subject-predicate pattern. Beck (1960, 86) further points out that in the *Critique of Practical Reason* Kant extends the scope of the distinction even more by speaking of analytic and synthetic imperatives.

Against these considerations we must set Kant's own classification of judgments into three species: categorical, hypothetical, and disjunctive (B95). He explains that "in the first kind of judgments we consider only two concepts, in the second two judgments, in the third several judgments in their relation to each other" (B98). Kant's explanation of analyticity is obviously tailored to fit the first of these three species of judgments, and nowhere is it altered to fit the different dimensions of the other two. This is a matter of some significance for appreciating the distance between Kant's conception of analyticity and that of many moderns. There is, for example, no obvious way for Kant to regard the judgment "If the Mekong is longer than the Danube and the Yangtze is longer than the Mekong, then the Yangtze is longer than the Danube" as analytic—although it would seem that this hypothetical judgment merely makes explicit something that is implicit in the relational concept *longer than;* it surely does not state any geographical information. Similarly, truth-functional tautologies, which are today often presented as a paradigm for analytic propositions, are either hypothetical or disjunctive in form and therefore do not fall within the scope of the concept for Kant. The valid formulae of modern symbolic logic would no doubt be ruled out on this ground too; but it is likely that such formulae would in any case be excluded from the range of Kant's distinction between the analytic and the synthetic on the ground that they do not express judgments.[1] Such exclusions are perhaps to be regretted, especially where they seem to preclude a logic of relations; but they do seem to be implied by Kant and they demonstrate, as Beth (1953/54) has argued in another context, the great distance between Kant's view and the views of modern logicians.

---

1. In the *Critique* Kant consistently speaks of "principles" of logic rather than of "judgments" of logic or "truths" of logic. His term for 'principles' is *Sätze,* which can also be rendered as 'proposition' or 'sentence'. The important point is that he uses *Urteil* in formulating his distinction between the analytic and the synthetic, but *not* in speaking about logical principles.

Kant does not retain the same terminology in his *Logik,* for in sections 36 and 37 he speaks of *analytische Sätze;* but he characterizes logical formulae in a way that makes it doubtful that they are to be regarded as *Sätze:* "Formeln.—Diese sind regeln, deren Ausdruck zum Muster der Nachahmung dient. Sie sind übrigens ungemein nützlich zur Erleichterung bei verwickelten Sätzen und der erleuchteste Kopf sucht daher dergelichen zu finden" (*Einleitung* x = *Weischedel* III.507).

I conclude, in what I take to be close agreement with Marc-Wogau (1951, 142), that certain judgments—though not the ones Robinson supposed—and certain other formulae, which we today might wish to count as propositions, do not fall within the scope of Kant's distinction between analytic and synthetic judgments. The distinction does apply unrestrictedly, however, to categorical propositions.

2.   Kant's Various Explanations

Kant first says that in an analytic judgment "the predicate B belongs to the subject A, as something which is (covertly) contained in this subject A" (B10). Either a judgment is analytic in this manner or "B lies outside the concept A, although it does indeed stand in connection with it" (B10). We are all perfectly familiar with the idea that something may be contained in something else, where the alternative is that the first thing lies outside the second. For example, if I put a wastebasket at the far end of my room and try throwing crumpled pieces of discarded manuscript into it, the result will most likely be that some of the paper balls will be contained in the basket and some will lie outside it. The difficulty which we have in understanding Kant's first explanation of analyticity is the difficulty of applying this familiar concept of containment in an unfamiliar context.

We know that in the case of physical objects there are limits to the application of the idea. If one of the crumpled pieces of discarded manuscript gets hooked on the top edge of the basket, or lies at the top of the heap above the plane of the brim of the basket, there is no absolutely definitive way of saying whether it is contained in the basket or lies outside of it. In general the concept of containment loses its clear dichotomous character whenever the putative container either lacks sharp boundaries or has boundaries that an object can straddle. It follows that Kant must have assumed that concepts all have "sharp boundaries," so that one can always say definitely whether one concept is "contained in" another or not, if containment is to serve as a definitive criterion of analyticity.

Concepts, whether sharp or not, are not literally contained in one another in the same basic sense in which paper balls may be contained in or lie outside of a basket. If we look at the matter with this familiar sense of 'contain' in mind, we shall have to say that Kant was speaking metaphorically. This metaphor, like any other, may have valuable rhetorical force and may even be instructive; but we cannot understand exactly what the explanation is meant to convey until we can put it in nonmetaphorical terms. Presumably Kant's recognition of this need is one of the reasons why he offered further explanations of analyticity.

Kant next presents the explanation in terms of identity:

> Analytic judgments (affirmative) are therefore those in which the connection of the predicate with the subject is thought through identity. (B10)

Again, it is necessary to be generous with Kant. The expression 'thought through identity' is not an expression which our ordinary familiarity with the language enables us to understand. There is no ordinary idiom according to which we speak of thinking something "through" something else. Nor is the German any less baffling: "Analytische Urteile sind also diejenigen in welchen die Verknüpfung des Prädicats mit dem Subjekt durch Identität . . . gedacht wird." What does Kant mean by saying that "all bodies are extended" is thought through identity?

Kant's odd phrase makes it clear that an analytic proposition is not the same as an identical proposition, although there is a very intimate connection between the two. Some years later, in his essay on the progress of metaphysics since the time of Leibniz and Wolff, Kant explicitly commented:

> A judgment is *analytic* if its predicate only sets forth clearly (*explicite*) what was already thought, albeit obscurely (*implicite*), in the concept of the subject. For example, that every body is extended. If one wished to call such a judgment "identical," one would invite confusion; for judgments of that sort contribute nothing to the elucidation of concepts which must be the aim of all judgment, and hence are said to be empty. For example, that every body is a bodily (in another word, material) substance. Analytic judgments are indeed *based* on identity and can be resolved into it; but they cannot *be* identical, since they require analysis and thereby contribute to the clarification of concepts, which would not be done at all if they were identical *idem per idem*. (1804, 20:322 = R 174–75)

But it is still obscure exactly how an analytic judgment is to be resolved into an identical proposition.

When Kant says that the judgment that all bodies are extended is "thought through identity," a part of what he means might be expressed by saying that this judgment is one which depends upon our acknowledging that the concept of a body is identical with the conceptual combination of a number of elements, one of which is the concept of being extended. To put it symbolically, in a symbolism suggested both by Parkinson (1960) and by Beck (1965, 74–91), we can say that analytic propositions are not of the form

$$\text{All } A \text{ are } B$$

but of the form

$$\text{All } A = BX \text{ are } B,$$

where X is a concept or a set of concepts which joins with B in a conceptual complex identical with A.

These symbolic representations of Kant's idea are doubly useful. In the first place they show how a judgment's being analytic depends upon its being "thought through identity," namely that the subject-concept is conceived as identical with a conceptual complex of which the predicate is one component. In the second place we can see in these symbolic representations the connection of which Parkinson speaks between the containment criterion and the identity criterion, in that the predicate must be "contained in" the conceptual complex with which the subject is conceived to be identical. Thus these two criteria go hand in glove, and separately they are simply aspects of one and the same idea.

Nevertheless there are still difficulties. One problem centers around the way concepts are "combined" in "conceptual complexes." Leibniz held, reasonably enough, that the predicate of every true proposition must be a part of the subject (*Gerhardt*, 2:52). Since this principle applies to synthetic as well as to analytic propositions—or at any rate to propositions Kant regards as synthetic and which Leibniz would acknowledge to be contingent—the manner in which concepts are "combined" in a Leibnizian subject must be different from the manner in which they are "combined" in the subject of one of Kant's judgments. Where the proposition involved is a contingent or synthetic one, let us call the manner of combination "Leibnizian combination" as opposed to "Kantian combination." The dilemma arises when we ask how one can tell, in a case where concepts are combined, whether the combination is Leibnizian or Kantian. The obvious answer is that the combination is Kantian if the judgment that might be framed from it is analytic. But this answer is not available to Kant, since it entails that we must know whether a proposition is analytic *before* we can apply the identity criterion or the containment criterion, and hence would make Kant's first two explanations of analyticity grossly circular.

Even if we knew the nature of this conceptual combination, the identity criterion would remain mysterious. *If* I conceive A as identical with *BX,* the judgment that all A are B is analytic. But how am I to know whether I *rightly* conceive A as identical with *BX* — that is, whether A *is* identical with *BX*? Such conceptual identity is by no means easy to understand, and nothing of Kant's work which we have as yet examined throws any light upon the problem. The passage quoted above from *Fortschritte* throws this problem into even sharper relief; for Kant's insistence on the distinction of analytic propositions from identical ones makes it perfectly plain that one can never have an adequate explanation of analyticity *just* in terms of identity, and hence that the heart of the problem is what the identity sign stands for in the symbolic representations, and how to tell whether a judgment can be "resolved into identity."

The third criterion of analyticity which we find in Kant is, or appears to be, a psychological one (Beck [1965, 77] calls it phenomenological), in that whether a proposition is analytic depends upon how we think it. We can already see a hint of this in the way in which Kant articulates the identity criterion, which emphasizes the way in which we think or conceive of the proposition. Kant subsequently remarks that an analytic judgment is one in which "the subject is only divided into constituent concepts which were always conceived [thought] as existing within it, although confusedly" (B11). This way of speaking surely makes it appear that whether a judgment is analytic depends upon the perspective or intention of the person making the judgment, and it would follow that a proposition might be analytic for one person and synthetic for another person.

One special obstacle to understanding these remarks is that Kant has elsewhere insisted (rightly) that general logic and psychology must be kept firmly separate, and in particular that matters of empirical psychology cannot bear upon matters of logic:

> There are therefore two rules which logicians must always bear in mind, in dealing with pure general logic:
>
> 1. As general logic, it . . . deals with nothing but the mere form of thought.
>
> 2. As pure logic, it has nothing to do with empirical principles, and does not, as has sometimes been supposed, borrow anything from

psychology, which therefore has no influence whatever on the canon of the understanding. (*KdrV* B78)[2]

Hence, what appears to be a psychological criterion for a general logical concept must simply be a manner of speaking. As a manner of speaking this seeming psychology can no doubt be harmonized with the other criteria for the general logical distinction between analytic and synthetic propositions. But there is a suspicious ambiguity about the remarks, and in any case we are left without any satisfactory explanation of the term 'analytic'.

A fourth way in which Kant presents the distinction has to do with the manner in which one comes to know the proposition in question. "It would be absurd to found an analytic judgment on experience" (B11). In framing an analytic proposition I do not need to "go outside" the subject-concept itself, according to Kant, for "I have already in the concept . . . all the conditions required for my judgment" (B12). But in the case of a synthetic proposition I must go outside the subject-concept, either to experience or to "the unknown = X," in order to know that the predicate is connected with it. In the example which Kant gives, the proposition "all bodies have weight," what one refers to beyond the concept of 'body' is empirical evidence to the effect that there is a constant connection between the cases where the concept 'body' is applicable and the applicability of the concept 'weight', or of some scale of weights.

It should be noted that this explanation suffers from the same sort of ambiguity as the previous one, in that the question can be treated either psychologically or logically. If it is treated psychologically, one makes an empirical study of how it is that certain people arrive at certain beliefs, taking into account their experiences and other beliefs which they had at the beginning of the period in question. If one discusses the matter logically, the question of how the person has arrived at a belief is left aside, and the discussion centers instead on the question whether the belief is justified and what principles are required to make such justification explicit. Kant's statement of this epistemological criterion should certainly be read as logical rather than psychological and hence as equivalent to the familiar dictum that an analytic judgment must be justified apriori.

---

2. There is a similar remark at the beginning of the *Logik;* see *Einleitung* i = *Weischedel* III.435.

Still, the matter is not easy to understand. If we admit that Kant's epistemological criterion has to do with justification rather than the psychological side of knowing, we must then ask how in practice such justification is going to be given. Kant says (B12) that the proposition that all bodies are impenetrable is analytic, whereas the proposition that all bodies have weight is synthetic. It is difficult to grasp and hold on to any firm difference in the way of knowing these two propositions; and some philosophers, among whom British idealists (Caird [1889] and Kemp Smith [1962]) and contemporary American philosophers (White [1950] and Quine [1953]) are prominent, maintain that the reason for the difficulty is that in the last analysis there is no difference to be grasped. Caird says that "all judgments are synthetic in the making and analytic when made" (1889, 1:269). Kemp Smith argues as follows:

> There is little difficulty in detecting the synthetic character of the proposition: all bodies are heavy. Yet the reader has first been required to admit the analytic character of the proposition: all bodies are extended. The two propositions are really identical in logical character. Neither can be recognized as true save in terms of a comprehensive theory of physical existence. (1962, 38–39)

It would, for example, be plausible for someone to maintain that he didn't have to go beyond the concept of a body to know that all bodies have weight; he might insist that if some visual object could not be weighed, then it must be an illusion rather than a physical body. By refusing to apply the concept 'body' where there was not an ability to assign some weight, even an indefinite one, he would be treating the judgment "all bodies have weight," which Kant regards as synthetic, as analytic. On the other hand, it is also conceivable that a person should regard the concept of a body as requiring only that there be a certain figure, volume, and mass, and holding in addition that the fact that such physical bodies are often resistant to touch or to the intrusion of other physical bodies is a mere accident, for which we have a large amount of empirical evidence. Such a person would be treating this judgment, which Kant takes to be analytic, as synthetic. Nothing that Kant says makes it clear why these alternative perspectives are not legitimate. If they are legitimate, their legitimacy raises again the prospect that a proposition which is analytic for one person may not be analytic for another person.

Kant presents his fifth account of analyticity when he says that to determine whether a certain predicate is contained in the subject concept, "I have only to extract from it, in accordance with the principle of contradiction, the required predicate" (B12). This reference to the principle of contradiction is very casual indeed, and is wholly omitted from the earlier version of this section (A7–8). Nevertheless Kant explicitly says later on that the principle of contradiction is the "highest principle of all analytic judgments," and "the universal and completely sufficient *principle of all analytic knowledge*" (B189–91).

One might be tempted to conjecture that Kant, in this later section, is putting forward a thesis about analytic propositions rather than explaining what they are, and that he refrained from putting any emphasis on the principle of contradiction in the earlier passage so as to ensure that his thesis would not be vacuous. Certainly it would be neater and more convincing to have the meaning of 'analytic' firmly tied down, in terms other than contradiction, before entering upon a discussion of the highest principle of analytic judgments. But Kant does not proceed in this manner. Instead he reformulates the principle of contradiction— "the proposition that no predicate contradictory of a thing (*Ding*) can belong to it" (B190)—specifically "in order that the nature of an analytic proposition be clearly expressed through it" (B193). We are justified, then, in taking what Kant says in this regard as an elucidation of the meaning of 'analytic'.[3]

Explaining analyticity in terms of contradiction raises the hope, especially in the mind of a student trained in modern logic, that the idea will now become precise and clear. We might, for example, say that the epistemological criterion is to be applied in conjunction with the criterion based upon contradiction as follows: if I can know that the proposition "all S is P" is true by showing that "some S is not P" can be reduced to a substitution instance of the form "p and not-p," the proposition is analytic; otherwise it is synthetic. Unfortunately such an interpretation does not fit Kant at all. Kant's formulation of the principle of contradiction—"that no predicate contradictory of a thing

---

3. Very able commentators differ wildly about this point. Richard Robinson chastises Kant for *not* explaining analyticity in terms of contradiction: "This was the obvious way for Kant to explain his distinction between analytic and synthetic statements, because it would have shown where he stood with Leibniz, it would have been a clear and sharp distinction, and it would have been true" (1958, 296). H. W. Cassirer goes to the other extreme, suggesting that Kant does the whole job in terms of the principle of contradiction: "In Kant's opinion, analytic judgments exhibit one characteristic in virtue of which they are differentiated from every other kind of judgment, namely that a denial of their truth results in self-contradiction" (1954, 110). Fortunately this is one of those controversies where it is not necessary to choose sides, for they are both wrong.

can belong to it" (B190)—is itself a howler from a modern point of view, since it assumes contradiction to be a relation between things and predicates rather than a relation holding between propositions. Nor does the interpretation fit Kant's examples. Following such a line it is very difficult to see how the judgment that all bodies have weight, or even the judgment that all bodies have volume, could ever be known to be analytic unless a definition were first supplied. Kant, on the other hand, as Beck has pointed out (1965, 61–73), regards analytic judgments as more basic than definitions and prior to them. In view of the examples Kant gives of analytic and synthetic judgments, he must have in mind some notion of "conceptual contradiction" rather than truth-functional contradiction. This fifth explication, therefore, does not remove the obscurity which surrounds Kant's concept.

There is a final explication of analyticity which can be constructed out of Kant's discussion of the role or function of the judgment in question. Kant says that an analytic judgment is illustrative or explicative, while a synthetic judgment is ampliative and therefore expresses a genuine bit of knowledge (B11, 13–14; *Prolegomena* 2). In discourse, explication is often required to make clear what we mean: we must sharpen our linguistic tools so as to be able to work more efficiently at building a body of science. The propositions in which we set out such explications are analytic propositions. The object of our inquiry, however, will always be some matter of substance rather than mere explication of terms; and the matter of substance must be expressed in a proposition which is not explicative but ampliative. We may then distinguish between analytic and synthetic propositions according as the propositions enter into an inquiry simply to elucidate or stipulate how some term is to be used, or what some concept is to be regarded as "including." Propositions which do not have this explicative function, but which do enter into the inquiry in some other important way, will be synthetic rather than analytic.

But in spite of its plausibility this sixth explanation of Kant's conception of analyticity is very puzzling. The proposition that analytic propositions are explicative would seem on its face to be a thesis about analytic propositions—that is, to be ampliative. But Kant does not seem to regard it as ampliative, since he does not give any reasons or evidence for it. Instead he assumes that any proposition we can call 'analytic' will, as a matter of course, have an explicative function. Sometimes what is presented as obvious is a fact so commonplace that it would be merely tedious to elaborate or defend it; but in this case what is at issue is surprising rather than commonplace, for form and function rarely go hand-in-glove so neatly in linguistic matters. So the explicative function of analytic judgments must be obvious for Kant because having such a function is part of his conception of an analytic judgment. But, on the other hand, it is precisely because form and function are so different that it is hard to credit Kant with the view that having a certain function in discourse forms part of the same conception as that for which containment of the predicate in the subject is the chief criterion, since containment seems to be a matter of logical form.

3. Interpreting What Kant Said

We now have to try to understand what Kant meant. We have before us six alternative formulations of the distinction between analytic and synthetic judgments, as this distinction is presented to us by Kant. They are based respectively on (1) containment, (2) identity, (3) psychology, (4) epistemology, (5) contradiction, and (6) explication. There is no indication in what Kant has laid before us that he regards these alternative formulations as diverging in any way from one another; but we can hardly accept without careful consideration his apparent view that all six formulations are equivalent. Beck (1965, 78), for example, has concluded that "we have to suspect here a fundamental failure on Kant's part to distinguish the logical from the phenomenological aspects of thought." He says further that "we can discern two criteria for analytic judgment," and that "Kant, in apparent disregard of their difference, uses first one and then the other as it suits his purpose."

I shall follow Beck in regarding the six formulations of the distinction between the analytic and the synthetic as various verbalizations of two competing criteria of analyticity. I have already noted ambiguities in Kant's presentation, and it will be convenient now to make explicit the radically divergent aspects of his notion of analyticity. Beck sees the contrast as one between the logical and the phenomenological aspects of thought, but one might also see it as one between the form of a judgment and its function. Roughly, the first, second, and fifth of Kant's formulations of the idea of an analytic judgment seem to be based on the logical form of the judgment in question. The third, fourth, and sixth formulations, on the other hand, seem to be based on the way in which the judgment is related to the human beings who make it, or who may make it. The distinction intended is between those features of a judgment or statement which might be set out schematically by a logician, without consideration of the circumstances in which the judgment was made; and those features of a judgment or statement which require consideration of the intent or purpose of the speaker, and of the surrounding circumstances and the verbal context to the extent that they throw light on the purpose served (the intent expressed, or the role played) by the judgment or statement.

Starting from this recognition of two competing strains in Kant's notion of the analytic, two ways to interpret Kant suggest themselves. One might, on the one hand, suppose that Kant was proposing a formal, logical concept, and then explain Kant by offering a clear, precise formal definition, emphasizing the first, second, and fifth of Kant's explanations. On the other hand one might suppose that Kant's conception of the analytic was essentially phenomenological or functional, and that the formalism has to do merely with symbolizing analytic statements, not with their essential character. I want to propose an interpretation along the latter line, but I shall first consider the attempt to give a formal, logical definition of 'analytic'.

Frege faced the lack of clarity and precision in Kant's discussion, and "to state accurately what earlier writers, Kant in particular, have meant" (1950, 3n) by the terms 'analytic' and 'synthetic', he offers the following definition:

> The problem becomes, in fact, that of finding the proof of the proposition, and of following it up right back to the primitive truths. If, in carrying out this process, we come only on general logical laws and on definitions, then the truth is an analytic one, bearing in mind that we must take account also of all propositions upon which the admissibility of any of the definitions depends. If, however, it is impossible to give the proof without making use of truths which are not of a general logical nature, but belong to the sphere of some special science, then the proposition is a synthetic one. (1950, 4)

This definition is admirable for its conciseness, its clarity, its continuity with Kant, and its harmony with recent advances in logic.

In Frege's discussion there is no question whether the epistemological considerations are a matter of psychology or a matter of logic. Frege has insisted that "we should separate the problem of how we arrive at the content of a judgment from the problem of how its assertion is to be justified" (1950, 3), and his definition makes it clear that in determining whether a proposition is analytic it is only the logical question that counts. Thus he avoids one of the most troublesome ambiguities in Kant's discussion.

The expression 'general logical laws', upon which Frege's definition turns, does not occur in Kant's discussion of analytic judgments, and the connection between the two may not be immediately apparent. The thread which ties the two together is Kant's mention of the principle of contradiction as a criterion for determining whether a judgment is analytic (*KdrV* B12). He also insists that the principle of contradiction "belongs only to logic" (B190), and "must be recognized as being the universal and completely sufficient *principle of all analytic knowledge*" (B191). It seems reasonable, therefore, to suppose that Kant would either regard the principle of contradiction as the only general logical law, or else maintain that all general logical laws can be deduced from the principle of contradiction. Such a view belongs to a more traditional theory of logic from which Frege had broken away: Frege's propositional and functional logic is a form of modern symbolic logic in which the principle of contradiction no longer has a preeminent position. In modern symbolic logic all valid formulae can conveniently be regarded as having the same status; although certain laws are primitive in some systems, they may be derived in others, and thus their ultimate status cannot be different or more fundamental than that of other general logical laws. The most obvious way for Frege to render Kant's distinction between the analytic and the synthetic serviceable within the framework of symbolic logic was to speak of "general logical laws" where Kant had spoken of "the principle of contradiction." And this is just what he did.

Frege's definition of 'analytic' provides a sharp and challenging presentation of the view that Kant's distinction is a matter of form. Its principal connection with Kant is via Kant's reference to the principle of contradiction, which belongs to the group of Kantian criteria which suggest a formal interpretation. General logical laws are based upon form alone, independent of any consideration of content or application; by regarding a truth as analytic if it has a proof comprising only general logical laws and a limited sort of definitions, Frege has clarified and emphasized the formal aspect of Kant's distinction. It is also possible to account for some of Kant's more phenomenological remarks within the framework of Frege's interpretation. Logical proof is a matter of form, but it also seems in a certain sense to be a way of knowing—that is, a way of ascertaining the cognitive acceptability of a string of symbols. Kant's epistemological criterion of analyticity can therefore be assimilated into Frege's interpretation; the same may be true for Kant's other ways of explaining analytic judgments.

In spite of the clarity of Frege's definition of 'analytic,' and the enormous influence it continues to exert through such philosophers as Russell, Carnap, Bergmann, and Richard Martin, there are sound reasons for not accepting it as an accurate account of what Kant meant. Two of these considerations are particularly powerful. The first is that Frege's definition of 'analytic' applies paradigmatically to logical formulae and tautologies, whereas Kant, as we have seen, did not include formulae within the range of his notion and regarded tautologies as of marginal significance. The second is that no Fregean conception of the analytic can have application to discourse in a natural language without relying on definitions; whereas Kant, as is made admirably clear by Beck (1965, 61–73), held that the relation between analytic truth and definition was quite the reverse, analytic truth being more fundamental than definition and prior to it. A third point has to do with a radical divergence not in the framing of the notion of the analytic but in its application. All those who have held a Fregean conception of analyticity have held that the laws of arithmetic are analytic, and some (e.g., Bergmann) have explicitly framed their definition to be able to hold this; whereas Kant maintained that mathematics, including arithmetic, provides the clearest example of synthetic apriori truth (B14–17). A final tangential point is that Quine (1951) and White (1950) have shown the Fregean view of analytic truth to be seriously deficient, and hence it would not do justice to Kant to interpret him as having intended it. I conclude, therefore, that the admirably clear concept of analytic truth put forward by Frege and refined by his successors, according to which 'analytic' is defined in terms of general laws of logic, is radically different from Kant's,[4] and I shall say no more about it.

A phenomenological or functional interpretation of Kant's conception of the distinction between the analytic and the synthetic — in other words, an interpretation which sees the distinction as turning on the job

---

4. The same conclusion is stated more generally and more sharply by E. W. Beth: "Eine geradedazu entgengengesetzte Haltung ist kennzeichend für diejenigen Philosophen [zitiert sind Frege, Heymans, Couturat, Schlick, Carnap, von Alster, und Scholz—NG], welche Kants Lehre und namentlich sienen Ansichten über dir Grundlagen der Mathematik kritisch gegenüberstehen. Diese Denker geben Begriffsbestimmungen, welche die von Frege gegebene typische repräsentiert werden. . . . Diese Begriffsbestimmung hat jedenfalls den Vorzug der Schärfe, sie hat jedoch . . . mit Kants Absichten nichts gemein und liefert daher auch keine Grundlagen für eine Deutung and Wertung Kants Ansichten." (1953/54, 254)

done in discourse by the judgment or statement in question, or on the role played by it—must begin by taking seriously what Frege left out of account, namely, Kant's third, fourth, and sixth explanations of what an analytic judgment is. These explanations are based on phenomenological considerations and on whether the statement made is explicative or ampliative.

There lurks in the background of any attempt to work out a phenomenological or functional interpretation of the analytic one very basic and very serious question that deserves to be considered separately as a prolegomenon to study of the larger problem. That is the question, which I raised in commenting on Kant's psychological and epistemological explications of analyticity, whether what is analytic for one person may be synthetic for another, or *vice versa*. It seems clear that one person may conceive a concept in one way and a second person conceive it differently, that two people may differ as to whether the connection between a subject and a predicate is thought through identity or not, and that our phenomenological and epistemological understanding of a concept changes as we learn more. If such considerations enter into the definition of 'analytic', it thus appears that whether a proposition is analytic may well vary from person to person and from time to time. Moving our attention from the phenomenological to the functional, it is equally beyond serious doubt that whether a proposition explains a term or concept depends in part on the circumstances in which it is propounded, for what is mere explication to one person may be real news to a second person and gibberish to a third. As Wittgenstein has said, "what today counts as an observed concomitant of a phenomenon will tomorrow be used to define it" (*PI* 79). A functional interpretation also suggests, therefore, that the status of a judgment as analytic or synthetic is variable rather than fixed. I wish to examine how this suggestion fits with what Kant says, and whether such variability would impugn the concept of analyticity.

Kant himself raised this question a decade before the publication of the *Critique*:

> If one had the whole concept of which the notions of the subject and the predicate are both parts, then synthetic judgments would be changed into analytic ones. The question arises to what extent this is something arbitrary. (Reflexion 3928 = *AA* 17.350)

Unfortunately he does not give a clear answer to the question—nor, indeed, is it clear even in the *Critique* whether such fluctuation entails that there is something arbitrary about our concepts. But in spite of Kant's reticence to speak for himself, the commentators seem largely in agreement that it is important for Kant that the distinction between the analytic and the synthetic be fixed and firm. This agreement needs to be reconsidered.

Marc-Wogau (1951) argues that Kant must hold the subject of an analytic judgment to be a definable concept, on the grounds that if this were not the case he would be forced to admit that a proposition such as "Gold does not rust" is analytic for some and synthetic for others. He then points out that there is no easy escape for Kant, for empirical concepts, far from being fixed and definable, evolve and develop in the course of scientific advance. This ingenious challenge to Kant is based simply upon pointing out that the following four propositions are not a consistent set:

1. The range of the analytic-synthetic distinction includes judgments whose subject is an empirical concept such as 'gold'.
2. It is impossible that a judgment or proposition might be sometimes analytic and sometimes synthetic.
3. To avoid such fluctuation in the status of a judgment, the subject of the judgment must be a definable concept; that is, it must be possible to give a complete exposition of the concept, and to know that the exposition is complete.
4. A property that is shown to be connected with an empirical concept may subsequently be taken as a characteristic [*Merkmal*] of that very concept, and hence empirical concepts are, by their very nature, open-textured rather than definable.

Marc-Wogau believes that Kant is committed to all four of these propositions, and that his conception of an analytic judgment consequently needs careful reevaluation. I find this a very powerful challenge indeed. Let us examine the four propositions Marc-Wogau has drawn together.

Beck (1965, 61–73) insists that (3) cannot be attributed to Kant, and that to suppose that definition must be prior to analysis is to misconstrue completely the role of analytic judgments in Kant's theory of knowledge. A concept that cannot be defined may nonetheless be analyzed, and hence analytic judgment has a broader range than definition. Beck's view is clearly borne out by the texts, for Kant says that "an *empirical* concept cannot be defined at all, but only *made explicit*" (*KdrV* B755), and that in philosophy "since the definitions are analyses of given concepts, they presuppose the prior presence of the concepts although in a confused state; and the incomplete exposition [*sc.*, through analytic propositions] must precede the complete [*sc.*, through definitions]" (B758). So (3) is thoroughly un-Kantian.

The remaining set of propositions, however, is still inconsistent. For if empirical concepts evolve in the course of scientific advance, the criteria for these concepts must change, and hence there can be no test for deciding once and for all time whether a putative characteristic is really a *Merkmal* of an empirical concept. Beck recognized this, and took the rather desperate line that Kant rejected (4). Beck summarizes his understanding of Kant on this point as follows:

> A concept cannot be arbitrarily widened through the accumulation of information. It can be replaced by another called by the same name; but of any given concept it can be decided what is implicit in it to be explicated by analytic judgment and what does not lie in it at all. (1965, 83)

The idea that a concept is unchangeable is an old and familiar one. Beck adopted his version of it from C. I. Lewis, who used much the same words and who explicitly acknowledged the Platonism of the idea (1929, 268–69).

It is possible, alas, that Kant held such a view of empirical concepts. Beck cites texts in which Kant distinguishes between the *concept* of water and various *notions* of water which change over time. The suggestion is that use of concepts is restricted (at best) to science, and that most of our talk dispenses with them. Such a view would leave a large gap in any general theory of meaning, and I am therefore doubtful that the passage Beck cites gives convincing reason for attributing this view to Kant. It would in any case be difficult to reconcile this view with Kant's statement that empirical concepts are undefinable. More important, the inherent implausibility of the view stands as an obstacle to any general acknowledgement that Kant intended it. Surely the concept of water which I have after learning the chemical composition of water is not just "another called by the same name," for the "new" concept has all, or almost all, the characteristics of the "old" one and practically the same range of application. Imagine the confusion which would result if instead of arbitrarily choosing the same name I had arbitrarily chosen a different one! The very idea of "another concept called by the same name" is suspicious where the concepts have roughly the same application, and suggests an inadequate philosophy of language. To fall back on it in the present context is neither a satisfactory way to meet the challenge posed by Marc-Wogau, nor, in the absence of firm textual support, does it do justice to Kant.

Another possibility is that Kant may not have held (1). Paton suggests this interpretation (although he does not adopt it) when he says the following:

> In dealing with analytic judgments Kant is primarily concerned with those in which the subject-concept is itself *a priori*. (1936, 84)

But this suggestion would also be a desperate one. It has never, to the best of my knowledge, been seriously maintained, and it conflicts with the fact, well established by Parkinson (1960), that the Kantian distinction is meant to apply unrestrictedly to all categorical propositions.

If these considerations are sound, it remains to give up (2), that is, to acknowledge that there can be a fluctuation in the status of a judgment on the basis of the surrounding circumstances, as would be suggested by a phenomenological or a functional interpretation of Kant's doctrine. The challenge thrown out by Marc-Wogau enables us to see it as a positive asset of an interpretation based on the role or use of judgments or on their phenomenology, so far as being faithful to Kant is concerned, that this way of understanding Kant excludes having each and every categorical proposition classified definitively as either analytic or synthetic. Paton's observation that few of the propositions which interest Kant have empirical subject concepts may explain why the possibility of this fluctuation has not been more widely noticed. It is worth noting that Paton does explicitly acknowledge the possibility of such fluctuation in the case of propositions whose subject-concept is empirical:

> Is this distinction of analytic and synthetic a subjective distinction, so that what is analytic for one man would be synthetic for another? Kant's language in places might suggest that the distinction is subjective; but this, I think, is true only where the subject-concept is empirical. (1936, 83)

One might object that Paton's apparent identification of variation with subjectivity, like Beck's apparent identification of variation with arbitrariness, casts unnecessary disdain upon what is acknowledged; but the substance of Paton's comment lends support to the contention that a notion of a variable distinction between the analytic and the synthetic, which allows for a proposition to be sometimes analytic and sometimes not, conforms to what Kant said.

This conclusion constitutes a reconstruction of Kant's views rather than an interpretation of them. I rather think that Marc-Wogau is closer to a true reading of Kant when he finds an inconsistency in the whole of what Kant holds to be true. The crux of the problem concerns what to say about judgments of the form

p is analytic.

Such a judgment belongs either to logic or to philosophy, both of which disciplines Kant conceived of as forms of knowledge. If *knowledge* is what is at stake, each judgment of this form must be definitively true or false, and must be true or false in virtue of relations holding among concepts—and so holding independent of variations in empirical circumstances. By embracing a variability of the analytic, phenomenological and functional interpretations save a good deal of Kant's views but inevitably give up the view that the discipline in which the distinction between the analytic and the synthetic is discerned is itself a branch of science or a form of knowledge.

Two paths of reinterpretation therefore suggest themselves, and both have been trod. The one lies in defining analyticity in terms of how the relations of concepts is conceived, or how a statement is intended, and is exemplified in C.I. Lewis's explanation of analytic truth in terms of experiments in the mind (1946, 251 and passim). Lewis's work is familiar and commanding, and has many merits as a contemporary restatement of Kant's idea of analytic truth. It is along this line that Beck's phenomenological account runs. I wish to turn my attention to the other path, which proceeds by explaining analytic statements in terms of the role or function those statements play in discourse. Wittgenstein referred to such a distinguishable use of expressions as a 'language-game' (*PI* 23). I propose to assume that making analytic statements is one such language-game and to inquire what the characteristics of this language-game are, other than the central one that statements used in this way are explicative. I shall argue that what Kant calls an analytic judgment is generally the same thing as what Wittgenstein calls a grammatical proposition; more specifically, that analytic judgments are all grammatical propositions, but that the two notions are not identical because synthetic apriori propositions are also grammatical. Using Wittgenstein to reconstruct Kant is suggested by the fact that in an important passage where Wittgenstein introduces the idea of a grammatical proposition (*PI* 247–252), he raises a question about the standing of Kant's paradigm, that a body is extended. The deeper reasons for proposing that grammar and analyticity are closely analogous will become apparent as we consider what it means to say that analytic judgments are explicative.

4.   The Explicative Function of Analytic Statements

We can, unfortunately, get only the barest hints from Kant himself about the explicative function of analytic judgments. He says that analytic judgments may be called explicative because they "add nothing through the predicate to the concept of the subject, but merely break it up into those constituent concepts that have all along been thought in it" (*KdrV* B11), and that such judgments "are very important, and indeed necessary, but only for obtaining that clearness in the concepts which is requisite for such a sure and wide synthesis as will lead to a genuinely new addition to all previous knowledge" (B13–14). Meager though it is, we shall have to follow the lead that is given in these brief remarks. Analytic judgments serve primarily for obtaining clarity in concepts, and for this purpose Kant says that they are "very important, and indeed necessary" (B13). It seems reasonable to ask what this clarity consists in, and why and for whom it is important and necessary.

Whom might such a clarification serve, and in what circumstances? In answer to the first part of the question, Kant suggests in the first edition that "the concept which I already have is . . . made intelligible to me" (*KdrV* A8), and in connection with the second part he says that the time for analytic judgments is when we wish to prepare the way for a "genuinely new addition to all previous knowledge" (B14). Both these points deserve examination.

If I have a firm grasp on the concept 'body'—that is, if I know all the rules of language pertaining to the word 'body'—then I am in a position to know that the judgment "all bodies are extended" is analytic. Kant says that then "the concept which I already have is . . . made intelligible to me" (A8), but it is difficult to see how this could happen. If I have the concept, it must *already* be intelligible to me, and cannot be *made* intelligible by the analytic judgment. A concept can only be made intelligible to me by an analytic proposition if I have at most a vague understanding of it and am in particular uncertain about that aspect of the concept which is made explicit in the analytic proposition. But if I have such a vague and uncertain understanding of the concept, I can hardly be in a position to warrant the proffered judgment as truly analytic. Thus, on the view Kant suggests, analytic judgments are useless when they are possible and impossible when they are useful. Perhaps Kant himself saw this absurdity, for he dropped the passage at hand from the second edition of the *Critique*.

An analytic judgment which I make might conceivably be useful to me personally, but a more typical case would be one where an analytic proposition is "important and indeed necessary" to some *other* person. This might be the case where you and I are discussing a problem and it becomes clear, either through my own admission or through my making clumsy or absurd remarks, that I have at best only a vague understanding of some expression you use. You may then make one or more analytic statements in order to clarify the expression for me. It is in this manner that an analytic proposition typically serves to convey to an uncertain reader or listener the clear understanding which the writer or speaker has of a concept.

When Kant said that analytic judgments help prepare the way for "a genuinely new addition to all previous knowledge" (*KdrV* B14), he must have had a scientific context in mind; for it is only in science that we can be sure of having a genuine addition to knowledge. Analytic propositions are important and necessary in such contexts because they enable scientists to explain to one another how they understand the concepts and terms which they use. For example, one might use the sentence "An acid is a proton donor" to make an analytic statement, and thereby explain the term 'acid'—at the same time (what is the same thing) conveying that proton donation is to be regarded as an *essential* property, or *Merkmal*, of acids. There is no reason to doubt that such elucidatory remarks occur in conversations among scientists; but they must be far more important, and indeed indispensable, in the education of scientists, where young apprentices are initiated into the "language" and vocabulary of the discipline.

It cannot be, however, that only scientists take advantage of this useful device. It would have been reasonable for Kant to be thinking primarily in terms of the advance of science when he propounded the distinction between the analytic and the synthetic, since he was then writing a book on the theory of knowledge. But many categorical judgments are made outside of any scientific context, and they too must fall under Kant's distinction. I can see no reason that judgments should not be made "for obtaining that clearness in the concepts" which is requisite for an accurate moral appraisal, or a sensitive aesthetic evaluation, or a sound legal decision—in general, a reliable judgment in any walk of life. It seems likely that analytic propositions, grammatical remarks, have a special importance in moral discourse because of the common tendency to lose sight of the logic or grammar of moral concepts in the press of a difficult or dangerous predicament, as is often illustrated in the Socratic dialogues, such as the *Euthyphro* or the opening third of the *Crito*. In all these other fields of endeavor, as in science, a large part of the employ for analytic propositions will be found in explaining technicalities and subtleties of the special "language" to laymen, and in training apprentices in the "language-game" of the discipline.

These thoughts about whom an analytic judgment might serve, and in what circumstances it might do so, help to reinforce the suggestion that an analytic judgment is basically "grammatical" in Wittgenstein's sense, a suggestion that is further reinforced when we examine the character of the clarification achieved through an analytic statement.

According to Kant the proposition "All bodies are extended" is analytic. The concepts involved in this proposition are those of 'body' and 'extension', but it is clear from Kant's discussion he is primarily concerned with the concept 'body', for he refers to extension as a "character" [*Merkmal*] of the concept 'body', and he mentions in the same breath that figure and impenetrability are also characters of the concept 'body' and bear the same sort of analytic relationship to it (*KdrV* B12). In this case, therefore, it is the concept of a body which is clarified by the analytic judgment.

What is the nature of such clarification? One feature of it is that it relates the concept being clarified to another concept, namely that of being extended. Another feature is that it presents us with, or makes clear, a rule pertaining to the use of the word 'body'—namely, that if anything is to be called a 'body' it must be extended; or, that if it can be called a 'body', then it can also be called 'extended'. A third feature is that this rule about the use of the word 'body' has to do with the inference possibilities pertaining to that word, and not with its morphological and syntactic possibilities. A fourth and most important feature is that the inference possibilities presented in an analytic judgment, unlike those which may be construed in a synthetic judgment, require no justification or verification. They can neither be confirmed by experience nor deduced from primitive truths, and hence may be called 'immediate'. Kant is explicit about this last feature when he says about analytic judgments generally that "in framing the judgment I must not go outside my concept" (B11). We may then summarize briefly by saying that the clarification achieved through analytic propositions consists in presenting immediate inference possibilities pertaining to some word which expresses the concept that is being clarified.

It is worth reflecting on the fourth feature, that the analytic judgment requires no justification. If someone were to demand justification for my statement that all bodies are extended, I could only say that that is the way the word 'body' is used, or (if he still protested) that that is the sense in which I should like to use the word. Such a response does not meet the demand for justification, but rather rejects it as an illegitimate demand. This rejection is accomplished by shifting the focus of the discussion. The original judgment is (or seems to be) about bodies, whereas my response is not about bodies but about the word 'body', or the concept 'body.' But the response is an apt one, even though it does not meet the demand for justification; for it not only fails to meet the demand but also indicates why the demand for justification cannot be met. Indeed, the very fact that such a response is apt shows that, when a statement is warranted just by the way we use its constituent words (or just by what its subject concept "contains"), it is inappropriate to ask that the statement construed as a statement about bodies be justified. We may, of course, be able to give some sort of justification for the remark we make about 'body', even though we cannot do so for our statement about bodies; but even here it is important to note that we need not be able to. As Wittgenstein puts it,

> If I have exhausted the justifications I have reached bedrock, and my spade is turned. Then I am inclined to say: "This is simply what I do." (*PI* 217)
> When I obey a rule, I do not choose. I obey the rule *blindly*. (*PI* 219)

Though this is important, it should not be surprising. Since the clarification achieved by an analytic proposition consists in presenting inference rules pertaining to the concept or the term in question, it is entirely reasonable that the only warrant required for such propositions should be how the concept or word is in fact employed.

Since the analytic proposition "All bodies are extended" serves to clarify the concept 'body' by presenting a certain rule pertaining to the use of the word 'body', and since the only relevant warrant for it *qua* analytic proposition is the actual or stipulated use of the word 'body', we may say that *in this sense* this analytic proposition is not "really" about physical bodies but about the concept 'body' or the word 'body'. But there is no sharp dichotomy between judgments "about bodies themselves" and remarks about the concept 'body' or about the use of the word 'body'. A statement that is "about bodies themselves" will presumably set forth some *essential* characteristic of bodies, rather than a contingent or accidental feature. If this characteristic is really essential, there must be an associated rule pertaining to the use of the word 'body' which prohibits this characteristic being denied even implicitly of anything that is called a 'body'. If this rule were known and could be accurately stated, its statement would presumably settle the same doubts as the original statement "about bodies themselves." *"Essence",* says Wittgenstein, "is expressed by grammar" (*PI* 371), and hence facts "about bodies themselves" can be expressed in terms of the "logical grammar" of the word 'body'. But there is also the correlative point that "Grammar tells us what kind of object anything is" (*PI* 373); and hence certain "grammatical" remarks about the word 'body' can tell us something "about bodies themselves."

If analytic propositions are about words and present a certain sort lof rule pertaining to the use of those words, it is reasonable to say that an analytic proposition is a kind of grammatical remark, and that the clarification it achieves explains a part of the grammar of the language. Grammar is a descriptive discipline (*PI* 496), the aim of which is to characterize a language by stating rules for the use of various sorts of linguistic expressions, the empirical accuracy of such a description being determined by whether a person would have to follow such rules in practice to speak the language competently. In a narrow sense only rules of morphology and syntax count as rules of grammar, but in the broader sense intended here rules pertaining to phonology and to entailments and incompatibilities may be included too, since following them in practice is obviously necessary for having a command of the language. Analytic truths express rules of this last sort, as do what Wittgenstein called "grammatical" remarks. Wittgenstein can therefore be read as representing in a new way what Kant rather cryptically referred to as the explicative role of analytic judgments.

I have so far based my interpretation of Kant on the last of the six accounts of the analytic-synthetic distinction which we earlier identified, and have tried to characterize making analytic statements as a particular language-game. It is impossible to deny that Kant's remarks on this subject are thoroughly ambiguous, in that they lend themselves to alternative interpretations; and hence that Frege's formal reconstruction of what Kant meant has a certain plausibility, and so has Lewis's way of explaining analyticity. At the same time one may insist that the view that making analytic remarks constitutes a distinctive language-game is easily compatible with all that Kant has said about the analytic and the synthetic. Indeed, at least one of his accounts becomes more readily intelligible on this interpretation.

Kant gave one exposition which appeared to be psychological, in that "the connection of the subject to the predicate is thought through identity" (B10) and the predicate was "always conceived as existing within [the subject], although confusedly" (B11). The two difficulties we had with these passages were that the idioms Kant uses are unfamiliar in both German and English, and that Kant has elsewhere (for example, *KdrV* B78) insisted that empirical psychology has nothing to do with general logic. But on the view that an analytic judgment functions as a kind of grammatical remark, in that it sets forth some inference possibilities pertaining to a word or phrase, these passages cease to be embarrassing. The connection between the subject and the predicate that is under consideration is not the result of the association of ideas, nor of any other empirical law, but is rather "thought all along" in the sense that it depends upon and is required by certain rules for using the subject expression. Prior to the articulation or the acceptance of the analytic proposition, the connection may be thought "confusedly" in that the relevant rules are followed in practice without ever being formulated. Thus it is not empirical psychology which bears upon general logic, but some special sort of grammar.

Thinking along these same lines, it is easy to see that the famous containment criterion of analyticity lends itself to functional interpretation, for the predicate will be "contained in" the subject whenever it is "always conceived as existing within it" because of some rule, recognized in practice, for using the subject term. The account based on containment is one of those which has lent weight to a formal interpretation of Kant's conception of an analytic judgment, and the association of this account with those based on identity and contradiction shows that there will be no difficulty applying what we said to these accounts. Indeed, we are now able to make better sense of Kant's special and puzzling formulation of the principle of contradiction, "that no predicate contradictory of a thing can belong to it" (B190). Following out the lines of our interpretation of Kant's notion, a predicate may be said to be "contradictory of a thing" (see *KdrV* B1090–91) when it is a logical contrary or the logical contradictory of a *Merkmal* of the thing, that is, of a predicate attributed to the thing by a judgment which serves merely to clarify our concept of the thing. Since such a judgment is the very sort that Kant calls 'analytic', this special formulation of the principle of contradiction, however untidy it may be from the standpoint of modern formal logic, does appear particularly congenial to Kant's conception of analytic judgment. Kant's remaining account of analytic judgment, based on how we know, offers no special difficulties, since it merely expresses that every analytic truth is apriori.

5.   Some Consequences

It remains to inquire how an interpretation such as I have been urging affects the application of Kant's concept. I shall limit myself to four points: that a proposition can no longer be assigned a definitive status as either analytic or synthetic, that the attacks of White (1950) and Quine (1953) cannot be effective against such a conception of the analytic, that the distinction between analytic and synthetic apriori judgments does not survive this reconstruction, and that what Kant said about mathematics remains highly problematic.

Rules of language undergo change, and therefore a statement that at one time is warranted simply by virtue of rules of language may admit of empirical evidence at an earlier or a later time. There are two reasons for this. The first is that grammar differs from logic in that it is descriptive rather than normative (*PI* 81–124, 496), and hence it lacks logic's ability to guarantee in advance that there will not be changes in its inference rules. Relevant changes may be particularly apparent in the case of scientific terms, whose definitions may change in the face of increasingly sophisticated criteria; but such changes may also affect even proper names (see *PI* 79). In addition to such changes in rules of grammar, there are also (this is the second reason) variations in the assumptions and guidelines that govern different moments of discourse, and these variations are reflected in a fluctuation in what counts as explicative. A statement which is explicative to one person may be ampliative to a second and gibberish to a third. Hence the view that analytic statements are explicative or grammatical entails that analyticity is relative to certain conditions and circumstances and that there may be a fluctuation between the analytic and the synthetic.

A conception of the analytic which makes analyticity relative and variable helps to stem the attacks of White and Quine on the analytic/synthetic distinction, but White (1950) argues against a variable distinction as well as a static one. Immunity from their attacks depends rather on the fact that analytic statements, as I have explained them, are *not truth-claims at all;* they are explications. Kant admits that they are not knowledge-claims when he says that they are explicative rather than ampliative; what I have added is that they are not truth-claims either. What White and Quine attack is the thesis that there is a fundamental cleavage in the realm of truth-claims rather than a cleavage between truth-claims and explicative remarks. Quine, for example, says that what he rejects is "a belief in some fundamental cleavage between truths which are *analytic,* or grounded in meanings independently of matters of fact, and truths which are *synthetic,* or grounded in fact" (1953, 20). But what Kant was proposing, if I am right, was not a "fundamental distinction between truths." It was a distinction relative to context rather than an absolute one, and one between language-games rather than truths. The shoe, therefore, does not fit—and the reading I have given to Kant in fact seems quite congenial to the pragmatism Quine espouses in his essay. Similarly, White's attack is against a "dualism" in the realm of truths, and no such dualism follows from Kant's doctrine if we interpret him as distinguishing two roles which statements can play in discourse and reasoning.

Distinguishing the analytic/synthetic distinction from the apriori/empirical distinction was one of Kant's most dramatic innovations. His version of critical philosophy depends on it, for philosophy, in Kant's view, needs to be both synthetic and apriori. If it is not synthetic, it will not constitute genuine knowledge, and will no longer be fit to be the queen of the sciences; and if it is not apriori, it will be forever dependent on new discoveries, and will be a result rather than a foundation of the empirical sciences. Descartes and the Rationalists rightly saw that philosophy cannot be empirical, that it has to be apriori; Hume and the Empiricists rightly saw that philosophy cannot be analytic, that it has to be synthetic. No one prior to Kant—so Kant, with considerable plausibility, claims—had seen how it was possible for philosophy, or any science, to be both synthetic and apriori. It is this imposing worldview that needs to be abandoned to accommodate the functional interpretation of the analytic.

The concepts at issue here involve matters of form, of function, and of warrant. By stressing these different dimensions differently, Kant ingeniously arranged for the two distinctions. If analyticity is like grammar, there is no longer this multiplicity of dimensions at our disposal. Grammatical explanations can take any form you like, even the nonverbal form of pointing (in the right circumstances, following the right question) to an object or a state of affairs. And neither knowledge nor proof has any place in the course of it, since it is uptake (grasping the use of the expression) rather than truth that is at stake. Out of the original trinity, therefore, we are left with function. Grammatical propositions are supposed to remove perplexities or confusions by describing or explaining uses of language. Sometimes that will be accomplished by what Kant thought of as a synthetic apriori proposition, such as "Every rod has a length" or "Every event has a cause." If such an expression has the effect of reorienting someone in the course of a discussion or dialogue, then it is serving the same function as a lexical definition, in spite of its *looking* like a very different sort of proposition.

This, too, even though it involves a severe wrench from Kant's most cherished conceptions, may prove to be a boon to Kantian critical philosophy, as I explained more fully in chapter one. Critical philosophy must be self-referential, as Bubner (1974, 1975) has pointed out. This is best achieved by aligning philosophical criticism with some established or familiar discipline. Kant tried to do this by arguing that synthetic apriori judgments are familiar in mathematics and physics, but the argument has not withstood the test of time. With grammar there is no such problem. If making grammatical remarks is a familiar use of language, as it surely is, then there is no problem whatever in seeing that there must be a grammar for this use of language just as for the others. Nor need there be anything synthetic apriori about this self-referential grammar. Abandoning Kant's commitment to the synthetic apriori enables us to strengthen the critical philosophy to which he gave such a historic impetus.

There remains the matter of mathematics. Kant discusses the importance for his own philosophy of his distinction between analytic and synthetic judgment in *Fortschritte,* where he says that it constitutes the first step forward in metaphysics since the time of Leibniz and Wolff (20:265 = R 23). Its importance lay in the fact that it permitted Kant to ask for the first time how there can be synthetic apriori judgments, which question led to Kant's transcendental philosophy (20:265f., 323 = R 22ff., 177f.). Mathematics provided Kant the most obvious case of synthetic apriori knowledge (B14–17), and it seems reasonable, therefore, that an account of analytic judgments which claims faithfulness to Kant should preserve Kant's findings that all mathematical judgments are synthetic. Beth (1953/54) has noted that a Fregean conception of the analytic is invariably associated with the thesis that arithmetic is analytic, and in this way departs radically from Kant on a crucial point.[5] My functional account of the analytic, on the other hand, preserves some of the plausibility of Kant's insistence that mathematics is synthetic; but too many issues are interrelated to allow Kant to be wholly vindicated.

In mathematics, as in any other discipline, there is a difference between definitions and explicative remarks on the one hand and axioms and results on the other—and this is true not only in arithmetic and geometry but in newer forms of algebra such as mathematical logic. Analytic propositions occur in mathematics, for it is necessary to clarify concepts and explain operations, and to do so carefully and exactly, if these concepts and operations are to be employed in investigating mathematical problems. But mathematical judgments themselves seem, on a functional account, synthetic rather than analytic; at any rate they seem ampliative (within mathematics) rather than explicative. They report results that are obtained by using mathematical concepts and operations. If a mathematician has understood the problem or question he has posed himself, he is not in need of any further clarifications or explicative remarks. What he is looking for is not an explanation of the question but an answer to the question. This is a very simple and obvious fact about mathematical research, and one that is independent of the question whether anything other than general logical laws are needed to prove mathematical truths. If, therefore, Kant intended his distinction between analytic and synthetic judgments to be based on the function or role a judgment serves in a conversation or in the course of an investigation, he had a plausible justification for asserting that mathematical judgments are synthetic.[6]

Kant, however, meant to be presenting a general philosophy rather than a narrow philosophy of mathematics. We must therefore inquire what the role or function of mathematics is with respect to the wider

---

5. In Frege's case we may note a suspicion that his difference with Kant may have been more terminological than substantive:

> [T]he more fruitful type of definition is a matter of drawing boundary lines that were not previously given at all. What we shall be able to infer from it, cannot be inspected in advance; here we are not simply taking out of the box what we have put into it. The conclusions we draw from it extend our knowledge, and ought, therefore, on Kant's view, to be synthetic; and yet they can be proved by purely logical means, and are thus analytic. (1950, 100–101)

6. Compare Hintikka (1965) and Stenius (1965), who both argue on grounds different from mine that arithmetic and numerical truths are synthetic in some sense, and both defend Kant's intuitions on this point.

search for knowledge and truth. In this wider context the matter is no longer so clear. Our scientific and everyday inquiry seeks ways for us to accommodate to the world around us, by learning about that world. Within this wider search mathematics has an indirect role to play. Neither arithmetic nor geometry tells us anything directly about the world—not about either physics or chemistry, nor about either geography or the weather. Mathematics instead provides structures for the special disciplines, so that scientists and laypeople can reason more effectively and move more easily from fact to hypothesis. It provides, as David Hawkins (1964) has said, the "language of nature." Unlike science, however, language is characterized by grammar rather than truth. From this wider perspective, therefore, mathematics does not appear as genuinely synthetic as Kant claimed. Taking both perspectives into account, the question whether mathematics is analytic or synthetic is exceedingly complex, and I doubt that any conception of analyticity will suffice to either vindicate or refute Kant decisively.

Some sort of functional interpretation of Kant's distinction thus appears to be viable. The crux of such a view is that the distinction to be drawn is between different ways in which statements or propositions function in discourse, rather than between different logical forms which propositions may exemplify; and that the function of an analytic judgment is to explicate its subject concept by presenting certain linguistic rules. A major difficulty for traditional Kantian philosophy— though a blessing in the eyes of some of his followers—is that synthetic apriori judgments appear to function in very much the same way. Because of their function, analytic propositions might be called 'grammatical,' although there may be some stretching of the term in doing so. According to this interpretation of Kant's famous distinction, the criterion of analyticity lies in the way in which the judgment is related to the human beings who make it, or who may make it. More specifically, what an analytic remark does is to clarify a concept by presenting immediate inference possibilities pertaining to some word or phrase which expresses the concept that is being clarified. Because analytic statements present rules governing uses of words and phrases, they are a matter of grammar, and they are equally about words and about things themselves. Although much remains to be clarified about the nature of grammar and of rules of language, to look upon making analytic statements as part of a distinctive language-game, and upon analytic and synthetic apriori statements as different from empirical or scientific statements in the same way that explications differ from truth-claims, helps to appreciate the soundness of some of Kant's puzzling or unappreciated remarks, though other familiar and distinctive features of his philosophy are jeopardized by this reading. There certainly are other concepts of analyticity than Kant's, but his is more relevant to contemporary discussions than one might have thought.

3

Schemata and Criteria

*Images are valuable aids to thought;
we study what is higher first 'in
images'. . . . Our ability to use visual
structure to understand nonvisual
structures . . . is fundamental to explanation in any field.*

—Iris Murdoch

1. Outline of the Issues

In this chapter I wish to sketch explicitly an important detail of the
parallel between Kant and Wittgenstein, namely that one needs more
than rules to master the use of concepts or the use of language. I shall
first give a summary sketch of the argument, and then consider
exegetical details, which are admittedly formidable.

Kant and Wittgenstein are both critical philosophers. Both disparage
speculative philosophy, and in particular both criticize certain contemporary philosophical disputes as in some way absurd. For both the
absurdity arises because of a misuse of words or concepts, and their
diagnoses are similar. Both hold that certain empirical conditions or
presuppositions are required for the felicitous employment of words or
concepts, and that the relevant conditions or presuppositions are
ignored by participants in speculative disputes. These conditions or
presuppositions are either rules for the employment or application of
words or concepts, or paradigms (exemplars) that contain or imply such
rules. Kant and Wittgenstein recognize that these rules differ radically
from the logical or semantic rules for words and concepts, that is, from
the rules which warrant ordinary inferences. Indeed, it is precisely to
impugn speculation based on such formal rules alone that Kant and
Wittgenstein invoke these other rules for the employment or application
of words and concepts: if we do not heed the conditions for the
employment of words or concepts, our reasoning may lead us to "a wheel
that can be turned though nothing else moves with it" (*PI* 271); or to

the "pure employment of reason," when, "in defiance of all the warning of criticism, it carries us altogether beyond the empirical employment of the categories" into "transcendental illusion" (*KdrV* B362, 352). It is schemata (Kant) or criteria (Wittgenstein) that invoke and specify these critical restraints. Both Kant and Wittgenstein regard these restraints (schemata/criteria) as involving phenomena (such as intentions and circumstances), rather than as semantic or logical or conceptual. But they must be very special phenomena, not the sort we ordinarily talk about, because of their role in determining the use of words or concepts. Clearly schemata and criteria are not only a bit mysterious and portentous, but they also have much in common in the service that they perform for Kant and Wittgenstein.

This brief sketch needs to be developed in greater detail, on both the Kantian side and the Wittgensteinian side, since 'schemata' and 'criteria' are concepts which have perplexed commentators and about which there is no settled reading. In order to maintain that there is a strong parallel between Kant and Wittgenstein in this matter, it is necessary to enter into exegetical disputes and to take sides in them. Even so the issues cannot be resolved in this chapter, and will come again in various forms throughout the chapters in part three.

2.   The Puzzling Relation of Schemata to Concepts

Let us first consider the case of Kant. One of the striking and puzzling features of his discussion of schemata is that he does not place it in Book I of "The Transcendental Analytic," which is called "Analytic of Concepts," where he explains the concepts and categories of the understanding, but at the beginning of Book II, "Analytic of Principles," which has to do with the use of concepts rather than with their constitution. The puzzle is that if concepts are adequately explicated by their definition, their analysis, and their relation to categories—all of which are set out in Book I—then why is it necessary to insist that they require schemata for their employment? And conversely, if schemata are necessary for their (felicitous) employment, how can it be thought that categories and definitions can give us the whole meaning of concepts?

One of the most effective presentations of this line of critical perplexity is to be found in Warnock's article in *Analysis* in 1949. Warnock asks whether one could be said to "have a concept" if one exhibited an inability to employ the concept in standard instances. He admits that we do not often speak of "having the concept of *X*," but he uses examples to argue that if it means anything, then I cannot be said to have the concept of '*X*' if I cannot use the word '*X*' in standard cases. For example, if a child calls his schoolmates 'blood relatives' but hesitates whether his sister is a "blood relative," we must conclude that he does not have the concept yet. If the child then proceeds to give a perfectly adequate verbal definition of 'blood relative,' we may wonder at his ability, but would be reluctant to count the definition as overriding the pragmatic evidence against his having the concept. Warnock's position, generalizing from this example, is uncompromising: "[I]f I cannot apply a concept then I have not got it. . . . [T]o ask how I can apply a concept that I have is to ask how I can use a word that I know how to use. And this is a silly question, brought on by illegitimately separating the application of concepts from having them" (1949, 80). Warnock rightly takes this line of argument to count against Kant's separation of questions of the employment of concepts from questions of their constitution and definition.

It might also be said that Warnock's argument, although it appeared prior to the publication of the *PI*, is highly Wittgensteinian in its identification of meaning and use. Wittgenstein's work is so wholly unlike that of Kant in style and organization that comparisons are difficult. If we take criteria to govern the application of concepts—say, in truth-claiming predications, or (more narrowly) in knowledge-claims—and if we take concepts to be determined by their "place in grammar" or their "use in the language," we can then ask how the specification or invocation of criteria is related to grammar in general. The answer must be that the criterion for an expression is part of its grammar, as Wittgenstein repeatedly indicated (*BB* 24, 56–57, 63–64; *PI* 182, 251–53, 572). So it looks as though Wittgenstein might join Warnock in criticizing the appeal to schemata as redundant and misleading.

This is not wholly right, for reasons that are sketched in the section that follows and explained more fully in chapters seven and fourteen; but one thing does seem right about it. For Wittgenstein every statement explaining or specifying the criterion for something must be a grammatical proposition (what Kant would call an 'analytic judgment'), whereas for Kant the status of a proposition setting forth the schema for a concept is highly problematic. It seems *not* to be analytic, since the schema for a concept, not being a concept or *Merkmal* at all, is not something which is contained within the concept, as a predicate may be; but it does not seem to be synthetic either, since it merely explicates the use of the concept and does not set forth any genuine knowledge. It really does seem to be a criticism of Kant's conception of schemata, in relation to his other leading ideas, that there is no satisfactory answer to the question whether the propositions setting forth the schemata of concepts would be analytic or synthetic.

3. The Subtle Distinction between the Use and Employment of Words

But however sound the criticism of Kant's radical separation of concepts from their use, it remains unsatisfactory to identify the meaning of a word with its employment or with its applications to phenomena. The word 'ghost' has a perfectly clear meaning even though there is nothing I can truly apply it to and no criteria which can be presented in an ostensive explication of it. Such a simple example, however, immediately reminds us that Wittgenstein did not identify the meaning of a word with its actual employment, its *Anwendung,* but with its *Gebrauch in der Sprache.* Wittgenstein's position therefore is somewhat problematic: its interpretation, saved from a simplistic error by a distinction between use (*Gebrauch*) and employment (*Anwendung, Verwendung*), will depend on how we understand the relation of use and employment and on what we understand criteria to be.

With regard to the relation of use and employment Wittgenstein's texts are obscure. A distinction between the two is observed but not heralded. In the first sections of *PI,* leading up to the remark in *PI* 23 about the countless ways in which we use words and sentences, what is at stake is the employment of expressions in concrete circumstances, that is, to the phenomena of life, so as to distinguish and identify such human activities as giving orders, making reports, judging, joking, and so forth. Some sections later, in *PI* 43, Wittgenstein gives his famous definition of the meaning of a word as its use in the language. It is clear that this definition is not a continued elaboration of the same doctrine set out in the first sections. This can be seen decisively by considering that the definition of *PI* 43 does not work at all for sentences or whole utterances. Wittgenstein does not speak of the meaning (*Bedeutung*) of a sentence at all; but if we were to do so, such meaning would be determined by the meanings of its component words and structures. Unlike a word, a sentence does not normally have a "use in the language." Also unlike a word, a sentence normally can be *employed* in certain circumstances and/or as part of certain activities. As Ryle once put it (adapting the famous distinction of Saussure's between *langue* and *parole*), words are the atoms of Language, sentences the units of Speech (1971, 2:408). This distinction is clearly respected in the *PI*, although Wittgenstein does not explicitly call attention to it.

A positive account of the relation of employment and use is more difficult to tease out of Wittgenstein's text. The best clue is that Wittgenstein begins with a discussion of the employment of expressions as part of an activity, and hence may believe that the meanings of words must be derived from the sense utterances have in their pragmatic employment.[1] Such an understanding of Wittgenstein's view fits with what he says about "Hand me a slab" in *PI* 19–20, and perhaps also with the *Tractatus* view that a name has meaning only in the context of a sentence (*TLP* 3.3). But this evidence is too thin to warrant the conclusion that Wittgenstein must reject the commonsense view that learning vocabulary and syntax is separate from—or at least separable from—learning the countless ways in which we make use of words and sentences.

Criteria have been at least as difficult for exegesis as uses. It is clear, however, that they cause some embarrassment for the preceding discussion, for they must *both* have to do with the application of words to phenomena *and* also be intrinsically connected with the meaning of the words. This double aspect of criteria threatens the distinction we have just made, and lends a certain plausibility to regarding Warnock's remarks as Wittgensteinian. Here, just as we earlier found Kant's position somewhat confusing for making a distinction between a concept and its schema, we find Wittgenstein's position confusing because of the absence of a clear distinction between the meanings of a word and the criteria for its application. Let us try to sort this out.

Criteria, as Cavell says, (1979, chs. 1 and 2) are standards of judgment. That is to say, they do not govern every sort of employment of words and sentences but specifically govern their use to make truth-claims. What the specification of a criterion does in such a case is to show what would count as evidence for or against the claim. Hence there are many utterances for which we neither have nor need criteria:

---

1. It becomes more difficult when one considers other texts as well, as Mason (1978) has done. In *On Certainty* 59–65 Wittgenstein talks about meanings of words, apparently having in mind tricky words such as 'know'. He suggests comparing the meaning of a word with the function of an official. He then remarks, "When the language-games change, the concepts change, and with the concepts the meanings of the words change" (65, translation modified). Mason spells out with unrelenting perspicuity the havoc this plays with *PI* 43. I discuss the issues further in chapter 12.

metaphors, jokes, avowals, greetings, and all other utterances such that neither the utterance nor a response to it depends on evidence. But since they are standards for judging, criteria do not—as Cavell points out against Malcolm and Albritton—determine the certainty of truth-claims. They determine instead the application of concepts or words used in making truth-claims, and this determination is a matter of grammar rather than judgment or knowledge. Hence asking for the criterion for something is always a grammatical rather than an empirical inquiry, and specifying the criterion for something is always a grammatical remark rather than a truth-claim.

It seems, then, that Wittgenstein can assign a clearer status to sentences describing criteria than Kant can to judgments describing schemata, but that this achievement is tarnished by a vagueness about the meaning of a word. In particular it is unclear whether the criteria for the use of 'X' in judgments and the explanation of 'X' in accordance with *PI* 43 are two aspects of the grammar of 'X', or whether the former is meant to be contained in or entailed by the latter. Certainly the difficulty of reading Wittgenstein on this matter means that we ought not to take Warnock's remarks against Kant, which identify meaning and application in judgment, as wholly Wittgensteinian. Walker is right to insist that one can distinguish between the verbal definition of a word or concept and criteria for recognizing instances of it, (1978, 90) even though it is obscure whether the distinction is between *Gebrauch* and *Anwendung* or between two aspects of *Gebrauch in der Sprache*.

We arrive, therefore, at five points, each of which is at considerable odds with common understanding, either of the issues or of the relation between Kant and Wittgenstein on them:

1. There really is a problem to be addressed. Knowing how to apply concepts or words in concrete circumstances is different from the logical or semantic knowledge of the place (or relations) of a word or concept within a system of words or concepts. The former can be developed without the latter, or the latter without the former, although it is only their combination that ensures a mastery of language or of making judgments.

2. Kant's work is more perspicuous than Wittgenstein's in recognizing the distinction of the pragmatic from the semantic component of words and concepts.

3. Wittgenstein's work is more perspicuous than Kant's in recognizing that our ability to apply concepts and words is an aspect of our

mastery of them, not something added to our mastery of concepts or words.

4. There are striking differences between Kant and Wittgenstein in terminology, but when these are discounted it is difficult to discern any differences of doctrine.

5. The recognition of schemata or criteria as an essential component or presupposition of making judgments is crucial to a project common to Kant and Wittgenstein, namely, the establishment of critical philosophy.

4. Schemata/Criteria and Understanding

In the years since this chapter was first written, one of the most interesting contributions to the issues considered here has been that of Hubert Schwyzer in his brilliant essay, *The Unity of Understanding, A Study of Kantian Problems*. Schwyzer does not set out to compare Kant and Wittgenstein. His book is rather, as the title indicates, a study of what understanding (*Verstehen*) is in Kant's *Critique of Pure Reason*. The result, however, is significant illumination of the overall context in which discussion of schemata is important.

In his book on Wittgenstein's later philosophy (1977), Roy Finch remarks that Wittgenstein successfully completes the overthrow of Cartesianism that Kant began; but he does not show in detail what Kant's shortcomings were nor exactly how Wittgenstein's work succeeds in overcoming them. Schwyzer's book is rather the obverse of this: it shows what the deficiences are in Kant's account of the understanding and how Wittgenstein's later work overcomes the gaps in Kant's premises and presentations, but without making any historic claims for Wittgenstein.

The scholarly quality of the essay is impressive. Schwyzer's reading of Kant differs from those of Bennett, Strawson, Stroud, Guyer, and others, and he reports and analyzes their views judiciously. There is never a survey of the literature; indeed, in the critical sixth chapter, which discusses consciousness as rule governed and therefore engages, implicitly, the vast literature about Wittgenstein on privacy, there is only one parenthetical reference to Kripke. Instead Schwyzer makes use of these other authors when it is essential for his argument that a common misreading of Kant be refuted. He cites Bennett and Strawson in this manner in the second and third chapters, Stroud in the fourth, and

Guyer in the fifth. With Bennett and Guyer he engages in extensive discourse, quoting them generously and confronting their readings of Kant at length. He is so forthright, so respectful, and so focused on his central theme in these confrontations that I would expect Bennett and Guyer to feel more honored than abused by his treatment of them. Schwyzer's style is elegant throughout. Not only does he take great pain to explain clearly what Kant means, he also articulates in relatively simple terms, employing a minimum of jargon, what the difficulties are that must be faced in the next stage of the essay.

The book is an attempt to get clear about the philosophical aims and convictions that are embedded in Kant's account of the nature of human understanding, and about the problems that it is designed to solve. Schwyzer finds these to be genuine problems, and Kant's account attractive; but "Kant's theory, as it stands, does not and cannot succeed in solving these problems" (1990, 1). The second chapter discusses the "Schematism," which is Kant's account of how concepts of objects are possible. Schwyzer insists on distinguishing this question from the question how functions of unity are possible, and he therefore (unlike Strawson 1966, Bennett 1966, Warnock 1949, and others) sees the "Schematism" as addressing a genuine and important problem, one that is connected with Kant's distinction (also disdained by the same scholars) between understanding and judgment. Here and in the next chapter he argues (against Bennett) that the understanding has dual complementary aspects, a "vertical" dimension realized in the recognition of objects and a "horizontal" dimension realized in the coherence and intelligibility of thoughts; and he finds that Kant fails to unify his accounts of these two dimensions.

Schwyzer focuses on three questions about the understanding: how and why the categories are (and must be) derived without any empirical input; how these nonempirical categories nonetheless apply to empirical objects; and how and why the categories are essential to self-consciousness. Readers will recognize that these are problems Kant discusses in the "Clue to the Discovery of all Pure Concepts of the Understanding," in the "Schematism," and in the "Transcendental Deduction," respectively. Each of Kant's discussions claims that these pure concepts are essential to some aspect of what is generally (not just by Kant) called 'understanding': coherence and communicability of thoughts, objective thinking, and consciousness of oneself as communicating coherently and objectively. At each crucial juncture in his essay

Schwyzer argues in detail against those who claim that these are not real problems. He restates the problems and shows how they are present for anyone who looks closely at the matter, just as Kant said they were, in spite of Kant's sometimes misleading way of formulating them.

But Schwyzer argues that Kant fails to demonstrate a unity in the understanding. That is to say, he fails to show that these three essential accounts of functions of the understanding are accounts of one and the same thing. The three sections of the *Critique* remain three separate accounts of the categories rather than three aspects of one unified account. One aspect of Kant's failure, for example, is that Kant's account cannot overcome the problem of privacy: it claims but does not *show* that there cannot be self-consciousness without the capacity to communicate what one is conscious of.

The fourth chapter discusses the "Transcendental Deduction," where Schwyzer again finds that Kant's text addresses a real rather than a spurious problem. He takes up the problem in the long fifth chapter, "Sentience, Apperception, and Language." One large barrier to reading Kant right on these matters is the conception (most recently argued by Guyer 1987) that Kant holds all consciousness to be self-consciousness. Schwyzer very carefully and convincingly refutes this reading, leaving Kant with a much more plausible view about the three functions of pure concepts. It is nonetheless an unsatisfactory view, because of a rather too Cartesian flavor to Kant's conception of following rules, the topic taken up in the long sixth chapter.

Kant rightly conceives understanding to be both spontaneous (that concepts cannot be generated through confrontation with what is given) and rule governed. The problem is how to understand what exactly rules are, especially in their relation to consciousness—whether they are embedded in theory or embedded in practice. Kant holds that all consciousness, since it conforms to the categories, involves following rules. He requires, however, that the rules (categories) be "in the understanding" without being objects of consciousness (for they would then require further categories to conform to); and this seems a contradiction. Schwyzer, following Wittgenstein, argues that the only way out of the difficulty is to view following rules as ineluctably and irreducibly practical; that is, as being first and foremost a matter of action (how to do things) rather than intellect (how to think about things). Once again we see the centrality of the remark Wittgenstein quotes from Goethe, "Im Anfang war die Tat." In this case the focus on *doing* as primary gives Schwyzer the basis for constructing a unified account of the three essential aspects of the understanding identified by Kant.

The key to Schwyzer's solution of the Kantian problem is to argue that the three aspects of understanding are all abstractions from the mastery of the use of language. The discursive dimension is assured because language is social, as is each instance of the learning of a language, and being able to speak intelligibly serves as a criterion to one's instructors and trainers of whether one has learned correctly. Much the same can be said for the objective dimension. The skill in question is learned in natural contexts where real things are at hand, and therefore discursive competence—at least at the elementary levels of language use—is inconceivable unless the criteria (schemata) for concepts are satisfied. It may well be, in spite of the arguments of Warnock and others, that a person could discourse competently about this or that without being able to recognize certain particular instances of it. (This happens all the time with things like violence and injustice, and less frequently with things like elm trees and poison ivy.) As for apperception, it hardly makes sense to suppose that one could discourse competently about something without knowing who was talking, and in that sense self-consciousness is also an implicit dimension of linguistic competence, or of mastery of the use of a language (*PI* p. 174). This Wittgensteinian solution of the problem revolves around an important contrast between Kant and Wittgenstein, but leaves intact the parallel between schemata and criteria.

4

From Categories to Language-Games

1. The Puzzling Character of Aristotle's Categories

Aristotle's *Categories* is an anomalous work. Anyone who wishes to systematize or categorize our thinking about thinking must puzzle about where to put the straightforward and seemingly unobjectionable remarks Aristotle makes, and what to make of his leaving them so obviously incomplete. His students and editors (and perhaps he himself) put them at the beginning of his *Organon*. That is of course the right place, except that putting them there answers none of the questions. In particular it leaves us just as perplexed about what *kind* of activity it is to distinguish categories, whether it is an activity that belongs to metaphysics or to linguistics, and in either case how it relates to the more familiar linguistic domains of grammar, logic, and rhetoric. Perhaps we shall never be able to answer the latter question without revising simplistic conceptions about dichotomies among those traditional domains, but we certainly need to ask the question. In what follows I shall spell out reasons for thinking that Wittgenstein follows more closely in Aristotle's footsteps than Kant, and that Wittgenstein's language-games can profitably be seen as a generalization of what Aristotle was doing in the *Categories*.

If Aristotle's *Categories* provides a classification of things and not of sayings, as is traditionally insisted, the things classified are at any rate "things that are said" (1a16). The *Categories* may therefore be regarded as presenting in rudimentary form results that might possibly be appropriately and more completely formulated in terms of current methods of linguistic or grammatical analysis, applied to a level of language or discourse that linguists and grammarians usually ignore. While Aristotle's methods for making his distinctions should not seem strange to a contemporary linguist, linguists do not in fact bother with the distinctions he was making. In that respect—and as traditional metaphysicians would certainly insist—he, like Wittgenstein, was applying the concept and method of linguistic description beyond its normal range, thus "making things belong to grammar which are not commonly supposed to belong to it" (*M* 276).

Both the name 'categories', which signifies predications or sayings, and the position of the work at the beginning of the *Organon,* which deals with matters of logic and language, reinforce a temptation to interpret the *Categories* linguistically. Although neither the title nor the position of the work in the corpus is directly due to Aristotle, they do show that the inclination to treat the *Categories* as at least partially linguistic goes back to the very earliest tradition of Aristotelian scholarship. This observation need not trouble philosophers. The determination that the categories can be given a linguistic interpretation—even the conclusion that they are linguistic, Ackrill (1963, 71) and Benveniste (1971, ch. 6) notwithstanding—would not suffice to show that they are not also (in some sense) metaphysical, nor that they are not universal.

2.   A Linguistic Interpretation of Categories

The most useful linguistic method to employ in this inquiry is distinctive feature analysis,[1] which has been used in several kinds of linguistic analysis. Passages in the *Categories* can be interpreted as employing a related method, if not an early version of the method itself.

This method is based on a complex presupposition: that nothing is linguistically significant (or real) unless it contrasts with something else, that what it contrasts with is an alternative possibility within a systematic array of possibilities, and that the possible alternatives are determined by binary (sometimes ternary, positive/negative/neutral; or at any rate finitary) alternation along a finite number of dimensions, called 'fea-

---

1. This method of analysis is due to Roman Jakobson more than anyone else. For an account of the method and its uses, see Jakobson, Fant, and Halle (1952); Chomsky and Halle (1968); or Householder (1971). Most recent linguistics textbooks have a discussion of features. It should be noted that in the standard versions the oppositions mentioned later in this chapter are always binary, with one of the binary pair being "marked" and the other "unmarked," the marked member being dominant. The idea that basic ideas always involve binary oppositions with one of the pair being dominant has been taken over into social criticism in structuralist and deconstructionist thought. This seems to me very heavy handed indeed. In what follows I have loosened the requirement that the oppositions be binary.

tures'. It is unlikely that all types of phenomena admit of a fruitful distinctive feature analysis. The method does not, for example, seem fruitfully applicable either to mechanics or to formal logic. Admitting of a distinctive feature analysis may be a distinctive feature of some types of linguistic phenomena.

In phonology there are, theoretically, a finite number of articulatory and acoustic dimensions along which spoken sound can vary. In the phonemic analysis of a given language, each phonological dimension is either relevant or irrelevant for the identification of given phonemes, and the relevant dimensions, or features, are either positive or negative. Phonemes can then be regarded as bundles (that is, simultaneous collocations) of distinctive features. The English phoneme /p/, for example, can be described as the simultaneous presence of one set of phonetic features (the positive ones) and absence of another set (the negative ones), with the remaining phonetic features (e.g., strident/ mellow) being nondistinctive or irrelevant. In semantic theory lexical meanings can analogously, though somewhat more precariously, be regarded as bundles of abstract semantic markers. J. J. Katz (1966) has been especially impressive in developing semantics from this perspective.

3. Categories Are Not a Matter of Semantics

Aristotle does not define the categories, but he is careful to say what is distinctive about each. Some features, such as contrariety and whether a predication in the category "admits of a more and a less," are specified either positively or negatively for each category. There seems to be no difficulty in regarding each of the categories as a bundle of features (some positive and some negative, as in the case of phonemes). What sort of thing the categories are would then depend principally on what sort of features occur in the bundles.

Aristotle's categories are derived from predication: they are the kinds or species of the values of the variables in the form "X is predicated of some a." This is not to say that every member of each category can be predicated of something, but only that it must be distinctively involved in such predication and that it is what it is because of this distinct sort of involvement. A 'this', for example, cannot be predicated of anything, but it may be the subject of a predication, either as a substance or as something inhering in a substance.

Katz (1966, 224–39) has suggested that Aristotle's categories be interpreted as abstract semantic markers which (1) are entailed by other semantic markers and (2) do not themselves entail other semantic markers. Even leaving aside epistemological questions that arise about the entailments between semantic markers, Katz's suggestion is implausible. His account does not fit what Aristotle listed as categories, for 'being-in-a-position' does seem to entail other markers, and 'when' and 'where' do not seem to enter into entailment patterns; it gives no place to the features that Aristotle singled out as distinctive, such as contrariety and whether the predicate admits of a more and a less; and it presupposes a full-blown logical apparatus instead of providing a basis for it. Since it is difficult to imagine a more sophisticated and detailed elaboration of this proposal than Katz has provided, it is reasonable to conclude that Aristotle's categories are not semantic categories.

4. Predication as a Speech-Act or Language-Game

Predication, or making truth-claims, is a genus of speech acts (language-games). Aristotle assumes it can be distinguished from other sorts, such as inferring, praying, commanding, imploring, promising, reciting poetry, and so on. Viewed linguistically, therefore, Aristotle's *Categories* form (in Searle's terms) a small subsection in the general theory of speech acts or (in Wittgenstein's terms) a partial description of a limited range of language-games.

It is certain that predication is more basic than some other sorts of language acts (such as inferring, which clearly presupposes predication), and there are considerations both from generative grammar and from common sense which suggest (falsely[2]) that it may be the most basic sort of speech act. What should be granted is that predication is basic to science and other truth-seeking linguistic activities, which no doubt accounts for the prominence Aristotle gave this use of language over the others he recognized. But from a linguistic point of view the very idea of

---

2. The background supporting this negative judgment includes Malinowski's insistence on the primacy of phatic communion, in the appendix to Ogden and Richards; Husserl's emphasis on the primacy of prepredicative judgments in *Formal and Transcendental Logic;* and Wittgenstein's introduction of language-games that involve no predication, in the early sections of the *Philosophical Investigations.*

some use of language being basic or foundational is suspect, since its significance as a particular use of language would depend on its having been recognized or identified initially as one kind of speech-act among many. Speech acts are distinguished from one another by two sorts of criteria, the circumstances in which they are appropriate and the sort of questions and comments that can be made in response to them.[3] I will call them both "discourse features," the first having to do with "discourse conditions" and the second with "discourse possibilities." The discourse features that Aristotle cites to distinguish the categories belong mainly to the second group.

Ackrill points out (p. 79) that "one way in which he [Aristotle] reached categorical classification was by observing that different types of answers are appropriate to different questions." This is true, and useful for seeing the overall design of the *Categories*. But the distinctive features that Aristotle cites are often based on the reverse insight, that different questions are appropriate to different sorts of predication. It may be useful to look at some examples: (1) "Substance, it seems, does not admit of a more and a less" (3b33). Suppose X is predicated of some a (someone says, "a is X"). It goes hand in hand with X being in the category of substance that no question can be raised whether a is more X than b or less X than a was yesterday. If the question could be raised, the predicate would belong to some other category, where this feature is positive or neutral rather than negative. If someone says, "a is more a man than b," the presence of the word 'more' shows the predication to be qualitative rather than substantial, even though 'man' normally signifies a substance. (2) A substantial predication involves not only *predicating* X of a but also *saying* X of a. The latter (but not the former) carries with it a commitment to predicate the definition of X of a; that is, both the genus of X and the differentia of X are also implicitly predicated of a, when X is *said* of a. This obviously shapes the subsequent discourse possibilities. For example, I can attack a substantial predication by contending that the definition of the predicate does not apply to the subject; but I could not attack a qualitative or quantitative predication in this manner. And conversely, the discourse possibilities determine the category; for if I can impugn a predication by charging that the definition of the predicate does not apply to the subject, then the predication must have been substantial rather than

---

3. This characterization holds for the work of Wittgenstein (*PI* 1–25, 304) as well as that of Austin (1975) and Searle (1969).

merely qualitative. The distinction between *predicating* and *saying* is subtle, but Aristotle got it right.

Each of Aristotle's discourse features governs a specific range of possible subsequent discourse. When a feature is positive, a certain set of responses (questions, challenges, comments, etc.) is open or permitted to predications in that category. When a feature is negative, another set of responses is open or permitted. From this point of view, therefore, categories involve or entail, in addition to distinct discourse conditions (which Aristotle largely ignores), distinct clusters of discourse possibilities.

One advantage of such a linguistic reading is that it brings the discussion of categories into a field of active scholarly research. It thereby makes possible a rational and potentially useful criticism of Aristotle's work. Within his category of substance, for example, discourse features can certainly be found to distinguish substances in the modern sense (gold, coal, mud, water, etc.) both from individuals and from natural kinds (species and genera)—perhaps (as John Corcoran has suggested) making use of the distinction between mass nouns and count nouns. There are, of course, reservations to be kept in mind. Although predication is a universal speech act, it is not clear that the discourse features which distinguish the categories are universal; nor is it clear what the import would be of their not being universal. Another ground of caution is that discourse features belong to the domain of rhetoric, whereas the categories have always seemed a matter of logic. A third caution is that the theory of speech acts, which perhaps has the potential for revitalizing rhetoric in the way that the theory of quantification revitalized logic, is itself in a youthful state, and its precise relation to other branches of linguistics remains as uncertain as does that of Aristotle's *Categories*.

5.   The Complaints of Kant and Ryle

Behind these specific issues there lurks the problem that this reading may turn Aristotle from a philosopher into a linguist or some sort of empirical scientist. It seems a betrayal of Aristotle to interpret him as engaged in an empirical rather than an apriori inquiry. Ryle (1971, 2:180) puts the point cautiously:

> The danger is, of course, that we shall be taken and shall unwittingly take ourselves to be talking grammar, as if it was all part of one topic to say

"Plural nouns cannot have singular verbs" and "The dotted line in '. . . is false' can be completed with 'What you are now saying . . .' and cannot be completed with 'What I am now saying . . .'".

Kant rises to the defense of philosophy with a more strident comment:

> It has not arisen rhapsodically, as the result of a haphazard search after pure concepts, the complete enumeration of which, as based on induction only, could never be guaranteed. Nor could we, if this was our procedure, discover why just these concepts, and no others, have their seat in the pure understanding. It was an enterprise worthy of an acute thinker like Aristotle to make search for these fundamental concepts. But as he did so on no principle, he merely picked them up as they came his way, and at first procured ten of them, which he called categories (predicaments). Afterwards he believed that he had discovered five others, which he added under the name of post-predicaments. But his table still remained defective. Besides there are to be found in it some modes of pure sensibility (*quando, ubi, situs,* and also *prius, simul*), and an empirical concept (*motus*), none of which has any place in a table of concepts that trace their origin to the understanding. Aristotle's list also enumerates among the original concepts some derivative concepts (*actio, passio*), and of the original concepts some are entirely lacking. (*KdrV* A81=B107)

With respect to these complaints against Aristotle, the key issue is whether Aristotle was proceeding on some principle. I have shown that he was, and that the principle is a thoroughly respectable one within linguistics. I suspect Kant would reply that this is not really a *principle*, since (1) it proceeds empirically rather than apriori, and (2) it provides no closure, no criterion for saying the list is complete. Rather than challenging these retorts I propose instead to note them as points of contrast with Aristotle, and to further delineate the contrast by considering Kant's categories and Wittgenstein's more Aristotelian language-games.

Kant's alternative, as is well known, is to base the table of categories on his table of judgments (*KdrV* A70=B95), in which he claims to have presented all the logically possible functions of unity (forms of judgment). The table of categories (A80=B106) is claimed to be derived from the table of judgments, and to be complete because that table is complete. His alternative to Aristotle, like Katz's interpretation of Aristotle, presupposes a full-blown logical apparatus within which and by means of which the categories can be defined. Kant is unquestionably correct in saying that this way of proceeding makes for a neat table and a closed system of categories. The system is not only neat and in tabular form but is also complete. But this is achieved by completely changing the nature of the enterprise, as Ryle acerbically notes:

> Kant's doctrine of categories starts from quite a different quarter from that of Aristotle, and what he lists as categories are quite other than what Aristotle puts into his index. Kant quaintly avers that his purpose is the same as Aristotle, but in this he is, save in a very broad and vague sense, mistaken. (1971, 2:176)

Kant's purpose could be described as an ideal language project based on analysis of propositions or judgments, rather than an empirical project based on their use.

Unfortunately Ryle proceeds in a way that has some of the same defects as that of Kant, including the crucial defect of treating the categories as an aspect or development of logic rather than as part of its background. He does not begin with a table of judgments. He begins instead with "sentence-factors" and "proposition-factors," where a factor is some part of a sentence or proposition, whether a word or a phrase. By means of this beginning Ryle avoids having a closed system, which he rightly conceives as an advantage over Kant. But he identifies categories with logical types, and says that a categorial sentence is one that specifies the logical type of some factor. Like Kant, therefore, he identifies categories analytically rather than contextually, and within the framework of logic (which is just assumed) rather than within some prepropositional domain of language, such as rhetoric. Again like Kant, therefore, Ryle changes the project hopelessly, from an empirical enquiry into the ways of words to a logical prescription of what they *must* be.

6.   Language-Games as Categories

Wittgenstein uses the word 'category' sparingly, but it does occur both in the early lectures after his return to Cambridge and in the very late remarks on certainty (*M* 295; *OC* 308). Though it is easier to associate these uses with Aristotle than with Kant, Wittgenstein did not wish to resurrect the concept. Instead he developed the concept of language-games, and he placed his discussion of them at the beginning of his *Philosophical Investigations,* as a kind of organon. He summarizes some of his points in *PI* 23:

But how many kinds of sentence are there? Say assertion, question, and command?—There are *countless* kinds: countless different kinds of use of what we call "symbols," "words," "sentences". And this multiplicity is not something fixed, given once for all; but new types of language, new language-games, as we may say, come into existence, and others become obsolete and get forgotten. . . .

Here the term "language-*game*" is meant to bring into prominence the fact that the *speaking* of a language is part of an activity, or of a form of life.

Here Wittgenstein insists on the open-endedness of the list of language-games, one of the features of Aristotle's categories that Kant most roundly condemned. He also emphasizes that what is primarily at issue is *doing* something rather than simply thinking or intending. This emphasis on action is what he had in mind when he quoted (as he did frequently) Goethe's line (from *Faust*, part 1), "Im Anfang war die Tat" (In the beginning was the deed).[4]

Wittgenstein's later work seems centered around "grammar," and by grammar he seems to mean the description of these language-games, or the rules implicit in them. As in Aristotle this grammar (description of "things that are said") leads into metaphysics:

Essence is expressed by grammar. (*PI* 371)
Grammar tells what kind of object anything is. (*PI* 373)

Perhaps the metaphysical dimension of language-games comes into play most clearly in connection with sensations:

"And yet you again and again reach the conclusion that the sensation itself is a *nothing.*"—Not at all. It is not a *something*, but not a *nothing* either! The conclusion was only that a nothing would serve just as well as a something about which nothing could be said. We have only rejected the grammar which tries to force itself on us here.

The paradox disappears only if we make a radical break with the idea that language always functions in the same way, always serves the same purpose: to convey thoughts—which may be about houses, pains, good and evil, or anything else you please. (*PI* 304)

Wittgenstein refers over and over to discourse conditions and discourse possibilities in distinguishing different ways in which language functions. The range of cases he discusses is different from Aristotle's, but

---

4. Winch (1987) has a useful chapter discussing the significance of this thought of Goethe's in Wittgenstein's later work.

there is nothing in what Wittgenstein says or in the way that he proceeds that casts doubt on Aristotle's work. If there are categories of which Wittgenstein would be critical, it is those of Kant rather than those of Aristotle.

From a metaphysical perspective Wittgenstein makes his greatest contribution to the philosophy of mind, through distinguishing different kinds of mental states and mental acts.[5] His discussions of sensations (including pains) (*PI* 243–315) and of "seeing as" (*PI* 2:xi) are the most famous; but even in these cases there has been relatively little consideration of how these fresh approaches to sensation and perception transform British empiricism, where the topics have been the central ones for centuries. In addition to these discussions, however, the second half of part I of the *Philosophical Investigations,* all of *Zettel,* most of *Last Writings,* and all of the *Remarks on the Philosophy of Psychology,* consist of elaborate contributions to the philosophy of mind—descriptive rather than hypothetical or explanatory contributions, but contributions nonetheless. Being descriptive is connected with a distinctly Aristotelian role, that of providing *categories* for understanding and describing our mental life. Here are some typical passages in which Wittgenstein characterizes, in part directly and in part contrastively, some typical human mental phenomena:

> Continuation of the classification of psychological concepts.
>   Emotions. Common to them: genuine duration, a course. (Rage flares up, abates, and vanishes, and likewise joy, depression, and fear.)
>   Distinction from sensations: they are not localized (nor yet diffuse!).
>   Common: they have characteristic expression-behavior. (Facial expression.) And this implies characteristic sensations too. Thus sorrow often goes with weeping, and characteristic sensations with the latter. (The voice heavy with tears.) But these sensations are not the emotions. (In the sense in which the numeral 2 is not the number 2.) (*Z* 488)

Here we find Wittgenstein setting out, in a most Aristotelian fashion, to distinguish two genera of psychological phenomena. The effort seems straightforwardly metaphysical, in that he is clearly trying to say just what sensations and emotions are; or at least what emotions are, by reference to what we already know that sensations are. It is naturalistic in that the phenomena are accepted as given. And the metaphysical criteria

---

5. Malcolm Budd (1989) gives a full and accurate account of Wittgenstein's categorization of mental states and mental acts, especially in pages 10–15 and 146–165.

are grammatical, since the point about localization expresses the grammatical rule that the question "Where do you feel that?" makes sense with respect to sensations but not with respect to emotions. The effort continues:

> What goes to make them [emotions] different from sensations: they do not give us any information about the external world. (A grammatical remark.)
>
> Love and hate might be called emotional dispositions, and so might fear in one sense. (*Z* 491)
>
> Consider the following question: Can a pain be thought of, say with the quality of rheumatic pain, but *un*localized? Can one *imagine* this?
>
> If you begin to think this over, you see how much you would like to change the knowledge of the place of pain into a characteristic of *what is felt,* into a characteristic of a sense-datum, of the private object I have before my mind. (*Z* 498)

Another person can very well know what I am feeling, if it is a matter of sensation, by observing me. The grammatical or logical connection between sensations and their localization, which pertains to the *essence* of pain and other sensations, conflicts with Cartesian dualism; it is flatly incompatible with both the privacy and the epistemic immediacy of mind and mental experience, as conceived by Descartes. It is a Cartesian, therefore, of whom Wittgenstein is speaking in the second paragraph of *Z* 498. Other grammatical contrasts between feelings and emotions follow shortly:

> To the utterance: "I can't think of it without fear" one replies: "There is no reason to fear, for . . .". That is at any rate *one* way of dismissing fear. Contrast with pain. (*Z* 501)
>
> Love is not a feeling. Love is put to the test, pain not. One does not say: "That was not true pain, or it would not have gone off so quickly." (*Z* 504)

These are passages in which Wittgenstein provides insight into what kinds of psychological things there are, by reference to discourse possibilities pertaining to the psychological predications we make. That this work follows the line Aristotle established in the *Categories* seems too obvious to require further comment.

Wittgenstein's relation to linguistics is as puzzling as Aristotle's. Both of them discuss language and language use in general terms, and do so with methods that are familiar to linguists. Neither of them, however, discusses the aspects of dimensions of language with which linguists and grammarians are generally concerned. They further, and more significantly, depart from classical linguists in that the features to which they refer are inextricably embedded in contexts of human action and interaction, resulting in a contextualism that is only superficially like the analytic methods of traditional linguistics. In the long run one principal advantage of a linguistic reading of Aristotle's *Categories* may be that it opens the way to Wittgenstein's grammar as a generalization of that work. Another may be that this perspective will in turn allow us to use an appreciation of Aristotle to read Wittgenstein differently from the conventional rendition of him as a radical departure from traditional philosophy.

Categories are transcendental requirements upon the objects of our consciousness—objects of imagination as well as objects of knowledge. Nothing can be an object at all without being a thing of some kind (category) or other. Something can be a substance, a quality, a time, a place, a quantity, and so on; but nothing can "just *exist*" without falling under any of the categories. For Kant, too, categories are inescapable, even though they are very different from what Aristotle thought to be inescapable. Wittgenstein's language-games belong to the same tradition. To have meaning, a sentence must be a move in some language-game or other: "Nur im Fluß des Leben haben die Worte ihre Bedeutung" (*LW* 1:913). If Wittgenstein borrows from Aristotle the naturalistic idea that the categories are found in experience and may very well change, he is more insistent than Aristotle that they are found in our *linguistic* experience rather than in the world of science. Thus he equally borrows from Kant the idea that they are human inventions, belonging to the spontaneous rather than the merely receptive part of our cognition and created somewhat arbitrarily rather than imposed on us by external or internal reality. Since they filter reality for us, categories by their very nature presuppose the reality they filter; it would be transcendental illusion (in Kant's sense) to suppose that they might constitute that very reality.

Language-games are Wittgenstein's categories, applicable to psychological as well as material reality. They are distinctly *human*, inconceivable apart from human lives and actions; but they are also ineluctable. That, carefully thought out, is not so very different from what Aristotle thought as well.

5
Wittgenstein's Reception in America

The standing of Wittgenstein's philosophical work in America is somewhat curious. On the one hand his prestige is enormous, and his presence as a figure in the philosophical landscape cannot be overlooked; on the other hand his impact has been minimal. Commentary on his work, which began as a trickle of articles in the 1930s, has become a flood of books. In the profession he no longer belongs to the narrow group of those who knew him; philosophers of every persuasion and background are expected to be familiar with his work. And in the humanities he is increasingly recognized as a philosopher to be reckoned with—for example, at my university the six philosophers selected for special attention in the Philosophy and Literature Program are Plato, Aristotle, Augustine, Kant, Heidegger, and Wittgenstein. There is no doubt whatever that Wittgenstein has been noticed in America, and there is every reason to believe this will continue to be the case into the foreseeable future.

On the other hand, Wittgenstein has no significant following. People recognize him, read him, cite him, and discuss him; but few take up philosophy in his manner, or modify their thinking in line with the main thrusts of his work. It may be the case in literature that there is no difference between being noticed and having an impact, but there certainly is a difference in science: Velikovsky's *Worlds in Collision* has been widely noticed, and continues to be discussed, but it cannot be said to have had an impact on modern science. In the same sense, one has to say that Wittgenstein has had little impact on such American philosophers as Carnap, Hempel, Feigl, Grunbaum, Quine, Chisholm, Goodman, Rawls, Kripke, Dworkin, Gewirth, Donagan, Kaplan, Searle—even though they have all noticed Wittgenstein. The exceptions are fewer: Black, Malcolm, Bergmann (selectively), Cavell, and Foot.

This curious state of affairs is to be explained, I believe, by a combination of three factors. The first is a concentration on subordinate details, such as the nature of objects, the picture theory, family resemblance, and the private-language argument. It is not that these details are not important: details are always important. But they are also subordinate to main thrusts. The second factor is that the main thrusts of his works have been ignored—the holism and the ethical thrust of the *Tractatus,* and the representation of philosophical remarks in the *Investigations* as part of the natural history of mankind. This leads into the third factor, for the neglect of main thrusts almost inevitably leads to a distortion of Wittgenstein's thought. So it is the concentration on details, combined with neglect of main themes and with distortions, which has minimized Wittgenstein's impact in America.

My assessment is in agreement with that of Marjorie Grene (1976), whose words are sharper and sadder and who includes Frege along with Wittgenstein in the circle of the misunderstood: "Even the so-called analytical tradition has in fact developed in response to typically English or American misreadings of two great European thinkers, Frege and Wittgenstein, whose work, thus misinterpreted, has been in each case cabined, cribbed, confined within the inflexible bonds of unquestioned, and unquestioning, empiricist principles" (11). In particular she accuses Russell and others of attempting to deny the *intensional* aspect of concepts that was important to Frege, and of ignoring the strain of mysticism obvious in the *Tractatus.* The target of her attack broadens out to include Quine, Dennett, and Føllesdal, as well as Russell. In what follows I concentrate more on metaphysical than logical matters, and I attack different philosophers; but my remarks complement rather than compete with hers.

The *Tractatus* is filled with intriguing details, and it is hardly surprising that they have attracted attention. Philosophers antecedently interested in causation, or probability, or universals and particulars, or identity, or Russell's paradox, or a dozen other problems, will find cryptic remarks on the subject, often presented as wholly definitive. It is entirely reasonable to explore the import and the cogency of such remarks. But at the same time it must be borne in mind that an exposition conducted within the framework of an independently defined problem, however valuable in other ways, is not likely to cast much light on Wittgenstein's philosophy. For *one* of the things Wittgenstein was doing was challenging the independent or antecedent definition of philosophical problems.

Typical of the "problems" on which there has been an interesting series of essays is the question whether the "objects" (*Gegenstände*) of the *Tractatus* are universals or particulars. The essays by Copi, Anscombe, Allaire, Proctor, and Keyt, for example (in Copi and Beard [1966]), all contribute significantly to the discussion of this issue. While these scholars do refer faithfully to Wittgenstein's text, they inevitably make it subordinate to the framework imposed by the "problem of universals." One of the issues in this debate, for example, is whether these can be "bare particulars"—quite an interesting question in its own right. But neither 'universal' nor 'particular', nor *a fortiori* 'bare particular', is an expression that occurs in Wittgenstein's text; so these studies have as much prospect of distorting as of illuminating Wittgenstein's text. And distortion does seem to have resulted. Black (1964, 57) and Pears (1986, 65) conclude that it is most likely that Wittgenstein deliberately skirted this issue—presumably on the grounds that it is a nonissue, in the sense that all the problems of philosophy can be resolved without saying anything about universals and particulars. In chapter seven I argue that one reason for this avoidance on Wittgenstein's part is his attempt to represent the new logic of Frege and Russell as independent of the Aristotelian idea of subject/predicate that is inherent in the terms 'universal' and 'particular'.

A more powerful demonstration of the distortion of Wittgenstein in the course of this debate over whether "objects" are universals or particulars is contained in articles in which McGuinness (1981, 1985) attacks the alleged metaphysical realism of the *Tractatus,* in particular the supposition that "objects" are real entities. Since objects can be neither universals nor particulars if they are not real, in which case the very plausible position argued by McGuinness cannot even be considered, these papers expose this particular concentration on details as a gross distortion of the *Tractatus.*

A second factor, besides concentration on details, is neglect of main themes. It is well known from the *Notebooks* and the *Prototractatus*—and the same can be said about the *Investigations*—that there were two distinct phases to Wittgenstein's composition of the *Tractatus:* careful attention to the details, and careful attention to their arrangement. In his footnote to the first proposition he explicitly draws our attention to the arrangement, saying that propositions numbered with decimals are comments on—so subsidiary to—propositions numbered with integers or with fewer decimals. So the order of propositions in the *Tractatus* is one key to its main themes.

The first proposition reads, "The world is all that is the case." This is one of the themes that has been neglected. Black remarks on Wittgenstein's metaphysical innovation here, in making the world consist of *facts* rather than things (1964, 27); and Curley draws our attention to powerful similarities between this opening metaphysical idea and the metaphysics of Spinoza (1969, 76–77). But I don't believe this primary metaphysical statement is cited once, as primary, in the whole long dispute over the nature of objects. For example, in his book *Ludwig Wittgenstein* David Pears, one of the ablest of Wittgenstein scholars, writes that "Wittgenstein's ontological conclusion is recondite. His view about the structure of reality was that it is composed of simple objects" (1986, 46). Though the paragraph continues, there is no mention of *facts* as that of which the world is composed. Even more astonishing is the neglect of this main theme by Norman Malcolm. The first three chapters of his book *Nothing Is Hidden* (1986) are devoted to expounding and criticizing the conception of the world and reality in the *Tractatus,* and yet he ignores this opening theme and the propositions which immediately comment on it. His view is that for the *Tractatus* the world is composed ultimately of objects (*Gegenstände*), but he never considers the first elucidation of the opening theme, "The world is the totality of facts, *not of things*" (1.1, emphasis added). Hence one of Wittgenstein's main themes is neglected just when it ought to be brought forth.

Another main theme is economy of speech. Wittgenstein says in his preface, "The whole sense of the book might be summed up in the following words: what can be said at all can be said clearly, and what we cannot talk about we must pass over in silence." We know from his correspondence with Engelmann and Ficker (Engelmann 1967) that he felt his book to have a moral or aesthetic import (it is not clear he would have distinguished between 'moral' and 'aesthetic'), and at least a part of it would presumably be found in this summary point about speech and silence. One might think that such a prominent point, identified by the author as central, would receive much attention. It has, indeed, been noticed more often than the opening proposition about the world; but that is to admit very little. Generally when this main point has been noticed, it has not been discussed; and it has often not even been noticed. Consider, for example, Russell's introduction to the *Tractatus.* Russell focuses on Wittgenstein's concerns about language, and gives a running summary of the contents. When he comes to the end of the *Tractatus,* where Wittgenstein states part of this main point that he called attention to in the preface, Russell brushes aside the counsel of silence, makes no mention of anything aesthetic or moral, and refers to Wittgenstein's acceptance of the "mystical." It is not altogether silly to regard a belief in something which cannot be articulated as "mystical," and Wittgenstein himself uses the expression. But Russell then proceeds to propose a logical device (metalanguages) to avoid Wittgenstein's mystical. He does not seek to understand or explain it, and he omits mention altogether of the idea that what can be said at all can be said clearly. Seeking to *avoid* one of Wittgenstein's main themes is altogether premature. What we really need to ask is what sort of insight Wittgenstein has here. Is it a rebuke to laziness? Is it a rebuke to common sense? Is it a rebuke to Kant? In what context could it be challenged or defended? What can be said in its favor? It is questions such as these that are omitted from Russell's discussion, as from most others.

Neglect of such main themes as these two, combined with energetic discussion of details, has led inevitably to distortion of the *Tractatus.* One of the distortions is that in this work Wittgenstein is a logical atomist. This view is extremely widespread, having originated with the earliest presentations of Wittgenstein's ideas by Russell, both in his introduction to the *Tractatus* and also in his "Lectures on Logical Atomism." Sometimes there are passages cited which might in isolation suggest a kind of atomism, but often it is simply taken for granted that Wittgenstein was an atomist. In 1964, for example, James Griffin published a volume called *Wittgenstein's Logical Atomism,* in which one might expect to find an explanation of this doctrine. In fact the book is an excellent exposition of the main lines of the *Tractatus,* full of helpful insight on difficult details, such as the influence of Hertz on the picture theory. But Griffin nowhere justifies his title. He just assumes that it is right and proper to refer to Wittgenstein's thought in the *Tractatus* as "logical atomism." In point of fact, there is no mention of "atoms" in Wittgenstein's book, and some of its trenchant remarks seem incompatible with atomism. As we have noted, for example, the book starts with the world—that is to say, with a certain totality, or "limited whole"— not with independent elements out of which a whole might be constructed. Holism is apparent again in the symbolism. A name does not have an independent or absolute meaning: "only in the nexus of a proposition does a name have meaning" (3.3). And although a proposition has sense, and more or less stands on its own as expressing a definite sense, "nevertheless the whole of logical space must already be given by it. . . . The force of a proposition reaches through the whole of logical space" (3.42). The holism reaches its most poetic eloquence in

Wittgenstein's remark (5.511) on the rather funny and arbitrary character of the symbols of formal logic:

> How can logic—all-embracing logic, which mirrors the world—use such peculiar crotchets and contrivances? Only because they are all connected with one another in an infinitely fine network, the great mirror.

An infinitely fine network constituting the necessary structure of language is obviously incompatible with atomism in that domain.

There are other passages in which Wittgenstein insists on the possibility of analysis (3.25, 4.221, 4.2211), and in which he makes clear that names are elements (3.2, 3.201, 3.26). These passages give a certain plausibility to interpreting the philosophy of the *Tractatus* as a kind of logical atomism—as Wittgenstein himself explicitly notes in *Investigations* 90–91. Nonetheless, this view seriously distorts Wittgenstein's thought. Wittgenstein insists on contextual understanding as firmly as on analytic understanding, and therefore he cannot possibly be an atomist in the philosophical sense.

The second most widespread distortion of Wittgenstein's thought is that he was an empiricist. This distortion, due in large part to the success of the Vienna Circle in America, rests in part on the *Tractatus* and in part on a famous remark he made to Schlick and Waismann. In the *Tractatus* he says,

> In order to tell whether a picture is true or false we must compare it with reality. It is impossible to tell from the picture alone whether it is true or false. (2.223–2.224)

It seems indisputable, given that all elementary propositions are models or pictures, that Wittgenstein intends the truth and falsity of elementary propositions to be determined empirically. It is this aspect of his thought on which the Vienna Circle seized. Their understanding was reinforced by the remark made to Schlick and Waismann, and used by Waismann in his articles in *Erkenntnis* and *Analysis:* "The sense of a proposition is its method on verification" (Waismann 1930). This slogan seemed just what was needed to shore up the central claim of logical positivism, namely that all significant questions which are not matters of formal logic are questions of empirical science.

Wittgenstein was never an empiricist about philosophy, although he certainly did at times agree with the positivists that there are no significant philosophical questions. He insisted emphatically, from his early work through the later, on sharply distinguishing philosophy from science. In the *Tractatus* he says, "Philosophy is not one of the natural sciences. . . . Philosophy is not a body of doctrine but an activity" (4.111–4.112). So if philosophy deals with questions of meaning, these questions cannot be scientific questions, however much certain passages may suggest this possibility. In the *Investigations* the activity which constitutes philosophy is identified as that of giving grammatical elucidations (*PI* 90, 232, p. 222), and there is again a sharp distinction between grammatical and empirical propositions. He warns of "something whose form makes it look like an empirical proposition but which is really a grammatical one" (251), and he contrasts grammatical with experiential propositions and grammar with facts (295). So Wittgenstein has also stood firmly against that blurring of the distinction between philosophy and science which empiricism and pragmatism generally represent.

There is an even more profound reason why it distorts Wittgenstein to conceive him as an empiricist, and as endorsing the idea that meaning is to be defined in terms of verification. The reason is that such a view puts epistemology back in the center of the philosophical stage. Descartes, with his famous doubts, made questions about what it is possible to *know* the first problem of philosophy, to which all other problems are subordinate. Giving priority to epistemology was endorsed by continental philosophers at least through Kant and by British philosophers at least through Russell. Wittgenstein stood against this conception of philosophy. In the *Tractatus* he says that philosophy is not a body of doctrine, or a set of truth-claims, but an *activity,* which "consists essentially of elucidations" (4.112). He presents the same general conception of philosophy in the *Investigations:*

> The work of the philosopher consists in assembling reminders for a particular purpose. . . . The philosopher's treatment of a question is like the treatment of an illness. (*PI* 127, 255)

Wittgenstein was, of course, perfectly *certain* of what he said in the course of this activity. But the ground of his certainty was not *knowledge.* At first, in the "Notes on Logic" of 1913, he thought it was logic; in his later work he spoke of it as grammar, or as natural history (*PI* 90, 413). He explicitly took up the problem of the relation of knowledge to certainty at the very end of his life, in remarks published as *On*

Certainty. While one must be cautious with remarks that Wittgenstein never revised for publication, the whole thrust of this work is an effort to resist labeling as knowledge certain statements (primarily those put forth by Moore in two famous papers) about which there is no doubt whatsoever. One remark underscores this thrust dramatically: " 'Knowledge' and 'certainty' belong to different *categories*" (*OC* 308). If what is certain beyond all doubt cannot be said to be *known,* then the theory of knowledge is not so vital to philosophy as Descartes, Hume, Kant, and Russell have thought. I will return to this issue shortly and then will discuss it more extensively in chapter ten.

Wittgenstein's later work has attracted even more attention than his *Tractatus.* The *Philosophical Investigations* is a major source and inspiration for "Ordinary Language Philosophy," just as the *Tractatus* is for Logical Positivism, and it has been on this work that the preponderance of recent attention has been concentrated. As was the case with the *Tractatus,* Wittgenstein prepared this work for publication by selecting, revising, and arranging remarks which he had previously presented in lectures and/or written down in notebooks. And as was the case with the earlier work, most of the commentary has focused on details and ignored the main thrusts signaled by the arrangement.

The details that have attracted most attention have been the remarks on sensation and "private language," those on ostensive definition and "family resemblance," those on following rules, the definition of meaning as use, and the long section on seeing aspects. Each one of these topics is important in its own right, and corresponds to one or more of the perennial problems of philosophy. Wittgenstein meant his remarks to be applied to these problems, so one can hardly object in principle to philosophers who try to make use of Wittgenstein's comments to resolve their traditional problems. And yet serious distortions result from failing to notice the main thrust which Wittgenstein signals by the arrangement he finally decided on after several false starts. What comes first in the *Philosophical Investigations,* as Hintikka and Hintikka (1986) usefully insist, is the discussion of the variety of uses of language, or of language-games. Let us look more closely at this neglected theme in Wittgenstein's later work.

The expressions 'use of language' and 'language-game' are employed by Wittgenstein as technical or quasi-technical terms. They are used interchangeably, and refer to natural (or ordinary) activities in which speech plays an indispensable role. Some of the examples he gives are obeying orders; speculating about an event; reading a story; guessing riddles; telling a joke; solving a problem in practical arithmetic; asking; thanking; cursing; greeting; praying; commanding; questioning; recounting; and chatting (*PI* 23, 25). Wittgenstein does not intend to *explain* these activities—only to describe them: "Philosophy simply puts everything before us, and neither explains nor deduces anything" (*PI* 126). He describes his own work—which is also a language-game—as a contribution to the "natural history of mankind" (*PI* 25, 415), natural history being a purely descriptive discipline devoid of theory as well as of explanatory or predictive power. Throughout his work Wittgenstein does not say that human beings *must* engage in these activities—only that they do so; and he avoids saying they *cannot* do other things, which they do not do—only that they do not. Wittgenstein's idea—the one that inspires "Ordinary Language Philosophy"—is that people do not ordinarily confuse one activity with another, one use of language with another; but that deep philosophical perplexities arise when such confusions occur. To resolve them and defend against them, Wittgenstein proposes to follow a motto from *King Lear:* "I'll teach you differences!"

We think, for example, that 'reports' are *reports*—different from commands and questions but all alike in *reporting* about some object or other. But Wittgenstein insists on differences. Whereas bank reports and battle reports can be checked for accuracy, there is no such check for reports of dreams (*PI* pp. 184, 222). That is to say, the only questions in the case of dream-reports can be about the honesty or truthfulness of the speaker:

> The question whether the dreamer's memory deceives him when he reports the dream after waking cannot arise, unless indeed we introduce a completely new criterion for the report's 'agreeing' with the dream, a criterion which gives us a concept of 'truth' as distinct from 'truthfulness' here. (*PI* pp. 222–23)

So reports of dreams are different from reports of battles or of bank balances. That is to say, since "*Essence* is expressed by grammar" (*PI* 371), dreams are not states of affairs or events; they belong to a different category.

First-person reports of pains are similar to reports of dreams in that there is no distinction between their truth and their truthfulness. But there are also differences. Pains are always present when we notice them, and are often present when we report them; whereas dreams, although they may be recurrent, are never present. So while some sort of memory is always a factor in reports of dreams, it is altogether absent in the case of very many ordinary first-person reports of pain (except for such memory as is involved in learning and mastering the use of language). Reports of pains, unlike reports of dreams, can be made in the third person—"She has a headache," which functions logically more like bank reports and battle reports—as well as in the first person. Furthermore a first-person report and a third-person report can be about the same pain, and can stand, say, in contradiction to one another. The grammar of pain reports is therefore very much more complicated than the grammar of dream reports, and the concept of pain accordingly more subtle than that of dreaming.

The subtleties of the concept of pain are significant because they are typical of those of consciousness in general, and problems about what sort of thing pain is are analogous to traditional problems about consciousness and sense data. Wittgenstein was as gripped by these problems as any other philosopher, and his remarks on them and elaborations of them have attracted untold critical and exegetical comment. The problems are many and varied, and none is intrinsically more interesting than the others. There are, however, two related problems which have been most troubling to philosophers with a different training and a different perspective: one about the metaphysical reality of sensations, and one about the epistemological value of sensations (that is, the relation of sensation-reports to knowledge-claims).

With regard to the metaphysical problem, Wittgenstein certainly knew that he was likely to be misunderstood. In section 304 he reproduces a dialogue with a philosopher who reads Wittgenstein with the conviction that pain must either be something real, like sticks and stones, or not:

> "But you will surely admit that there is a difference between pain-behaviour accompanied by pain and pain-behaviour without any pain?"
> —Admit it? What greater difference could there be?—"And yet you again and again reach the conclusion that the sensation itself is a *nothing*."—Not at all. It is not a *something*, but not a *nothing* either! The conclusion was only that a nothing would serve just as well as a something about which nothing could be said. We have only rejected the grammar which tried to force itself on us here. (*PI* 304)

In an effort to cut short this misunderstanding, he then in the next paragraph refers to the central theme which he had stressed in the opening paragraphs:

> The paradox disappears only if we make a radical break with the idea that language always functions in one way, always serves the same purpose: to convey thoughts—which may be about houses, pains, good and evil, or anything else you please.

Reporting a pain (one's own present pain) is at the same time an expression of pain. It is a completely different use of language from reporting a traffic accident, different from reporting someone else's pain, and different from reporting a dream. That is to say, this use of language typically makes sense in different circumstances, it is integrated with different activities, and different sorts of questions and responses are appropriate to it. Questions analogous to those which test whether sticks and stones are real or illusory lead only to confusion here.

Being half logical and half metaphysical, this central point is subtle. At the same time it requires early recognition and application; for if the problems are already defined in some traditional way, the confusions against which Wittgenstein aims to protect us have already occurred. If, for example, it is assumed that the philosophical problem is whether "reality" is characterized by spatio-temporal location (materialism) or by indubitability (modern idealism), it will then appear that Wittgenstein must be either a behaviorist or a Cartesian—whereas his point is precisely that both these views confuse one use of language with another. It is in this way that neglect of Wittgenstein's central point has led to distortion of his thought even when his texts are cited.

The epistemological problem has been given renewed prominence by Kripke's lively book, *Wittgenstein on Rules and Private Language*. It is in many ways a splendid book, original, highly readable, and wonderfully persuasive in developing a paradox about rules.[1] He also is a careful reader: he cites Wittgenstein with accuracy, and notices some points which others have sometimes missed, such as that both sensations (psychology) and equations (mathematics) are critical test cases for what Wittgenstein has to say about rules. And yet a more grievous misunderstanding of Wittgenstein's later work is hard to conceive. For what Kripke calls 'Wittgenstein's Paradox' is an epistemological paradox,

---

1. But it should hardly be surprising that not everyone admires the book. For a searing attack, see Baker and Hacker (1984).

concerning what we cannot "know" and presuming a concept of "knowledge" or "knowing" already established—a sceptical paradox; and he attributes to Wittgenstein a "sceptical" solution. It is, therefore, a paradox which traps a philosopher caught in the Cartesian tradition of modern philosophy, according to which problems of knowledge are primary problems, to be confronted first as a necessary preliminary to other problems. And the "sceptical solution" is the response of a philosopher who remains within that same tradition, where every significant declarative sentence must be either known or not known. Kripke has, in other words, wrenched Wittgenstein back into the tradition which he constantly and repeatedly repudiated from 1913 until his death in 1951.

To appreciate the enormity of this distortion, one must understand that the main achievement of Wittgenstein's work, if he has achieved anything, has been to overcome the three-hundred-year hegemony of epistemology over logic and metaphysics in Western philosophy. It is an unchanging theme in his work. In his 1913 "Notes on Logic" he wrote: "Philosophy consists of logic and metaphysics: logic is its basis" (*NB* 106), problems of knowledge being omitted entirely. He continues his disparagement of epistemology in the *Tractatus:* "Theory of knowledge is the philosophy of psychology" (4.1121)—obviously implying that the legitimate problem is only what causes our beliefs, not what justifies them. The identification of a countless variety of "language-games," or uses of languages, allowed him to back off from this extreme position in his later philosophy. That is to say, it allowed him to recognize legitimate questions about the justification of belief without according them priority. In *On Certainty,* written during his last years, he reverts to powerful traditional terminology: " 'Knowledge' and 'certainty' belong to different *categories*" (*OC* 308). Doubts and knowledge-claims, scepticism and science, belong to the same *"category."* But they are not primary. They are based on certainties. And these certainties are immune to doubt, lying "beyond being justified or unjustified" (*OC* 359), as a part of the natural history of mankind.

The part of "natural history" of concern to philosophy is the kind of grammar discussed extensively in other chapters—that is to say, descriptions of the uses of languages characteristic in human life, where such descriptions are not idiosyncratic, culturally specific, dependent on theories, or in need of theoretical constructs. To make grammatical explanations is itself a normal, ordinary use of language. So while philosophy is critical and exposes transcendental metaphysics as nonsense, it is also self-referential, and describes critical philosophy as a specialized form of an ordinary language-game. This is what philosophy always has been: Plato's dialogues, for example, are easily read as forays against limits of language or as studies of the aporia which results from confusing two different uses of language; and it is instructive to see Aristotle's *Categories* as a careful grammatical description of differences among different sorts of truth-claims, as was done in greater detail in the previous chapter. Thus while Wittgenstein's philosophy is critical, it is not hostile to philosophy as such, and not an attempt to replace traditional philosophy with Freudian therapy or with Derridean deconstruction.

If Wittgenstein were to become influential as well as important, one would see certain lines of thought replacing those now dominant in American philosophy. Philosophy itself would be both critical and self-referential, rather than alternating between dogmatism and nihilism. This would be achieved in part by a sharp contrast between science (theoretical and explanatory, and sustaining both prediction and engineering) and philosophy (untheoretic and purely descriptive). The pure descriptions of philosophy would focus on the "natural history" of humans, insofar as this consists in characteristic activities, which distinguish humans from nonhumans in that they involve mastery of the use of language. Thus philosophy would focus on grammar rather than on logic, on what is rather than on what must be. Philosophical puzzles would be resolved contextually (understanding things in relation to a larger whole) rather than analytically (understanding things in relation to constituent elements). Philosophy itself, as other activities, would be seen as part of "this complicated form of life" of those who "have mastered the use of a language" (*PI* p. 174). At present this influence is as little felt in America as in Europe. On both sides of the Atlantic we still have the impact of Wittgenstein's thought to look forward to.

PART TWO

WITTGENSTEIN'S EARLY WORK

6
The Metaphysics of the *Tractatus*

1. The Problem of Dualism and Metaphysical Realism in the *Tractatus*

The most striking feature of the metaphysics of the *Tractatus* is an apparent dualism: the world is one irreducible reality, and its substance is another sort of thing altogether. The world is the totality of facts, not of things, and serves as the metaphysical grounding for truth. The substance of the world is composed of objects, not facts, and serves as the metaphysical grounding for meaning. The metaphysical dichotomy has a direct consequence with respect to human expression, or what we can picture to ourselves. Facts can be explicitly expressed or stated, and therefore the world can be described. Objects, on the other hand, cannot be expressed or said but can only be shown or named (3.221), and therefore the substance of the world cannot be described. The "correct method in philosophy" (6.53) also reflects the dualism, since it consists not only of the very famous silence with respect to the substance and limits of the world, as well as its value or meaning (7), but also of saying what can be said, namely, factual propositions which describe the world. There is, in addition, a direct consequence with respect to ethics. Happiness consists in being in harmony with the world, which is a difficult challenge for each of us because of the stubbornness of facts. Happiness could not possibly consist of simply being in harmony with the *substance* of the world, since the substance of this world is the same as the substance of any possible world, and therefore conforms as well to our wishes and fantasies as it does to facts. There is no more ethical challenge to conforming to the substance of the world than there is to being satisfied with fantasies.

Dualism is intrinsically unsatisfactory, since it seems to exclude the kind of perspicuous overview at which philosophers always aim, and has rarely been mentioned in connection with the *Tractatus*. One may therefore hope that the dualism is only apparent, and that one of the two aspects is really in the final analysis subordinate to the other. Such reductive interpretation began with the first publication of the *Tractatus* and has become standard. At the very birth of the *Tractatus* Russell conceived of it as a form of logical atomism, with the objects serving as the atoms. So deeply ingrained did this conception become that when James Griffin published his fine expository book, *Wittgenstein's Logical Atomism*, he did not even bother to defend this characterization of the work, nor say explicitly what the atoms are. More recently Pears (1987), Malcolm (1986), and Bradley (1992) have echoed Russell and Griffin by characterizing the metaphysics of the *Tractatus* exclusively in terms of the objects. While there are very substantial differences among these five readings of the *Tractatus,* they are alike in attributing to young Ludwig a monistic metaphysical realism, in which the objects are the only ultimate and irreducible elements of reality.

This is, furthermore, not the only monistic reading of the *Tractatus.* Two others are those of Wolniewicz and of McGuinness. Wolniewicz (1990) notes that Wittgenstein assigns a dependent status to objects (*TLP* 2.0122), and he therefore argues that the *Sachverhalte* (atomic facts, states of affairs) are the "atoms" of Wittgenstein's "logical atomism." A further consideration in favor of *Sachverhalte* as Tractarian atoms is that they are the indisputable elements of the only method of analysis explicitly developed in the *Tractatus,* namely, truth-functional analysis. The view of Wolniewicz is arguably closer to Frege than the standard British reading, partly because of the priority given to *thoughts* or propositions rather than to their parts, and partly because of bypassing epistemological issues; at any rate it surely has, at first blush, an equal plausibility.

While the reading of Wolniewicz remains atomistic, that of McGuinness does not. He has written several articles challenging the "so-called realism" of the *Tractatus,* and in a recent one (1985) he explicitly extends his claim of nonrealism from the objects to the facts, and hence to the world. If there is nothing real, there can be no atoms, but his conception still seems monistic: roughly, that if objects are not real, facts cannot be either.

I shall endeavor to show the shortcomings of all these monistic readings of the work.

At first glance there is no denying the dualism. It is there in the very first pages, it is deeply motivated by the main theme of the book (about the possibility of language, especially in regard to the categorial difference between the meaning and the truth of propositions), it has a prominent place in the closing paragraphs, and a metaphysical difference between *fact* and *possibility* is essential to the ethical views Wittgenstein expressed in the *Notebooks*. I believe that it cannot be explained away, but constitutes instead an indispensable and much-neglected aspect of the *Tractatus*. At the same time I am not sure that this unbridgeable duality need be seen as a genuine metaphysical dualism, since (as the work of McGuinness helps us to see) there are not two sorts of reality involved. In the following essay I will discuss its relation to dualism in Frege. In this present essay I wish to consider in some detail its textual basis, its integral role in the main theme of the work, its implication for the current dispute about the alleged realism of the objects of the *Tractatus,* and what it suggests about the continuity of Wittgenstein's thought.

2. The Textual Expressions of Dualism or Transcendental Idealism

Wittgenstein's dualism is the result of his attempting to come to terms with more obvious dichotomies that pertain to the primary subject matter of the *Tractatus,* namely, how propositions are possible, or how it is possible for us to *say* things. With respect to this primary subject matter the difficult problem (as Wittgenstein had learned from Frege and Russell) is to keep in mind that propositions can just as well be false as true. Wittgenstein begins his account of propositions with a discussion of "pictures" in 2.1: "We make pictures of facts for ourselves." He quickly makes clear that what a picture presents is only a *possibility,* and that there is therefore always the possibility of falsity:

> A picture represents a possible situation in logical space. (2.202)
> What a picture represents is its sense. (2.221)
> The agreement or disagreement of its sense with reality constitutes its truth or falsity. (2.222)
> In order to tell whether a picture is true or false we must compare it with reality. (2.223)
> It is impossible to tell from the picture alone whether it is true or false. (2.224)

Whatever other problems there may be about the nature of pictures, it is clear from these passages that it belongs to the essence of a picture to leave open the possibility of falsity as well as truth. One may no doubt *show* things directly and absolutely, but no account of *saying* something can dispense with the true/false dichotomy.

There are further dichotomies in these passages. One is that between reality (*Wirklichkeit*) and possibility. Reality is fairly easy to understand. In 2.063 Wittgenstein says, "The sum-total of reality is the world." Since the world has previously been identified as consisting of the totality of facts, including negative facts, we see that *facts, reality,* and *world* stand together on one side of the dichotomy. This conforms well with common sense. Each of these words refers in ordinary discourse to something that exists and stands pat, as it is, whether we like it or not—that is, what we need to accept and come to terms with.

Reality grounds both truth and falsity, by comprising both positive and negative facts. Contrasted with reality is possibility. A picture represents a possibility of truth or falsity. The actual truth or falsity itself is determined by reality, and that leaves open the question of what it is that makes it possible for the picture to be *either* true *or* false. There is some indication of an answer to this question contained in the above passages, where the possible situation represented by a picture is identified with its sense. But what is the relation between possibility and reality?

One suggestion, elaborated by Bradley (1992), is that possibilities are themselves facts. If this were the case, then we could avoid a metaphysical dualism, for we need acknowledge nothing other than the domain of facts, the actual world. We do often think along this line, regarding possibilities as objective realities, which we are obliged to acknowledge and with which we are obliged to come to terms as much as with any other facts. Wittgenstein's initial emphasis on the world as the totality of facts might lead us to expect that he would follow this line of thought. Yet he does not. Nothing is more important for understanding the *Tractatus* than to realize, as McGuinness (1989) puts it, that possibilities are entirely different from facts. The main reason for this is that the sense of a proposition is something entirely different from its truth. The sense of a picture or proposition must be entirely definite even though its truth be unknown. If the truth of a picture is fixed by its relation to reality, the world, its sense must be fixed by relation to something else—although not another kind of reality, for reality is already a totality of what is real. Wittgenstein gets out of the dilemma looming here by making the sense of pictures depend on their relation to the *substance* of the world. More particularly, the sense of a picture or elementary proposition depends on the correlation of its constituent names with objects (3.202–3.22, 5.4733), the totality of objects making up the substance of the world (2.021).

So sense and possibility do not depend on the world of fact but rather on the objects which make up the substance of the world. Wittgenstein presents his argument in concise form:

> Objects make up the substance of the world. That is why they cannot be composite.
>
> If the world had no substance, then whether a proposition had sense would depend on whether another proposition was true.
>
> In that case we could not sketch any picture of the world (true or false). (2.021–2.0212)

While this argument is by no means entirely convincing, especially since Wittgenstein later (*PI* 242) rejects its conclusion without rejecting its major premise, it does show irrefutably that Wittgenstein at this time accepted the substance of the world as something different from the world itself, because of what he perceived as the necessity of grounding *sense* in something other than *truth*. It is not at all clear that the substance of the world constitutes another *reality* than that of the world, but it is at least something different.

The Tractarian conception of substance as providing an account of other possible worlds, or possible facts other than those which are real, is made clear in the next passages (*TLP* 2.022–2.023):

> It is obvious that an imagined world, however different it may be from the real one, must have *something*—a form—in common with it.
>
> Objects are just what constitute this unalterable form.

The cogency of this point is not immediately clear, in part because the notion of an "imagined world" occurs in only one other (unrelated) passage (6.1233) in the *Tractatus*. Perhaps some unexamined phenomenological idea underlies the standing of such an "imagined world." Throughout the *Tractatus,* however, Wittgenstein focuses on *language* rather than on phenomenology. In the context of language, an "imagined world" is one that is represented in pictures or propositions, and its status is therefore the same as that of the *sense* (not the truth) of pictures or propositions. The unalterable form, on this view, would simply be that which makes it possible for pictures to have sense. Since objects serve this purpose by being the correlates of names in elementary propositions, the final sentence above then becomes just as obvious as Wittgenstein takes it to be.

The standard monistic interpretations proceed by construing states of affairs (*Sachverhalte*) as concatenations of objects (2.01, 2.03; compare 4.22), and facts as existing states of affairs (2.04, 4.2211). The idea is that the transitivity in these relations then allows a reader to conclude that objects are the ultimate constituents of reality, since they are the constituents of existing states of affairs. The relation between the world and its substance—between reality and possibility—is then that the latter is the basis for the former, and hence the ultimate foundation of what is real. This is a very powerful but nonetheless mistaken line of thought, as can be seen from the fact that it leaves *existence* (i.e., reality) wholly unexplained. It fails to take into account (1) that objects lack independent standing, and (2) that states of affairs are possibilities rather than realities.

(1) For objects—or anything else—to be the ultimate constituents of reality they must have independent standing. If they are dependent on something else, that something else will have a more fundamental sort of reality—the something else will be that in terms of which the objects are explained and/or identified. Tractarian objects fail this test. They cannot be conceived independently of their role as constituents of *Sachverhalten*. Wittgenstein makes this dependence clear first in his initial discussion of objects and later in his discussion of the simple signs whose meaning is objects:

> It is essential to things that they should be possible constituents of states of affairs. (2.011)
>
> If I can imagine objects combined in states of affairs, I cannot imagine them excluded from the *possibility* of such combinations.
>
> Things are independent in so far as they can occur in all *possible* situations, but this form of independence is a form of connexion with states of affairs, a form of dependence. (It is impossible for words to appear in two different roles: by themselves, and in propositions.) (2.0121–2.0122)
>
> Only propositions have sense; only in the nexus of a proposition does a name have meaning. (3.3)
>
> It is only in the nexus of an elementary proposition that a name occurs in a proposition. (4.23)

Since names are proxies for objects in propositions (3.22), the dependent status of names in propositions must reflect a similarly dependent status of objects in states of affairs, as is in any case indicated by the first two of these passages. Those two passages (2.011, 2.0121–22) have not always seemed decisive; Pears (1987, ch. 5) has a long discussion which concludes by dismissing the straightforward reading I give them here, and Malcolm (1986, 1–2) is equally unimpressed. But Wittgenstein makes clear that we do not learn language through learning name–object connections, and thereby buttresses the dependent status he has assigned to names and objects:

> The meanings of primitive signs can be explained by means of elucidations. Elucidations are propositions that contain the primitive signs. So they can only be understood if the meanings of those signs are already familiar. (3.263)
>
> If objects are given, then at the same time *all* objects are given. (5.524)
>
> We can describe the world completely by means of fully generalized propositions, i.e. without first correlating any name with a particular object. (5.526)

The first of these remarks has been much discussed, and I do not propose to offer any light on the mysterious workings of these elucidations; I cite the remark to show that learning name–object correlations is not what Wittgenstein had in mind as the primary way of learning names. The other two remarks, less frequently cited, are more decisive in rebutting the suggestion that the meanings of names are learned by rote or by one–one correlation. The objects which come to mind as obviously conforming to *TLP* 5.524 are colors, phonemes, and cardinal numbers. It is clear that I cannot learn the meaning of the numeral '37' without learning other numbers, and that if I learn the numbers I effectively learn *all* of them. A similar conclusion holds for colors and phonemes, because of the dependence of color-words and of phonemes on a *system* of contrasts. It is equally clear that none of this learning consists in learning name–object correlations of the 'Fido'–Fido sort. In systems such as those of numerals and color-words, names have a role but no obvious priority.

The final remark quoted above (5.526) suggests that learning the meanings of names might not be necessary at all, a rather surprising comment in view of what Wittgenstein has said earlier. Perhaps the context would need to be further examined; but, even so, we cannot avoid the implication that the meaning of names is not absolutely ultimate for an account of either language or reality.

(2) There has been much ink spilled discussing whether states of affairs (*Sachverhalte*) are atomic *facts* or atomic *circumstances* (*possibilities*). Black (1964) takes note of the controversy, marshalls arguments on each side, and concludes that *Sachverhalte* are atomic *facts*. The strongest evidence for this view is *TLP* 2.04, where Wittgenstein says that existing *Sachverhalte* are the world; *TLP* 2.0124, where he refers to "possible" *Sachverhalte*; and *TLP* 4.2211, where Wittgenstein seems to obliterate the sharp line between reality and possibility:

> Even if the world is infinitely complex, so that every fact consists of (*besteht aus*) infinitely many states of affairs (*Sachverhalte*) and every state of affairs is composed of infinitely many objects, there would still have to be objects and states of affairs.

It is impossible here to deal adequately with this issue and its large literature, but Black's realist account of states of affairs cannot be wholly right. It may well be that Wittgenstein sometimes thought of states of affairs as facts, or as what makes up facts; the texts confirm this much. Anyone determined to avoid a dualistic reading of the *Tractatus* is bound to do so as well, and to maintain further that states of affairs (and hence objects) are the very *constituents* or stuff of facts. Perhaps Wittgenstein himself was sometimes pulled toward such a monism, but it is beyond serious dispute that he presents an irreducible dualism in the opening pages of the *Tractatus*. It is inescapable, furthermore, that some states of affairs *do not exist* and therefore cannot be facts. The fact, in such a case, is the nonexistence of the state of affairs. When the state of affairs exists, the *fact* is not the state of affairs as such but rather its *existence* (*TLP* 2). States of affairs are possibilities, not facts; they belong to substance, not to the world.

Wittgenstein certainly confuses matters when he speaks of existing states of affairs as facts (rather than the existence of those states of affairs); when he speaks of "possible states of affairs" and must be understood to refer, redundantly, to a sort of "possible possibilities"; and even more when he speaks of facts as "consisting of" states of affairs. These remarks do suggest the transcendental realism with which Black, Malcolm, and Pears tax him. But that reductivist doctrine is blatantly incompatible with Tractarian dualism, and such admittedly puzzling hints of transcendental realism cannot erase the clear-cut metaphysical dualism with which the *Tractatus* begins and ends, and which both Pears and Malcolm ignore. The *Tractatus* speaks this way rarely, otherwise speaking only of the existence and nonexistence of states of affairs as facts.[1] The latter way of speaking perspicuously represents states of affairs as possibilities—as they *must* be, since they are represented in false statements and descriptions of imaginary worlds, and since we must be able to understand propositions without knowing whether they are true or false. States of affairs belong to the domain of substance rather than that of reality. It is the existence and nonexistence of states of affairs, not they themselves, that are facts and hence elements of reality.

There is a troubling air of circularity in the argument just given, one that I find typical of the unsettling impact of the *Tractatus.* The dualism of the opening pages is threatened by the suggestion that the substance of the world consists of the elements out of which the world is constructed, and this reductivist reading is rebutted by insisting on the dualism. Perhaps it is just as well to be a little unsettled by any reading of a text later attacked by the author himself. Nonetheless the dualistic reading, which conforms closely to the influence of Kant, Schopenhauer, and Frege, as well as to both the opening and closing pages of the text, seems confirmed by this further consideration of key ideas, and also helps to read the text more fluently.

3. Supporting Exegetical Considerations

Four additional themes distinctive of Wittgenstein's early work have been mentioned above. They are the opposition between the ego and the world, the ethical point of the work, the dramatic closing words of the *Tractatus,* and its Kantianism. Even a brief discussion of these further themes will demonstrate that an appreciation of the metaphysics of the *Tractatus* is not confined to its first few pages. It takes in the whole thrust of Wittgenstein's early work, and its import extends especially to an appreciation of what it was he tried to do better during his second period at Cambridge in the thirties. The sharp opposition between fact/reality on the one hand and sense/possibility on the other is not expressed in quite the same way in Wittgenstein's other writings, but it does not entirely disappear either. Although Wittgenstein's ideas were

---

1. To speak of the existence of states of affairs, rather than of existing states of affairs, requires more words and more grammatical complexity. Since the *Tractatus* is a work in which words are pared wherever possible, I incline to weigh more heavily the usage which involves some circumlocution, however slight. The troublesome passages might then be thought of as shorthand expressions, used where careful circumlocution would mar the force of the language. Such a suggestion must be employed with caution, however, since Wittgenstein wrote with great care and revised extensively.

never fixed and settled, neither the dramatic changes in style and basic ideas nor the other matters that came to be at issue ever pushed aside the questions about language and meaning that dominate the *Tractatus,* or entirely nullified the astonishing insights of that work.

In *TLP* 6.373 Wittgenstein says, "The world is independent of my will." This remark is one of the few that he culled from the *Notebooks* entries that begin in July 1916. The quoted remark comes from 5.VII.16, when there were also remarks about death and about good and evil that are included in the *TLP* 6.4s. Three days later he writes, "There are two godheads: the world and my independent I." Here again is a duality, but the duality is not necessarily the end of the matter; for in spite of an attraction toward pantheism, he is unwilling to identify God and the world, if the world is conceived (as in *TLP* 1–1.1) as the totality of facts:

> The meaning of life, i.e. the meaning of the world, we can call God . . . To believe in a God means to see that the facts of the world are not the end of the matter. (*NB* 4–8.VII.16)

While this seems to expand beyond dualism, I am not convinced that a "God" so conceived is really a substantial independent entity. God seems rather to be a kind of perspective, or a way of seeing things. On 1.VIII.16 he writes, "How everything hangs together, is God. God is, how everything hangs together." Here God seems identified with facts (see *TLP* 4.5), in a sort of pantheistic view reminiscent of Spinoza, with whose work the *Tractatus* exhibits many interesting parallels that are discussed more fully not only in chapter eight but also, in a different and very stimulating context, by Edwin Curley in his *Spinoza's Metaphysics.* I frankly do not know how to come to terms—ontologically, in the context of the *Tractatus*—with these references to God and godheads. The minimal view is that there remain at least two independent entities: the world of facts and the subject or Ego with its will; God is perhaps a third but is more likely some meaning or perspective or aesthetic appreciation with which the subject comes to terms with the world. This gives us a rather different dualism from that of the first pages of the *Tractatus,* but one arguably compatible with it.[2]

---

2. Hodges (1990, ch. 7) argues that the two dualisms are ultimately, and significantly, incompatible. On the general topic of the opposition between the self and the world, as well as on the tension between the logical and the ethical dimension of transcendence, there is much stimulating discussion in Hodges's study, *Transcendence and Wittgenstein's*

These entries are interesting partly for the light they throw on the *Tractatus,* partly for their focus on ethics and the meaning of life, and partly for their alternating stress on some all-embracing reality and on some inescapable dichotomy. Both overall unity and its impossibility seem to have import for ethics, or for the meaning of life. Thus he characterizes will (21.VII.16) as "first and foremost the bearer of good and evil." This remark has overtones of Kant, for whom morals required a sharp metaphysical dualism, and in particular of the famous remark with which Kant begins his *Foundations of the Metaphysics of Morals:* "Nothing in the world—indeed nothing even beyond the world—can possibly be conceived which could be called good without qualification except a *good will.*" If the world referred to in *TLP* 6.373 is reality (as it ought to be, since the remark was retained in the *Tractatus*), then good and evil are not real (as they were not for Spinoza)—although they continue to have vast importance for humans, just as linguistic meaning does.

Many of the remarks in this section of *Notebooks* speak about happiness. Consider, for example, the following:

> And in this sense Dostoievsky is right when he says that the man who is happy is fulfilling the purpose of existence. (6.VII.16)
>
> A man who is happy must have no fear. Not even in the face of death.
>
> Only a man who lives not in time but in the present is happy.
>
> In order to live happily I must be in agreement with the world. And that is what "being happy" *means.* (8.VII.16)
>
> It seems one can't say anything more than: Live happily! (29.VII.16)
>
> I keep on coming back to this! simply the happy life is good, the unhappy bad. And if I *now* ask myself: But why should I live *happily,* then this of itself seems to me to be a tautological question; the happy life seems to be justified of itself, it seems that it *is* the only right life.
>
> But this is really in some sense deeply mysterious! *It is clear* that ethics *cannot* be expressed!
>
> But we could say: The happy life seems to be in some sense more *harmonious* than the unhappy. But in what sense??
>
> What is the objective mark of the happy, harmonious life? Here it is again clear that there can be no such mark that can be *described.*
>
> This mark cannot be a physical one but only a metaphysical one, a transcendental one. (30.VII.16)

"*Tractatus,*" although its neglect of Spinoza is a major weakness of the work. He argues that there are deep incoherencies in the *Tractatus,* especially between the metaphysical self and the ethical self, and between logical and ethical transcendence.

These ideas have obvious affinities with the work of Spinoza and Schopenhauer, and well-known roots in the latter, who is one of the few persons mentioned in these pages of the *Notebooks*. Our focus is on Wittgenstein's metaphysics, and we therefore need to note the metaphysical dualism. Here Wittgenstein invokes a transcendental realm to provide the mark of happiness, rejecting thereby the two obvious alternatives, that there is no such thing, and that it is a matter of fact.[3] That is to say, we see here, as in the case of language (sense and reference), that something of overwhelming importance to us as humans does not belong to the world of factual reality; its objective mark, its criterion, is transcendental.

Throughout these variations in the way that the fundamental dualities are characterized there are two invariants: the world of fact is the one genuine reality, and the stupendous matters which oppose rather than fit into that reality are vital to human life.

In his letters to Engelmann and Ficker, Wittgenstein stressed the ethical import of his work, and to Ficker he intimated that it was what was unstated in the *Tractatus*. That work itself ends with a famous remark about leaving things unsaid, based on a distinction between what *can* be said and what *cannot* be said. It is not often noticed that this final remark, taken in conjunction with what is said in 6.53 about the correct method in philosophy, is an exact parallel to the metaphysical dichotomy with which the book opens. About the world we can and should talk, about the substance of the world (as well as some other things) we cannot and must not.

These considerations suggest that Wittgenstein was Kantian in the main lines of his thought. Kantianism was attributed to Wittgenstein by Stenius in 1960, is a main theme of Morris Engel's book (1971), was stressed by Janik and Toulmin (1973) and Kenny (1973), and the idea has been discussed off and on since. Most recently Pears (1987) has been forceful in insisting on the Kantian character of Wittgenstein's *Tractatus*. Pears begins (p. 20) his detailed exegesis of the early work with the words, "When Wittgenstein's philosophy is put in a Kantian frame, most of its main lines stand out clearly." Later (pp. 94–96) he

---

3. Hodges (1990, 173ff.) argues vigorously that happiness is "contingent on an actual distribution within the totality of facts" (173), thereby rejecting the idea that happiness requires a transcendental mark. I take it that this is not exegesis and implies no disagreement with me about what Wittgenstein says, but rather a shift from explaining Wittgenstein to contesting (rather superficially, I think) some of his premises.

makes illuminating use of Wittgenstein's Kantianism in his discussion of Wittgenstein's indifference to certain problems about sense-data and solipsism. I am much indebted to Pears for this encouragement to think of Wittgenstein as having Kantian roots; or perhaps better, as being in the critical tradition. I differ from him both in holding that the later work is even more successfully Kantian, and also in giving a Kantian interpretation to the metaphysics of the *Tractatus,* as is evident in the fuller discussion earlier in chapter one.

With respect to the dichotomies that dominate the metaphysics of the *Tractatus* and Wittgenstein's early work in general, the first thing to say is that there is only one reality, the reality of the factual world. Set against this reality are things vital to our human efforts to come to terms with reality: meanings (*Gegenstände*), sense (*Sachverhalte*), logic and logical form, significance, good and evil, will, happiness, beauty, and so on. These things are transcendental, since they do not belong to the world of fact; but they are not real. Wittgenstein's *Tractatus* is not, as Pears concludes (p. 9), "a clear paradigm of uncritical realism." On the contrary, it is a thoroughly critical metaphysics combining factual realism with transcendental nonrealism.

4. The Argument of Pears That Objects Are Atoms of Reality

Pears (1987) characterizes the metaphysics of the *Tractatus* as a kind of atomism, in which the "atoms" are objects (*Gegenstände*) rather than atomic facts (*Sachverhalte*). A substantial part of his argument for this reading consists of rebutting two alternative conceptions of objects, which he views as "opposite extremes." I am not comfortable with this way of stating the issues. It takes a special perspective to see these alternatives as opposite extremes, for they are extremes on only one dimension, namely, degree of identification with the contemporary views of Russell. It is doubtful whether, in discussing Wittgenstein's metaphysical views, it is prudent to focus on this dimension. Russell had at best a secondary interest in ontology, subordinating its questions, along with the rest of metaphysics, to epistemology. Russell strove to achieve some sort of monism—he called it "neutral monism" in the early twenties—but whether he achieved it depended on whether the monism in question could be assimiliated to the theory of knowledge.

Wittgenstein did not share Russell's belief in the primacy of epistemology. The Kantian dualism of Frege and Schopenhauer—*object* and *function* being the basic ontological categories in the one case, *idea* and *will* in the other—provides a more plausible perspective for discussing the *Tractatus* than the one which sees the two alternatives as "extremes." Within the perspective that he adopts, however, Pears's arguments are careful, and therefore worth considering.

Pears first takes up the alternative which identifies the metaphysical elements of *Tractatus* with those of Russell's logical atomism, namely, sense-data.[4] Here his arguments are persuasive. He points out that the evidence for this reading, now that we no longer have to read the *Tractatus* without benefit of other writings by Wittgenstein, is to be found in writings from the late twenties and early thirties in which Wittgenstein discusses "phenomena" and "phenomenology." These later passages will count as evidence for the view in question only if one agrees to two premises, (1) that the passages refer to the *Tractatus,* and (2) that the "phenomena" are sense-data. Pears shows that neither premise is convincing, and that the second really has very little plausibility at all. The presentation has special authority because of Pears's detailed exposition of points where Russell's influence was decisive and because of his straightforward exposition of relevant aspects of Kantianism. Particularly useful are the considerations he advances to show that Wittgenstein's starting point, unlike Russell's, was Kantian rather than empiricist. For Kant, and therefore for the Continental tradition nurtured on Kantian terminology (including Schopenhauer and Frege), "phenomena" are not (as with Russell) contrasted with *material* objects but with *transcendental* objects called "noumena." While this fine combination of attention to detail and attention to the broad philosophical influences may in turn throw doubt on the perspec-

---

4. By far the most impressive development of this alternative is Merrill and Jaakko Hintikka's book, *Investigating Wittgenstein,* which Pears cites in this connection but whose arguments he does not reconstruct—rightly, since they would have taken him too far off track. Here I follow him in that omission. Suffice to say that the arguments of the Hintikkas are remarkably elaborate; they are not confined to the chapter Pears cites (chapter 3, the longest of the book), but are extended in the next chapter to attempt to explain some puzzling positions Wittgenstein takes in the *Tractatus.* These arguments are stimulating but not convincing. Besides the weaknesses which Pears identifies, the case presented also involves (1) a dubious estimation of Wittgenstein's commitment to epistemology as a clue to metaphysics, (2) confusion of relativity with relativism, (3) complete omission of the very powerful influence of H. Hertz (which is not phenomenological in any sense) on the formation of the picture theory, (4) omission, in their long discussion of Frege's influence on Wittgenstein, of any mention of Frege's antipsychologism, and (5) failure to mention the difficulty of understanding the holism of 3.45 and 5.524(1) if objects are sense-data.

tive which Pears himself adopts, it has here that happy consequence that his rebuttal of this alternative is indeed definitive.

Pears's treatment of the other alternative is less successful, and his defense of the alleged realism of simple objects therefore unconvincing. The other alternative is a position first sketched by Ishiguro (1969) and more recently elaborated and extended by McGuinness (1981, 1985). The central point of this alternative is that the meaning of names (simple signs) cannot be determined independently of or prior to their use in propositions, but only through such use. Though there must be objects whenever names have meaning, these objects do not have objective or metaphysical reality, nor do they fix the meanings of names prior to and independently of the use of names in sentences. They are not the ultimate constituents of the world because they do not even belong to the world. They belong instead to language, that is, to our practice of making pictures of facts. They are among the presuppositions of language. Therefore they do not have the reality of facts, of the world.

The argument for this alternative rests partly on texts and partly on exegesis, as does Pears's rebuttal. Neither case is entirely convincing. Pears neglects the subordinate role given to objects and to names in *Tractatus;* McGuinness shows an unconvincing disdain for the elements of realism which Pears stresses, particularly in his 1985 paper.

What Pears most neglects—and Malcolm (1986) and Bradley (1992), too—is *TLP* 1–1.1:

> The world is all that is the case.
> The world is the totality of facts, not of things.

Pears says instead that "the *Tractatus* begins with an account of objects" (p. 111; see also pp. 7, 9, 13), which he refers to as its "opening ontology" (p. 112). Presumably he does not regard *TLP* 1–1.1 as presenting an ontology, but it is difficult to see why not. Black calls this ontology of facts a great metaphysical innovation on Wittgenstein's part. Certainly the wording in *TLP* 1–1.1 straightforwardly expresses a metaphysical realism whose elements are facts rather than objects. It takes not only an extraordinary subtlety but downright intellectual contortion not to read this as an ontology.

Pears makes the further point that the account of objects in the 2.0s precedes Wittgenstein's introduction of pictures in 2.1. This point has no merit whatever. Taken in conjunction with Wittgenstein's explanation of the numbering scheme, the relative numbering counts for

Ishiguro and McGuinness rather than for Malcolm and Pears. Wittgenstein says, "The decimal numbers assigned to the individual propositions indicate the logical importance of the propositions, the stress laid on them in my exposition" (*TLP* 1, n). Since pictures are introduced in a remark with only one decimal, they have a greater "logical importance" than have objects, the account of which is given in remarks with an apparently supernumerary decimal place. The reason the subordinate remarks numbered 2.0s occur before 2.1 is no doubt the one offered long ago by Stenius, namely that the rhythm of the *Tractatus* has subordinate remarks both before and after main remarks; the former to pave the way, the latter to elaborate. Certainly, as all parties agree, the ontology of simple objects is indissolubly connected with our making pictures of facts. It is not, however, the primary ontology of *Tractatus*.

The subordinate status of objects, as indicated by the numbering scheme, (both that the ontology of facts is presented first and also that the ontology of objects is presented with an extra decimal), is connected with the metaphysical dependence discussed earlier. Ordinarily we can imagine that a table or an automobile might cease to exist and everything else remain the same, or that another apple or pencil should exist. Wittgenstein's objects do not have such independent possibilities of existence. Their status is instead like that of things we do not consider "objects" at all—like colors or phonemes or numbers, for example. With numbers and phonemes, as with Wittgenstein's objects, if I am familiar with one I must be familiar with the whole range; they do not have the possibility of being conceived independently of one another.

The subordination of objects to facts and the dependent status of objects are incompatible with the atomistic reading of the *Tractatus* given by Pears. Pears neglects these phenomena, and his defense of an atomistic reading of the *Tractatus* therefore fails. Atoms which constitute the ultimate reality of a contingent world would have to be both independent and simple. Russell's atomism, based on sense data, satisfies this requirement. In the *Tractatus* states of affairs are in a sense independent—not, to be sure, conceptually independent, since each presupposes all the others ("the whole of logical space" of *TLP* 3.42), but independent in reality, since each can exist or not exist while everything else remains the same (*TLP* 2.062, 5.134–5.135).[5] Though

---

5. As mentioned above, this is one plausible ground for B. Wolniewicz's claim (1990) that *Sachverhalte* are Wittgenstein's logical atoms.

independent, however, states of affairs are not simple. Objects are simple but not independent. Therefore there are no Tractarian atoms.

A second difficulty in Pears's rebuttal of Ishiguro and McGuinness is his treatment of possibility. Taking objects as real leads him to speak of the "real possibilities" inherent in each object (103, 111). The first trouble here is that an "unreal possibility" can only be an impossibility. To speak of "real possibilities" in a metaphysical or absolute sense is therefore sheer nonsense. A deeper problem is, as McGuinness (1989) has said, that a possibility is something entirely different from a fact, and it is facts that constitute reality. To speak of "real possibilities" inevitably confounds fact and possibility and thereby betrays one of the basic dualities of the *Tractatus*. It also makes Wittgenstein a hopelessly traditional sort of metaphysician—which is perhaps just what is intended, for widely differing reasons, by others who have, like Pears, found the ultimate reality of the *Tractatus* to consist of *possibilities* rather than *facts*. Malcolm and Bradley both read the *Tractatus* this way, but for totally different reasons.

Malcolm's book *Nothing is Hidden* traces the whole of Wittgenstein's work, treating the later work as a completely new philosophy that overturns the earlier work. In this picture Wittgenstein is portrayed as a kind of romantic hero, like an intellectual Heracles, say, doing things that no ordinary mortal could reasonably hope to achieve. I have no doubt that Wittgenstein was a genius, but he was also human. Unlike heroes, whose achievements are confined to myths and romances, humans work in the real world. If they achieve anything, their achievements take place in a context of the traditions and activity of other humans. "No Poet, no artist of any art," said Eliot in "Tradition and the Individual Talent," "has his complete meaning alone." If it were the case that Wittgenstein constructed a wholly original philosophy, essentially divorced from what other philosophers had ever attempted, and then returned after a decade to create *another* wholly original philosophy, the main thrust of which was to overthrow his earlier effort—that would indeed be a heroic achievement, and such are the terms in which Malcolm portrays Wittgenstein. Since I regard him in more modest terms, I take it that Wittgenstein's work was directed at problems he inherited from the tradition of Western philosophers, especially from Kant, Schopenhauer, Frege, and Russell, and that his return to philosophy in 1929 resulted in a refinement and improvement of his earlier thought rather than a repudiation of it.

The plausibility for Malcolm's version of Wittgenstein stems from his (mistaken) assessment of objects as the ultimate elements of reality in the metaphysics of the *Tractatus*. Objects *do* determine possibility, and if they were the ultimate reality, reality would indeed ultimately consist of possibilities rather than of facts, as Malcolm assumes. Here is a passage that expresses clearly Malcolm's line of thought:

> According to the *Tractatus,* if a name is assigned to an object, the use of the name in sentences must duplicate the form of that object. The possibilities of combination of that name with other names, in sentences that have sense, are determined by and exactly match the possibilities of combination of that object with other objects. Language does not *create* what is thinkable. What makes sense in language is based on the possible combinations of the simple elements of reality.
>
> There is profound difference here between the *Tractatus* and the *Investigations.* In the latter work a distinction *is* drawn between what is 'conceptual' or 'grammatical' on the one hand, and what is empirical or contingent on the other. Wittgenstein speaks of 'grammatical propositions', or 'grammatical differences', and of the 'grammar' of a word. But in this second philosophy he rejects the idea that the grammar of language is determined by some underlying reality. (1986, 14–15)

It is apparent that Malcolm takes the objects to have reality that is prior to language, to our making pictures for ourselves of facts (*TLP* 2.1). In this respect his position is similar to that of Pears, and like Pears he disparages (1986, 28–33) the suggestion of Ishiguro and McGuinness that, far from being metaphysically prior, the forms of objects derive from the requirements of our making pictures of fact. Nothing Malcolm says strengthens Pears's arguments against Ishiguro and McGuinness, which I have already found to be unsatisfactory on both textual and philosophical grounds.

Bradley (1992) has an entirely different motivation for a reading of the metaphysics of the *Tractatus* that follows the main line of Malcolm's. He reinterprets the *Tractatus* from a metaphysical perspective based on formal modal logic and possible-world semantics. The theme is that the *Tractatus* contains a "possibilist" rather than an "actualist" ontology.

> What is primary, for him, is always something complex: an object's having a property, or two or more objects' standing in a relation; in short, a state of affairs. Another way of expressing the point is to say that the metaphysically simple objects of Wittgenstein's ontology are not to be thought of as what Copi once called "absolutely bare particulars".

Rather, each simple object . . . is indissolubly and polygamously wed-
ded to several *formal* properties, each of which is "part of the nature" of
that object. (1992, 79–80)

The arguments made for this unusual view are challenging and rewarding throughout. The argumentation is careful, making extensive use of
the *Notebooks* as well as of the text and deploying critical assessments of
the logical work of Lewis, Adams, Carnap, Rescher, Stalnaker, and
Armstrong in their relation to Wittgenstein. His suggestion is that
Wittgenstein, in spite of saying that this world has its substance in
common with any possible world and that its substance consists of
simple objects, nonetheless admits of possible objects that might be the
substance of another world but not the actual one. More generally
Bradley takes possibilities as given and says (79) that Wittgenstein
"needs only to import existence"; whereas Wittgenstein begins with the
actual world of existing facts. An unconvincing argument against the
standard reading of 2.022–2.023 (43–47) involves confusing objects
that we talk about with the objects of the *Tractatus,* and also using the
Notebooks as a source for the ontology of the *Tractatus.* Nowhere is there
an acknowledgment that Wittgenstein begins with actuality, with the
world as the totality of *facts*—nor is there any recognition of how silly
the moral goal would be of trying to be in harmony with possibilities.
Philosophically what is most missing is any recognition of how actuality
is different from possibility, and of the connection of possibility with
making pictures and thereby with meaning rather than truth. This is
hardly satisfactory as a reading of Wittgenstein. It is a little distressing,
too, that by means of this reading Wittgenstein is pressed into doing
service for the very sort of swashbuckling metaphysical speculation he
was dedicated to rein in.

5. The Kantian Character of Wittgenstein's Work

Missing from Pears's discussion of Ishiguro and McGuinness is the rich
appreciation of Wittgenstein's Kantian starting point, which he so
effectively employs elsewhere. The Kantianism consists partly in beginning with a dichotomy, and more specifically focusing on a dichotomy
between what is *given* to us humans and what we *do* with what we are
given. In the *Tractatus* the first striking duality is between facts and

objects—two different kinds of entity. This is a metaphysical duality, a dualism. It is connected with another duality that is, like the first one, both obvious and problematical, that between the world (1, 1.1) and our making pictures of the world (2.1). This second duality is the Tractarian analog of Kant's distinction between the passive receptivity of the senses and the active spontaneity of the intellect. What remains the same in Wittgenstein's analog is the sharp contrast between what is willy-nilly given to us and our human action when we confront the given. What changes is the framework, since Wittgenstein discards Kant's epistemological focus, replacing it with a logical and metaphysical one. It is true that Wittgenstein says that the pictures are facts, and hence part of the world. But they are facts only as signs, not as symbols. Insofar as a picture is a fact, it is so only as a combination of signs, not as a determination of truth-possibilities. Since sense is unsayable, the sense of pictures is not a matter of fact—and we make pictures for ourselves *because they have sense.* Since *we make* pictures, our making of them introduces an element of intentionality or will that cannot be reduced to fact or idea, a Tractarian harbinger of Wittgenstein's later emphasis on Goethe's line, "Im Anfang war die Tat." It is this feature of pictures that is essential to them, that determines their truth-possibilities. However problematic, this duality between fact and picture, between the world and language, is not only a central feature of the *Tractatus* but also as thoroughly in the Kantian tradition as his distance from Russell and other empiricists on problems of sense-data and privacy.

Another relevant duality is that between meaning and truth, which Wittgenstein owed more to Frege and Russell than to Kantian tradition but which he used to reinforce his Kantian perspective: all pictures have meaning, but only some are true. Lying behind this duality is the possibility of false propositions, which Frege and Russell rightly emphasized. If there were no false propositions, and no possibility of them, then perhaps meaning could be assimilated to truth, pictures to facts, and language to the world. But some propositions are false, and it is important that *any* picture *can* be false. The duality of truth and falsity can thus be seen as holding the others fast and preventing their subtleties and complications from leading toward monistic assimilations. The human agency which creates propositions (meaning) is fallible; its products have no necessary connection with truth, which is determined by reality (facts) rather than by human agency.

These rather Kantian dichotomies presented in this brief sketch have a rather straightforward application to the metaphysics of the *Tractatus.* The work begins with an explicit commonsense realism.[6] The world of facts is there, independent of will and idea. About the reality of the world there are no grounds for doubt: the world is not inferred, but stands there as our starting point. McGuinness (1985) therefore surely draws his argument against the alleged realism of the *Tractatus* too far when he extends it to impugn the reality of facts—as he himself would perhaps agree, since he has more recently (McGuinness, 1989) emphasized that possibilities are entirely different from facts. The *facts* would be the same whether we picture them to ourselves or not. We do, however, make pictures of facts for ourselves, for one another (*TLP* 2.1). Our pictures, our propositions, contain something which is not just "there" and which therefore does not belong to reality, namely, that which invests our words with *sense* and connotes *possibility.* For although our picturings and our utterances are facts (*TLP* 2.141), their sense is not. For young Ludwig this means that *objects* and *states of affairs* belong to an entirely different realm from that of *facts*—and, since there is no reality other than that of facts, that they are not real at all (although they are humanly indispensable). It follows, contrary to Russell, Griffin, Pears, Malcolm, Bradley, and Wolniewicz, that neither *Gegenstände* nor *Sachverhalte* can possibly be "atoms" out of which facts are constructed.[7]

Since there is only one reality in the *Tractatus,* one could perhaps say that it is after all monistic rather than dualistic. Fine. Just remember that *Sachverhalte* and *Gegenstände,* though not real, are *indispensable.* Their status is therefore not unlike that which Kant assigns to the forms of

---

6. Ishiguro endorses this point, as she made clear in her contribution to the 14th International Wittgenstein Symposium (1990; see also 1989). Her understanding of the *Tractatus* is thus substantially different from that expressed by McGuinness in his 1985 paper, though the stress McGuinness later puts on the radical difference between facts and possibilities (McGuinness, 1989) seems also to endorse the sort of dualism for which I have been arguing.

7. This conclusion might seem so very plausible in view of Wittgenstein's general aim, the texts cited, and commonsense distinctions like that between reality and possibility, that one may overlook how difficult it has been to achieve. It would be hard to exaggerate the importance of Ishiguro's essay in 1969. Until that time the discussion of the metaphysics of the *Tractatus* was largely confined to whether its objects were universals or particulars, the presupposition being that they were of course atoms of some sort and therefore elements of reality. This presupposition stemmed from Russell's introduction to the *Tractatus,* and was surely a main reason for Wittgenstein's dislike of that introduction. The presupposition went largely unchallenged until Ishiguro's essay. The main question then became whether *Gegenstände* have any kind of reality at all. Pears and Malcolm continue to insist that they do. Ishiguro's negative answer has since been endorsed and elaborated by Rhees, Kenny, McGuinness, Schulte, and most recently Ishiguro herself.

intuition and categories of the understanding, "transcendental ideality."[8] So long as one recognizes the overwhelming importance of these
things, their absolute indispensability to us, and that they are not of the
order of factual reality nor reducible to that order—then one can say
what one chooses about whether this is "monism" or "dualism." In any
case it is not a variety of atomism at all.

---

8. Kant himself at one time characterized such a view as dualistic: "The transcendentalist
idealist . . . may well be an empirical realist, or, as he is called, a *dualist* . . ." (*KdrV* A370).
The remark is not, however, repeated in the second edition.

7
Dualism

1. The Apparent Dualism of the *Tractatus*

Wittgenstein's *Tractatus* is, as we saw in the previous chapter, built on an apparent metaphysical dualism, the world being one irreducible and unconditioned starting point and its substance another. Although dramatic, its presence has often been masked by the view (due originally to Russell) that in the *Tractatus* Wittgenstein is a logical atomist. The first problem with this view is to say just what the atoms are supposed to be. The objects (*Gegenstände*) are simple but dependent; they cannot even be thought of separately from the combinations in which they can occur (2.0121). The states of affairs (*Sachverhalte*), on the other hand, are independent but not simple. Even if this first problem about whether *Sachverhalte* or *Gegenstände* are atoms could be overcome, the atomism could not account either for the need for *context* or for the *totality* which is an essential feature both of the world and of the language which mirrors it (*TLP* 1.1, 1.11, 1.12). The context principle stated in 3.3, which Wittgenstein adopted from Frege, seems flatly incompatible with any sort of atomism:

> Only propositions have sense; only in the nexus of a proposition does a name have meaning.

This is especially so in view of the vast framework upon which propositions and symbols depend, according to 3.42 and 5.511:

> A proposition can determine only one place in logical space: nevertheless the whole of logical space must already be given by it.
> How can logic—all-embracing logic, which mirrors the world—use such peculiar crotchets and contrivances? Only because they are all connected with one another in an infinitely fine network, the great mirror.

These remarks summarize the case made in the previous chapter against treating the *Tractatus* as a philosophy of atomism. Here my object is to explore the incompatible view that the *Tractatus* is a form of dualism. I wish to bring the metaphysical dualism of the *Tractatus* into view, so as to consider its source, its function, and what became of it in the later work of Wittgenstein.

The dualism of the *Tractatus* is "linguistic" as well as ontological, in three ways:

1. The distinction between objects and facts is mirrored in the dichotomy between two sorts of signs, names, and sentences.
2. There is a corresponding semantic distinction between sense (*Sinn*) and reference (*Bedeutung*); only names have reference and only sentences have sense.
3. A sharp dichotomy between meaning and truth is thereby achieved, since it is correlation of names with objects that determines meaning and correlation of sentences with facts that determines truth.

The last point is central to Wittgenstein's early work. His problem (*TLP* 2.0121, 2.0122–2.023) is to provide a general account (with details to be supplied by special sciences) of ordinary statements we make to one another, and in that connection his insistence that the *meaning* of statements (their sense or *Sinn*) must be settled by reference to a domain wholly independent of the facts that settle their truth (or falsity) is an important reason for the dualism of the *Tractatus*.

In this essay I want to make a limited contribution to understanding how Wittgenstein came to adopt dualism in this particular form, and what happened to it in his later work. My main idea is that the doctrine is due primarily to Frege, but that the details—which are obviously not Fregean—come from Wittgenstein's attempt to revise and perfect Frege rather than to follow him slavishly. I shall therefore not be examining Wittgenstein's dualism in a critical or comprehensive or comparative manner; the chapter belongs more to the history of philosophy than to systematic metaphysics. But the history, at the same time, is partly speculative. Nor will the history be even minimally balanced, since I largely omit consideration of the profoundly important influence of Russell on the development of Wittgenstein's thought at this time. And finally, I shall treat Frege in a general, superficial, and derivative manner,[1] since I refer to him to establish the framework for

---

1. The texts of Frege on which I rely are in Frege (1952), especially pages 21–78, and Frege (1964), especially sections 0–4 and 26–32. Among the commentators I have profited from David Bell's *Frege's Theory of Judgment*, from the essays by Michael Dummett and by

Wittgenstein's dualism rather than to enter into the fascination of Frege's own work.

2. Frege's Dualism

Frege's dualism of objects and concepts is at first glance rather ordinary. One might suppose objects to be individuals and concepts to be universals, and thereby see Frege's dualism as simply another version of familiar medieval metaphysics. But Frege's dualism was highly original in its motivation and development, and it was its originality rather than its ordinary features that interested Wittgenstein. What is most striking is that Frege does not explain and develop his dualism by examining reality (the world) but by examining language. Indeed, his starting point is mathematical symbolism rather than ordinary language. Frege was convinced (rightly) that a productive symbolism requires two irreducibly different sorts of signs. Since they cannot be ultimately and decisively distinguished by their shapes or their mode of meaning, they must be distinguished by their referring to two irreducibly different sorts of reality. Therefore there must be two sorts of metaphysical entities. This is the argument in a nutshell as Wittgenstein must have seen it. Three prominent dichotomies are involved, whose complex interrelations I shall attempt to describe as briefly as possible.

The first dichotomy concerns symbols or expressions. Every expression is either a proper name (*Eigenname*) or a function-name (*Funktionsname*). By a 'proper name' Frege does not just mean what we ordinarily think of as a proper name, but rather any singular referring expression. Thus, 'the author of *Persuasion*' is a proper name, according to Frege's terminology, as well as '*Persuasion*' and 'Jane Austen'. *Eigennamen* are "complete" expressions, which is to say that they are "saturated." Frege's main criteria for whether an expression is saturated are grammatical: declarative sentences are saturated; noun phrases which are either proper names (in the ordinary sense) or definite descriptions (beginning with the definite article 'the') are saturated; and noun phrases which are either pluralized or introduced by the indefinite article 'a' or by 'one', 'some', 'any', 'each', 'no', or 'every' are not saturated.

Peter Geach in Klemke (1968), by Montgomery Furth in Frege (1964), and by David Shwayder in Schirn (1976). The article "Subject and Predicate" in the *Encyclopedia of Philosophy* (New York: Macmillan, 1967) is also useful.

Frege recognizes (1952, 45) that these grammatical criteria are not perfect, but he is confident that they can be grasped by any reader who meets him halfway.

Expressions of the other sort are "unsaturated names," that is, "function-names" or predicates; they are operators or incomplete symbols and cannot be fully understood in isolation from other symbols. His starting point (1952, 21) is "what is called a function in mathematics"—or rather the name of a function, since Frege insisted that a function must be distinguished from both its name and its value-range. Such an expression, when properly attached to it, turns one proper name into another proper name. If, for example, we consider the sentence

(1) The author of *Persuasion* is Jane Austen,

it is obvious that the expression 'the author of' is a function-name, since it turns the proper name *'Persuasion'* into another proper name. Frege maintains that the expression 'is Jane Austen' is also a function-name, on the ground that it turns the proper name 'the author of *Persuasion*' into another saturated expression, the sentence itself. Thus grammatical predicates are one sort of function-name. It can readily be seen that a grammatical predicate is unsaturated; but taking predicates to be operators requires construing sentences as proper names. Frege acknowledges that this seems unnatural, but he nonetheless embraces it. Predicates are those function-names which result in a sentence when they are attached to a proper name. They therefore stand for concepts and are called 'concept-words'. Sentences, in turn, express thoughts and stand for truth-values:

> We thus see how closely that which is called a concept in logic is connected with what we call a function. Indeed, we may say at once: a concept is a function whose value is always a truth-value. (1952, 30)

In addition to steadfastly maintaining that concept-words are function-names, he says something further about them which is both very sensible and very problematic. He insists that they are essentially predicative (1952, 43, 46, 50). This is sensible, because, for example, it is the essentially predicative nature of the phrase 'is Jane Austen', not its being unsaturated, that differentiates it from phrases like 'the author of'. We might be tempted to explain the difference by saying that the predicative expression can turn a name into a sentence, whereas the other phrase can only turn it into a complex proper name (a noun phrase). But such an explanation is not open to Frege, for two reasons. The first is that he takes sentences also to be complex proper names. The second is that it would be grossly circular for him to do so, since sentences are precisely those complex proper names whose function-name component is predicative (i.e., is a concept-word). Since being predicative can in no way be reduced to being unsaturated, we must conclude that it is never really explained by Frege at all, but is employed by him as a basic undefined notion in terms of which he distinguishes predicates from other operators—and thereby also distinguishes (on the side, so to speak, rather than as an integral part of his program) names of truth-values from names of other objects.

The second dichotomy is Frege's famous bifurcation of modes of meaning into sense and reference: an expression *expresses* its sense (*Sinn*) and *stands for* its reference (*Bedeutung*). The first thing to notice is that some distinction between modes of meaning is altogether necessary for Frege. His incisive and perceptive attack on formalism (1952, 182ff.) could be turned back against himself if he were to treat a perceptible difference in the signs themselves as basic. Difference in mode of meaning should, therefore, lead to—not follow from—a fundamental distinction between kinds of expressions. But at this point we meet a paradox. For the power of Frege's thought is due in large part to the fact that he employs the sense-reference distinction in a way that is altogether contrary to that which seems to be required by his distinction between the two basic sorts of expression.

Roughly speaking, sense (*Sinn*) is the mode of meaning characteristic of operators in general and predicates in particular, and reference or denotation (*Bedeutung*) is the mode of meaning characteristic of names. This is a more or less intuitive way of understanding the difference between the sense and reference of expressions; Dummett argues in two essays in Klemke (1968), against the mainstream of commentators but I believe convincingly, that Frege takes for granted this ordinary intuitive meaning. (See also Bell [1979] and Shwayder [1976]). This ordinary distinction can be confirmed by considering what is required to know that a simple proposition is true or false, such as

(2) Eliot is a poet.

If the first word, the proper name, prevents me from saying whether the sentence is true or false, the remedy is not to be found in an attempted account of the sense of semantic implications of this word, of its entailments and incompatibilities *vis à vis* other words, but only through identifying Eliot—that is, connecting a person with the name which he bears and which stands for him in (2). If, on the other hand, the trouble is over the concept-word 'is a poet,' it is to be resolved by explaining what sense the phrase expresses—for example, by elaborating entailments ("A poet is a writer") and incompatibilities ("Poetry is not prose"); that is, the semantic implications of the expression. All of this is very ordinary, and I believe it needs no argument. What Frege then does explicitly is to argue that both proper names and operators have both sense and reference. The sense of a sign, he suggests, is the mode of presentation of the *Bedeutung,* or that "wherein the mode of presentation is contained" (1952, 57). Senses, like referents and expressions, can be either saturated or unsaturated (1952, 54).

Thus, while Frege's doctrine of sense and reference certainly incorporates some of our ordinary intuitions, it is on balance a bewildering turnabout from a naïve point of view. And it is just this untidy complexity that has been most attractive and most influential in Frege's theory. Its first and most famous consequence is that it enabled Frege to account for the significance of identity statements such as (1). If proper names had just reference and the whole story about the names 'Jane Austen' and 'the author of *Persuasion*' were that they refer to the same person, (1) would be a worthless tautology. Frege explains that its significance comes from the fact that the two names, which do have the same reference, have different senses. Since arithmetic consists in significant part of identity statements (equations), this result is of the greatest importance. A second and closely related consequence is that there can be names that have a sense but no reference—such as 'Mr. Pickwick', 'the philosopher who accepted all of Frege's dualism', and sentences (3) and (4) that follow—though there cannot be reference without sense, since every sign must always present its referent in some manner or other. A third consequence that is very attractive has to do with complex proper names, such as sentences or definite descriptions, and involves what Furth (1964, xvii) calls "Basic Principles of Sense and References": that the sense of such a name depends just on the sense of its components, and its reference depends just on the reference of its components. Thus a sentence has reference if and only if each of its components has a reference; its reference is either the True or the False, depending on whether the object denoted by the subject falls under the concept denoted by the predicate. A sentence has a sense if and only if each of its components has a sense, and it is then said to express a thought (*Gedanke*). It follows that (2) expresses a certain thought and has reference, namely, it refers to the True. On the other hand

(3) Mr. Pickwick is a poet, and

(4) Eliot is a slithy tove

both lack reference—(3) because there is no reference (in Frege's sense) for the proper name 'Mr. Pickwick', and (4) because the concept-word 'is a slithy tove' does not stand for a concept. A sentence (*Satz*) therefore lacks a truth-value (reference) if and only if one of its components lacks reference.[2] This is an attractive result. So the sense-reference dichotomy, while it cannot serve to distinguish the two basic sorts of expression, is at the heart of some of Frege's most powerful contentions.

The third dichotomy is Frege's metaphysical dualism, his division of reality into objects and functions. These ontological categories correspond respectively to the two kinds of expressions, proper names and function-names, and serve as the ultimate explanation of how the two sorts of expressions differ. Thus Frege says, "I call anything a proper name if it is a sign for an object" (1952, 47), and Furth concludes that denoting an object and denoting a concept are two *different* modes of meaning (1964, xxix). Objects are complete and saturated. Functions (including concepts), on the other hand, are denoted by function-names in general and by linguistic predicates in particular, and like their linguistic counterparts they are incomplete and unsaturated. Both objects and concepts are real and objective, and both are denoted by names; they differ just with respect to saturation or completeness. With respect to the status of sense Frege is less forthcoming, and I have depended on the fine discussion of Shwayder (1976) for treating the two sorts of sense as metaphysically distinct on the level of semantics rather than ontology. Without delving further into what other complications

---

2. The principles of sense and reference are a bit more complicated than I have represented them here. See Furth (1964) for an incisive statement of them; another statement can be found in Shwayder (1976). This second dichotomy is more complicated than at first appears because of interaction between sense and reference. Both Shwayder (1976) and Bell (1979) point out that the reference of a sentence is determined by its sense as well as by the references of its components. Wittgenstein eliminates this complication by never talking of the reference of a sentence or the sense of a component, but the interaction between sense and reference figures in his explicit reference to Frege's principle in *TLP* 5.4733:

Frege says that any legitimately constructed proposition must have a sense. And I say that any possible proposition is legitimately constructed, and, if it has no sense, that can only be because we have failed to give a *meaning* to some of its constituents.

there may be, we may summarize Frege's view by means of the following diagram, in which an asterisk signifies the point of a metaphysical dichotomy, and the uneasiness of the metaphysics can be seen in the fact that the asterisks do not line up vertically:

FIGURE 1. *Frege's Dualism*

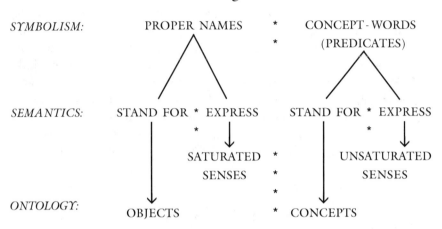

Frege has been treated with a curious combination of respect and avoidance. His distinction between sense and reference has been one of the most influential of this century, and the other two dichotomies are intriguingly associated with it; but I know of no one who has accepted all three. Wittgenstein, in the *Tractatus,* comes close. He presents a dichotomy at each level, and the two sorts of entities are correlated with the two sorts of symbols. There are, however, three features of Frege's theory which would seem to be defective from any point of view, and two others which are unsatisfactory from the point of view which Russell and Wittgenstein shared at the time they worked together. It helps to see a motivation for Wittgenstein's dualism if we suppose that he saw these defects and tried to "perfect" Frege's underlying idea by overcoming them.

Perhaps the most universally unsatisfactory feature of Frege's theory is that sentences are proper names of a sort. Frege did not shrink from this conclusion, but regarded it as one of the virtues of his theory. Treating sentences as names enabled him to formulate a theory of truth, which he regarded, not unreasonably, as better than not having a theory of truth at all. Nevertheless, the radical difference between names and sentences has been a standard feature of logic and the philosophy of language since the time of Plato, for good reasons. Frege's treatment of sentences as names undermines this crucial distinction as surely as Cratylus's treatment of names as truth-bearers. In spite of its ingeniousness, this aspect of Frege's theory cannot be regarded as satisfactory.

The second feature of Frege's theory to which there would be general objection is that it posits some very odd objects. Since sentences are names, for example, they must refer to some object or other. One might think that what a sentence refers to is the fact which it expresses; but this will not do at all, partly because it would be just as odd to regard a fact as an object as it is to regard a sentence as a name, but principally because there would be nothing for false sentences to refer to. According to Frege, each sentence refers to either the True or the False, and therefore the True and the False are genuine objects. Another consequence of Frege's theory is that the concept *horse* is not a concept but an object, since the expression 'the concept *horse*' is (in Frege's sense) a proper name rather than a concept-word. Following out this line of reasoning, Frege concludes that there is an abstract object, a "concept-correlate" as Wells (Klemke 1968, 17) calls it, associated with each concept, a consequence which seems a most profligate multiplication of entities. The paradoxical character of Frege's theory at this point has been a major factor in keeping others from following him.[3]

The third shortcoming in Frege's position is his apparent abandonment, or neglect, of one of three fundamental principles he had embraced with great fanfare a few years before he wrote the papers which set forth the three dichotomies. This is the "context principle," as it has come to be called, that a word has meaning only in the context of a sentence. Frege announced the principle in the preface to his *Foundations of Arithmetic,* and he used it forcefully in the course of his polemic in that book.[4] Six years later there were few traces of the principle; and though he never renounced it, he never restated it. It remains a powerful and influential—although controversial—principle, and Frege's own views about it are unclear, since he only abandoned it and did not criticize it. It is clear that to have retained the context principle after 1890, Frege would have had to resolve at least four questions: (1) whether it applies to proper names or to function-names, or to both; (2)

---

3. According to Grossmann (1969), Frege was mistaken in thinking that he was committed to these first two consequences. Bell (1979, ch. 1) comes to nearly the same conclusion, with reservations.

4. Frege (1950), x, 71, 73. Frege uses the phrase *"bedeuten etwas"* for "have meaning"; he had not yet made his distinction between *Sinn* and *Bedeutung.* Shwayder (1976) and Dummett (1976) argue that the rule of context was abandoned after 1890, but Sluga (1977) demurs.

whether it applies to sense or to reference, or to both; (3) how to reconcile it with his ontology, since any ontological entity which serves as the meaning of a word would presumably do so independent of context; and (4) how it can be reconciled with the treatment of sentences as names, for it would seem that a sentence could have meaning only in the context of a sentence, and so on *ad infinitum*. After Frege's famous papers in 1890, the range of the context principle is undetermined with respect to the distinction between *Sinn* and *Bedeutung* as well as that between names and predicates, and it seems *prima facie* incompatible with his account of sentences and with his ontology. Anyone impressed with the context principle, as Wittgenstein surely was, must remain hesitant to accept Frege's dualism until these questions have been resolved.

The fourth defect in Frege's view, one which might not be so generally shared, is that the three dichotomies do not line up with one another. Since reference is the mode of meaning characteristic of names, one would perhaps expect Frege to say—as Plato (*Theatetus* 201e–202c) suggested much earlier and as Russell (1918) and Wittgenstein (*TLP* 3.221, 3.3) were to say a short time later—that a genuine proper name has only reference, and no other mode of meaning. As we have seen, the power of his theory comes because he says precisely the opposite of this, in dealing with the problem of the Morning Star and the Evening Star and with statements of contingent identity in general. Both Russell and Wittgenstein objected to this lack of tidiness, and held that names have only reference. Wittgenstein was no doubt also disturbed by the violation of clean aesthetic lines, of *Übersichtlichkeit,* that results from this lack of congruence among the three dichotomies.

There is a fifth feature of Frege's theory which might be generally approved but which is a serious defect from the point of view of Russell and Wittgenstein, namely that it gives too much prominence to the subject-predicate distinction. Russell believed that the new logic which Frege inaugurated provided an alternative to subject-predicate logic. If that claim is to be convincing, the fundamental concepts in which the new logic is explained should not themselves be derived from the distinction between subject and predicate. Frege's distinction is not directly drawn from that distinction in exactly those terms, since Frege himself takes as his starting place a function and its argument rather than a predicate and its subject. But when Frege moves away from mathematics and begins discussing language and ontology, this particular qualification seems to be merely verbal: the distinction between saturated and unsaturated expressions seems little more than a metaphor for the subject-predicate distinction. We noted in particular that Frege's way of proceeding leaves the predicative nature of concepts (on which he insists) wholly unexplained; and therefore the idea of predication (that very Aristotelian idea of which Russell complained) appears as an unexamined foundation of Frege's semantic and logical theory. Of course, quantified sentences do not have a subject-predicate form in Frege's scheme, and that is certainly the main point. But if the three dichotomies could be refined so as to eliminate the implicit reliance on the idea of predication in Frege's papers, this would certainly be a great improvement from the point of view of the new logic. In his *Tractatus* Wittgenstein presents such a refinement.

3.   How Wittgenstein Reworked Frege's Dichotomies

The *Tractatus* accepts a dichotomy on each of the three levels on which Frege presented one, but there are some striking differences. On the level of symbolism Wittgenstein's dichotomy is between sentences and names; on the level of semantics it is between sense and reference, just as Frege's was; and on the level of metaphysics he presents an ontological dualism of facts and objects. These revisions of Frege's dualism are motivated primarily by a wish to give prominence to sentences, and in part by a concern, characteristic of Wittgenstein, to ensure aesthetic elegance in the set of dichotomies.

It is to Frege as much as to anyone that we owe a twentieth-century tendency to regard sentences or propositions, rather than propositional components (nouns and verbs), as the most fundamental units in semantics. In this respect Wittgenstein used Frege against himself. He used Frege's context principle, in ways that Frege did not intend, to transform Frege's dichotomy at the level of symbolism. He applied the principle specifically to names, which Frege regarded as saturated. Frege could not have applied this principle to proper names if he repeated it at all after 1890. The effect of the rule of context is to make the expressions to which it applies incomplete or unsaturated. Thus Russell could readily apply the principle to definite descriptions and to the other expressions which he called "incomplete symbols," and the later Frege could have applied it to function-names and predicates but not to proper

names. We might then present Wittgenstein's revision of Frege in the
following way: there are indeed both saturated and unsaturated expressions, but only propositions are saturated, and all names (all parts of
propositions, whether proper names or predicates) are unsaturated. This
perspective helps to explain why the distinction between proper names
and predicates, so prominent in Frege, drops out of sight in
Wittgenstein's *Tractatus*. (See Shwayder [1976] for a contrary view.)

When the principle is applied to names, it implies a radical difference
between names and sentences. If a sentence were itself a sort of name, as
Frege maintained in the 1890s, it would not have meaning unless
embedded in some other sentence, and so on *ad infinitum*. In that case
we would *never* be in a position to say that any name has meaning.
Wittgenstein gives great prominence to Frege's principle (*TLP* 3.3),
altering it slightly so that it applies specifically to names. Accepting this
principle, as amended and incorporated into *TLP*, entails that if there
are to be just two fundamental sorts of expressions, and if names are one
sort of expression, the other basic sort of expression *must* be sentences.
So names become opposed to sentences rather than to predicates, and
there is no longer another sort of component (predicates, relations) with
which names are contrasted, nor is it necessary to contrast one sort of
name with another.

This result, that names are to be contrasted in the first instance with
sentences rather than with verb phrases, can also be derived by applying
the basic principles of sense and reference to the problem of truth. Frege
had worked out an alternative to a correspondence theory of truth. But
the basic principle of reference, that the reference of a complex depends
just on the reference of its components, can be seen to imply a
correspondence criterion of truth. Whether a proposition is true
depends, according to this principle (and assuming the True or the False
to be the reference of each sentence), just on whether the referents of its
components (that is, the objects and the concepts) are arranged corre-
spondingly in the real world. Once the matter is put this way, it appears
that the basic distinction among symbols must be between words and
sentences. For both nouns/objects and verbs/concepts there is a
one-to-one correspondence of the name with its referent, whereas for
sentences/states-of-affairs it is *configurations* that must be matched—on
the basis of a coordination of their components. To put the point in
other words, as long as nouns and verbs both have *reference*, the
difference between them is secondary to the difference between them (as

components) and sentences, which have *sense* that is necessarily derived from the reference of components.

Except for retaining the dichotomy between proper names and predicates, this revision of Frege's doctrine is essentially congruent with the so-called Picture Theory of Meaning of *TLP*, whose possible origins we can thus see to lie in Wittgenstein's reworking of the implications of Frege's principles of sense and reference. Though historical evidence is lacking, such an account is at least as attractive—for a historian much more so—than the familiar story that the idea came to him while contemplating a diagrammatic form for reporting traffic accidents. It should be thought of as supplementing rather than as replacing the account of the role of Hertz's *Principles of Mechanics* in the development of the Picture Theory, which is persuasively documented by Griffin (1964, 99–102) and by Janik and Toulmin (1973, 139–45).

Since both the basic principles of sense and reference and also the context principle are profound and profoundly Fregean, it would be reasonable, for Wittgenstein as for us, to suppose that any modification of Frege's dualism which they both imply must be a refinement and perfection of Frege's leading ideas rather than an attack on him. Wittgenstein duly records his respect for the "great works of Frege" (*TLP*, preface), and Wittgenstein's sense of carrying on Frege's work probably accounts for the disappointment with which he concluded that Frege did not understand a single word of his work (*Letters* R37).

The elegance that results from Wittgenstein's transformation of the dualism is a striking achievement. Only names have reference, and only sentences have sense. In each case the semantic correlate of the symbol has a separate status in the metaphysics. The reference of a name is the object that it stands for in the context of a sentence, and the sense of a sentence is the state of affairs that it depicts. Names no longer have both sense and reference, Wittgenstein having adopted other solutions (see *TLP* 2.0201, 3.24, 5.53n) to the problems that were worrying Frege, about definite descriptions and identity statements. Objects, furthermore, can only be named; they cannot be described or put into words. Facts, on the other hand, can be described, but they cannot be given names. The one kind of symbol can *stand for* an object but cannot *depict* or *express* it, whereas the other kind of symbol can *depict* or *express* a state of affairs but cannot *stand for* it. Thus Wittgenstein retained a fundamental dichotomy at each of the three points where Frege introduced them; but he slightly revised the dichotomies and lined them up so that the split on any one level corresponds exactly with that on the other two. We can illustrate this as follows:

FIGURE 2. *Wittgenstein's Dualism (Tractatus)*

SYMBOLISM:	NAMES	*	SENTENCES
SEMANTICS:	↓	*	↓
SEMANTIC RELATION:	STAND FOR THEIR	*	EXPRESS THEIR
SEMANTIC OBJECT:	REFERENCE	*	SENSE
SEMANTIC ACHIEVEMENT:	MEANING	*	TRUTH-VALUE
ONTOLOGY:	OBJECTS	*	FACTS

Through this transformation of Frege's dualism, Wittgenstein overcame all five of the defects. The elegance and symmetry are obvious, sentences are sharply distinguished from names, the context principle is reinstated, neither truth-values nor any other strange sorts of things are objects, and the subject-predicate form drops entirely out of sight—which never happened in any of Russell's work, in spite of the vehemence of his attack on subject-predicate logic.

Although there is no question that Wittgenstein committed himself to the sharp dichotomies that have been discussed and to the necessity for both facts and objects, and although the literature of his early work often focuses on the question of objects and names, Wittgenstein himself gave a decided and emphatic prominence to facts, sentences, and sense, over against objects, names, and reference. It is helpful to keep this fact in mind when one is reading the whole of Wittgenstein's work, the *Investigations* along with the *Tractatus*. The evidence for it is clear-cut. Wittgenstein begins with his ontology of facts, which Black (1964, 27) calls his outstanding metaphysical innovation. He not only mentions facts first, but what he has to say about facts he says in sections numbered with whole numbers and only one or two decimal places. When he comes to discuss objects, on the other hand, they are discussed in at least two decimal places, beginning with proposition 2.01. This numbering, particularly at the beginning of the book, has a significance because of Wittgenstein's explicit statement, in a footnote to the first proposition, that "the decimal numbers assigned to the individual propositions indicate the logical importance of the propositions, the stress laid on them in my exposition." We find similar evidence when Wittgenstein comes to discuss pictures, sentences, and names. Pictures are introduced first at 2.1, sentences at 3.1, and Wittgenstein again introduces an extra, apparently superfluous, decimal place when he explains simple signs (names) in 3.201. This impression about the prominence given to facts and sentences over objects and names can be confirmed by reading just those *Tractatus* propositions numbered with either whole numbers or only one decimal place. In such a reading objects are not mentioned until 3.2 and names until 3.3, and in each case the simple element is subordinated to the composite. There is further confirmation in that language is the totality of sentences, not of names, just as the world is the totality of facts, not of things. So Wittgenstein not only trims up Frege's distinctions, but he also, contrary to Russell, gives prominence to the composite over the simple and to the whole over the parts. The reasons he does so may remain somewhat obscure, but appreciating that he does so enables us to see more clearly the transition to his later philosophy.

4. The Dichotomies in Wittgenstein's Later Work

What becomes apparent when the dichotomies are set out in Wittgenstein's way, with the prominence given to facts and sentences, is that the vulnerable flank in the schema is where names and simple objects are found. Since he had already subordinated them to sentences and facts, it was only natural that Wittgenstein should ask, when he returned to philosophy after nearly a decade, whether the logic of language really requires that there should be "names" (symbols that have only reference and are components of sentences) and "simple" objects. No topic is more prominent in his later work. And yet it is not easy to say what Wittgenstein's attack on his earlier view of "names" and "objects" implies. In particular it is not easy to know what it implies about the ordinary distinction between words and sentences. Does his attack on names and simples undermine all aspects of the radical dualism, leaving us no radical distinction between words and sentences? Or does he simply blast away at the metaphysical foundations, leaving the distinction intact at the other levels?

In the one publication that he personally prepared from his later work, the *Philosophical Investigations,* the first topic he takes up is the view that the basis of language is naming; in other words, associating certain words with certain objects. The discussion extends through *PI* 45, with Wittgenstein showing the limitations of the view, developing a method for examining the issues, and presenting an alternative account of how words have meaning. The discussion merges into a discussion of simple objects at *PI* 39, which becomes the focus through *PI* 46–64. By the end of these remarks the notion of absolutely simple objects has completely collapsed, and with it the whole conception of words which have meaning solely by being correlated with such objects. Wittgenstein's dualistic metaphysic in the *Tractatus* achieved independent basis for truth and for meaning, in facts and in objects, respectively. In the later work, with the ontological dualism obliterated, truth and meaning can no longer be kept independent of one another. For there to be language at all, there must be agreement in judgments as well as in definitions, and we must come to realize that this is a much less serious threat to the autonomy and validity of logic than it might appear to be (*PI* 242). One might almost say that the foundation walls are supported by the whole building (*OC* 248)—without this inverted priority impairing the serviceability of either the walls or the building.

Does the distinction between sentences and words, or that between sense and reference, survive this onslaught on the metaphysical foundations? The answer is not obvious. In the opening remarks of the *Investigations* Wittgenstein treats words as sentences and speaks interchangeably of "words" and "sentences." In the language-game of the builders (*PI* 2ff.), for example, the utterance of a single word conveys a whole message, the utterances which convey messages have no grammatical complexity, and there is no provision at all for combining the words of the language into larger expressions. Thus no distinction between words and sentences is possible within the language-game of the builders; and Wittgenstein's remark that we could imagine this limited "language" as "the whole language of a tribe" (*PI* 6) is (if the tribe is human) stretching imagination very far indeed. Later (*PI* 19–20) he says that we tend to think that 'Slab!' is really short for the four-word sentence "Hand me a slab!" just because we have certain contrasting possibilities in mind, such as "Send me a slab!", "Hand him a slab!", "Hand me two slabs!", and "Hand me a pillar!"—as if the articulation of the sentences is of no fundamental importance. A few paragraphs further on (*PI* 23), he reinforces this impression that there is no fundamental distinction to be made between words and sentences, when he speaks of "countless different kinds of use of what we call 'symbols', 'words', 'sentences'." We certainly get the impression that the dualism is being dismantled at the level of the symbolism as well as at the level of metaphysics.

On the other hand one must wonder how a philosopher who had been profoundly impressed with the difference between sentences and words could ever possibly come to ignore the profound difference between them, or come to regard the grammatical articulation of sentences as a superficial feature. And as might be expected, more careful scrutiny reveals traces of the old dichotomies. These traces are (1) continued use of *Sinn* and *Bedeutung* consistent with the distinction in the *Tractatus;* (2) a definition of meaning (*Bedeutung*) which applies only to words; (3) a generally observed distinction between two sorts of use, *Gerbrauch* and *Verwendung;* and (4) a recognition of differences between intentional significance (depending on aim or purpose) and conventional significance (depending on rules and customs).

1. Wittgenstein's continued recognition and employment of a difference between *Sinn* and *Bedeutung* is perhaps the most telling trace, one that is more apparent in the German than in the English version. Hallett (1977, 206) calls attention to it in discussing *PI* 117: "Note that here as elsewhere in the *Investigations,* Wittgenstein speaks of the *Bedeutung* of an individual word, and of the *Sinn* of a sentence, not vice versa . . ." This regularity (which is partially obscured in the English translation) exactly follows the basic semantic distinction of the *Tractatus.* It is true that the distinction is employed in the *Investigations* without fanfare; it is true that Wittgenstein was fighting against the bewitching simplicity and elegance of his earlier work; it is true, too, that he strove to avoid jargon, so that his translator's slurring of the terminological distinction may have served his wishes. Yet the terminology survives, and suggests that, however much Wittgenstein struggled against his earlier views, he continued to recognize two basic sorts[5] of linguistic expressions (sentences and words) with different sorts of significance (*Sinn* and *Bedeutung*).

---

5. The "countless kinds" referred to in *PI* 23 are all species of one genus, since the principle of division given there does not begin to get at what linguists recognize as different kinds of words. It is clear that the latter distinction is missing because of deliberate omission rather than ignorance, since a more conventionally linguistic elaboration of the different kinds of words is sketched in *Eine Philosophische Betrachtung,* Wittgenstein's German-language revision of the *Brown Book* (*Schriften,* 5:123).

2. In the *Investigations* the celebrated definition of meaning as use is put this way in *PI* 43:

> For a large class of cases—though not for all—in which we employ the word "meaning" it may be defined thus: the meaning of a word is its use in the language.

Quite apart from the cautious qualification "though not for all," there are four striking things about this definition. The first, from which all the others follow, is that it concerns words rather than sentences or utterances. The second is that it defines *Bedeutung* rather than *Sinn* or *Meinen*. The third is that it defines *Bedeutung* in terms of *Gebrauch* rather than of *Verwendung* or *Anwendung* or *Nutzen*. The fourth is that the "use" in question, in contrast to the sort of "use" stressed in *PI* 1–25, is use within a language rather than within activities or language-games. In view of these four points, the definition of *PI* 43 can constitute only part of the conception of "meaning as use." It applies only to words and phrases, that is, to components that remain available for employment in an indefinite range of utterances. It does not, and cannot, apply to utterances themselves. In the preceding sections Wittgenstein has been at pains to show how the sense (*Sinn*) of an utterance or sentence depends on its use (employment—*Verwendung*) in the context of an activity; the definition of *PI* 43 does not summarize those preceding remarks but simply leaves them to one side. In this definition, therefore, we do not have an overthrow of the *Tractatus* but another vestige of its radical dualism. The meaning (*Bedeutung*) of each word is now to be grounded in a use in the language rather than in a correlation with an object—an important refinement—but the new definition remains conspicuously faithful to the distinction between sentences and words and between *Sinn* and *Bedeutung*.

3. The number of German words which are rendered into English by the noun 'use' (*Gebrauch, Verwendung, Anwendung, Benutzung, Nutzen*) makes it difficult for one who reads the translation to see the vestigial dualism of Wittgenstein's usage. Wittgenstein is not wholly consistent, and it is well known that he avoided allowing his ideas to depend on jargon; but as Finch (1977, 27ff.) and Hallett (1977, 206) have pointed out, a pattern can nonetheless be discerned. *Gebrauch* (and sometimes *Verwendung* or *Verwendungsweise*) signifies a regular use according to rules, whereas the other words generally signify a use determined by something other than (or in addition to) rules—say, the aim or purpose or point of the agent. There is no aim or purpose to the "use of a word in

the language," and no specific date or place for it. It is only some particular employment of a word (or sentence) that can have an aim or purpose or can be located at a specific place or time. For example, 'slithy' is used by Lewis Carroll in *Jabberwocky,* but it has no use in the language, whereas 'slimy' has a use in the language but is not used in *Jabberwocky.* The word 'slithy' has *Verwendung* in *Jabberwocky* but no *Gebrauch in der Sprache;* 'slimy' has *Gebrauch in der Sprache* but no *Verwendung* in *Jabberwocky.* Of course 'slimy' also has *Verwendungen* in actual speech, and this makes the question of "uses" of words and sentences too complicated and difficult to capture in a simple formula or in a single paragraph. Perhaps, in view of there being at least five German words employed, we should anticipate more than two kinds of use. In any case Wittgenstein's texts need to be examined more closely than I can do here, and the subtleties taken into account, as is done brilliantly in one respect by Mason (1978). Here I mean to make only a single point: the "use" of 'slithy' in *Jabberwocky* is radically unlike the "use" of 'slimy' in the language, and Wittgenstein's terminology reflects this difference, at least to some extent.

4. The "use" of 'slithy' can be explained by reference to Lewis Carroll's intents and purposes, but not by reference to the (lexical) rules of the language alone; the "use" (meaning) of 'slimy' can be explained in terms of rules and practices, but not in terms of any particular person's intents and purposes. The two kinds of "use" are therefore connected respectively with intentions and with conventions. It is, furthermore, the distinction between conventions and intentions, between practices and acts, which furnishes the dimensions of human reality in which the two senses of use are ultimately grounded. In this scheme, "customs," "practices," "institutions," "uses" take over the role assigned to simple objects in the *Tractatus:* though the rules which define them have an uncertain (and perhaps transcendental) reality, they provide the substratum which makes speech and action possible at all. This distinction does not identify two ontological categories, two sorts of ultimate reality, since conventions and intentions must be involved in any instance of human activity. It is, however, a perfectly real and thoroughly familiar distinction, which Wittgenstein never denied. In particular, his famous attack on a certain conception of intentions—as being originally intelligible independent of rules or practices, and as thus being the ultimate basis for rules and practices—is in no way an attack on the ordinary distinctions between acts and practices and between intentions and conventions. On the contrary, the two kinds of use, associated

respectively with conventions and intentions, are generally distinguished by Wittgenstein, are evidenced by his generally using different words for them, and form an integral component of the vestigial dualism of his later work.

If this account is right, Wittgenstein's later position might be summarized in the following schema:

FIGURE 3. *Wittgenstein's Later "Dualism"*

SYMBOLISM:	WORDS	*	UTTERANCES
		*	
SEMANTICS:	HAVE (OR LACK)	*	HAVE (OR LACK)
		*	SENSE (*SINN*)
	MEANING	*	
	(*BEDEUTUNG*)	*	
	i.e.	*	i.e.
	HAVE (OR LACK) A	*	HAVE (OR LACK)
	USE (*GEBRAUCH*)	*	EMPLOYMENT
	IN THE LANGUAGE	*	(*VERWENDUNG*, ETC.)
		*	OR POINT
		*	(*ZWECK, WITZ*) IN
		*	HUMAN ACTION
		*	(IN THE STREAM
		*	OF LIFE)
		*	
HUMAN		*	
DIMENSION:	RULES, PRACTICES	*	ACTS, INTENTIONS

5. Summary

I conclude that Wittgenstein continued to employ basic dichotomies of the dualism of the *Tractatus*. He disguised them, he spurned fixed terminology, he denied them any metaphysical foundation, and he insisted that the distinctions might shift from here to there; but the distinctions are still present. Whether this pattern of symbolic and semantic distinctions still constitutes a dualism is harder to say. Everything now seems human—sometimes social and sometimes individual but always human. Ontological categories are thus replaced by dimensions of human activity. Metaphysical "objects" now become "use in the language," a kind of social reality.[6] Acts and intentions, though they may require a social context, are individual rather than social. Rules and practices make actions possible, just as objects make facts possible; and the problem of the status of rules and whether they are in an important sense transcendent, as Hintikka (1981) has persuasively argued, is parallel to the problem of the status of objects *vis à vis* the world of the *Tractatus*. It is surely true that Wittgenstein never succeeded in reducing the one dimension to the other and continued to respect their difference in the subtle ways I have enumerated. Hence, a kind of dualism remains. It is muted, undefined, unacknowledged, denied by his closest students, and far removed from Frege, but ineluctably present. A principal theme of his later work is that of infinite multiplicity, of "countless different kinds of use," and of intermediate cases to refute dichotomies. Yet the exorcism was not wholly successful, and the ghost of the dualism, Frege *invictus,* still lurks in the pages of the *Investigations.*

This is perhaps as it should be. Frege's radical dualism was untenable, but the insight behind it cannot be wholly transcended. Frege was right that there must be two irreducibly different sorts of expressions. Wittgenstein was right, too, in the *Tractatus,* to realize that the fundamental dichotomy must be between words and sentences; and he was right again, in the *Investigations,* to realize that the dichotomy does not require a special ontology, and indeed cannot profit from one.

---

6. This transformation needs to be traced more fully. Here it must suffice to point out that already in the *Tractatus* (*TLP* 3.328) there is a use-condition of meaning (that a sign has no meaning if it has no use) which is presented as a subsidiary comment on the rule of context (*TLP* 3.3). The identification meaning and use is repeated in Wittgenstein's comment on Occam's razor (*TLP* 5.47321). For further discussion see Ishiguro (1969) and McGuinness (1981 and 1985).

8
Pantheism

1. Pantheism in Wittgenstein's Early Work

In reading the *Tractatus,* one gets the impression that Wittgenstein, having resolved to his satisfaction the problems about language, logic, science, and mathematics, sets these painstakingly articulated findings in a disproportionately skimpy setting. There are perfunctory remarks about the world and somewhat more elaborate ones about substance at the beginning, all highly original as well as austere and perplexing. At the end he hurries even more than usual through ethics, aesthetics, and religion—as if the silence was already coming upon him prematurely. The *Notebooks 1914–1916* help a good deal in understanding this skimpy setting. They give little direct indication of the ontological overture, apart from their frequent reiteration that there must be simples of some sort if the sense of expressions is to be determinate, but they give a fuller treatment to the other topics. This is particularly true of the latter half of 1916, when this parcel of topics seems to have become uppermost in Wittgenstein's mind. Though it is exceedingly difficult to know what to make of what are in effect discarded notes, some of the entries are just too interesting to ignore. I wish to consider what light they throw on his thought at roughly the *Tractatus* period, and in particular on the ontology that apparently springs up full grown at the beginning of the *Tractatus.*

Two of the three sentences entered on the first day of August, 1916, read as follows:

> Wie sich alles verhält, ist Gott.
> Gott ist, wie sich alles verhält.

They express what God is in terms very like those used in the *Tractatus* to say what the world is or what a fact is, and therefore they suggest either a pantheism of sorts or else a change of mind in the intervening two years. The second alternative has a superficial plausibility, but in the absence of other evidence of a change of mind it must be wrong. In a way, these sentences are typical of what Wittgenstein suppressed when he extracted material for the *Tractatus* from the *Notebooks,* just because of their concern for what God is. Over a two-month period (*NB* 11.VI.16, 8.VII.16, and 1.VIII.16) the word 'God' occurs twelve times, each time in an attempt to say what God is. The whole attempt is given up in the published work, the only remnant of it being the guarded remark in 6.432—"God does not reveal himself *in* the world"—which might reasonably be said to presuppose some notion of what God is but which can hardly be counted as an attempt to *say* what God is. Since there is a whole interconnected set of remarks in the *Notebooks* that are nowhere repudiated, other than by being omitted from the published work, it is at least reasonable to hold that Wittgenstein simply opted for silence on this matter. Such a view fits well with Wittgenstein's known piety, and I think it can be supported by consideration of relevant texts.

At first glance it might seem from some of the published text that the opposite is true, that Wittgenstein had changed his mind, at least with respect to the entries quoted above. The full text of *Tractatus* 6.432 is as follows:

> *How* things are in the world is a matter of complete indifference for what is higher. God does not reveal himself *in* the world.

Taken as a whole, this section could appear to be a repudiation of the entries of 1.VIII.16, especially as the latter are translated by Miss Anscombe:

> How things stand, is God.
> God is, how things stand.

But closer inspection shows that the German expressions are not so similar as the translators make them appear. In particular the *Notebooks* entries refer to a totality, signified in the German word *alles,* that Miss Anscombe has omitted to translate, and they might better be rendered as

> How everything hangs together, is God.
> God is, how everything hangs together.

In the passage from the *Tractatus,* on the other hand, the German clause "*Wie* die Welt ist" could equally well be rendered as "*How* the world is," rather than "*How* things stand." But it is not the wording so much as the primary reference of the two passages that confirms that they do not conflict. In the *Notebooks* the reference is to a totality, God being identified not with how this stands and how that stands but rather with how *everything* stands (or hangs together). In *Tractatus* 6.432, on the other hand, the reference is not to a totality or a hanging-together-of-everything, but to the details of the arrangement, that is, to how this stands and how that stands.

Besides the fact that he did not repudiate these notions expressed in the *Notebooks,* there are two considerations that count in favor of the view that Wittgenstein, when he wrote the *Tractatus,* still held to what he expressed on 1.VIII.16. One is the special respect he expressed for totality in the *Tractatus,* regarding generality as pointing to a "logical prototype" (*TLP* 5.522) rather than just indefinite conjunction or disjunction. The world, too, is a totality, as he says in the very first proposition, and when conceived as a totality it surpasses rational comprehension:

> Nicht *wie* die Welt ist, ist das Mystische, sondern *daß* sie ist. (*TLP* 6.44)

Though there may possibly be other explanations for this remark, it seems to indicate a sort of pantheism in that the attitude expressed toward the world conceived as a totality—that is, when one regards it as a limited whole rather than focusing on details of it—is an attitude that is paradigmatically appropriate toward God. Furthermore, the remark of 6.44 is the sort of thing that Wittgenstein would reasonably have been led to say if he still had in mind the ideas set down on 1.VIII.16. The other consideration is similar: there is a conception of God presupposed by *Tractatus* 6.432, such that God cannot be revealed *in* the world, and one of the simplest conceptions that might be so presupposed is that God is the whole of the world; for it seems obvious, as was first pointed out to me by Richard Henson, that God cannot both *be* the world and also be *in* the world. These two considerations are, of course, not definitive. They are only sufficient to allow us to put aside the all-too-easy comment that Wittgenstein must have changed his mind, and to explore a little further the nature of Wittgenstein's pantheism and what the consequences are of supposing that these remarks in the *Notebooks* express Wittgenstein's views through the *Tractatus* period.

There is an ambiguity about the entries of 1.VIII.16 that is not important in itself but that deserves to be mentioned both because it might cause confusion and because it is connected with one of the distinctive features of Wittgenstein's pantheism. What is identified with God in the entries quoted might be either a collection of all the facts there happen to be, or a single fact—a kind of world fact, so to speak—comprising how everything hangs together with everything else. These different ways of explicating Wittgenstein's words conjure up different pictures, but I do not think that they signify genuine alternatives in the context of the *Tractatus,* since the propositions that express the facts in question will by their very nature show how all the facts involved are related to one another. What makes a difference for Wittgenstein is not how the totality is conceived, given that it is a totality that includes all facts, but rather that it is such a totality. One important feature of Wittgenstein's pantheism depends on the critical significance of such a totality, namely, the distinction between what is in the world and what is higher. A fact of the world is always one fact among many, whereas what is higher, or divine, leaves out nothing that pertains to the all-inclusive totality, the world as a limited whole.

The distinction between what is in the world and what is higher seems at first incompatible with the view that it is the world that is divine, but Wittgenstein held both these views in both the *Notebooks* and the *Tractatus.* In the *Notebooks* the view that the world of fact is divine is clear from the entries already quoted. The view that what is higher is distinct from the facts of the world is clear in the entries of 5.VII.16, particularly the ones that are a preliminary version of *Tractatus* 6.43, and in the following entry:

> To believe in a God means to see that the facts of the world are not the end of the matter. (8.VII.16)

In the *Tractatus,* Wittgenstein's view that what is higher is not to be found *in* the world is clear from 6.432, quoted earlier, but it is equally clear that what is higher does have to do with the world rather than with anything otherworldly:

> If the good or bad exercise of will does alter the world, it can alter only the limits of the world, not the facts. . . . In short the effect must be that it becomes an altogether different world. It must, so to speak, wax and wane as a whole. (*TLP* 6.43)
> Feeling the world as a limited whole—it is this that is mystical. (*TLP* 6.45)

Wittgenstein's pantheism, therefore, differs from some others in that the divinity of the whole is not inherited by component parts of that whole. This is certainly one of the most distinctive aspects of Wittgenstein's view, and one that makes it difficult to follow him, as will be seen later.

Needless to say, Wittgenstein's pantheistic conception of God is difficult to reconcile with the dominant features of a personal God. Nevertheless he says in the *Notebooks* (11.VI.16) that we can call God the meaning of life or the world (he identifies the two—see *TLP* 5.621) and connect this with the comparison of God to a father. Later (17.X.16) he also speaks of "a will that is common to the whole world," which could, I suppose, be thought of as God's will. I shall have no more to say about these matters.

2. Wittgenstein and Spinoza

Pantheism calls Spinoza to mind. Once called to mind, Spinoza's *Ethics* presents striking parallels to Wittgenstein's *Tractatus*—or, more accurately, to what is presented jointly in the *Tractatus* and *Notebooks* for the latter half of 1916, if Wittgenstein is taken to be a pantheist. There are, to begin with, certain obvious and apparently superficial similarities in structure, in particular that the works consist of a few main chapters that are broken down into numbered propositions. I doubt there is anything philosophically profound in this style. It is simply a style which they shared and which each may well have adopted for the same reason, namely, out of a determination (no doubt morally admirable) not to allow his passion to find the truth about important matters to be corrupted by the flowing rhetoric that so easily comes to dominate long paragraphs. It is an austere style, reminiscent of Socrates in ways, and in keeping with rather monkish lives. Spinoza and Wittgenstein both chose to live more simply and more austerely than they need have lived, and both were fearful of the danger of corruption involved in professional philosophy and in what is usually expected in connection with a university appointment.

It is far more significant and more useful for understanding Wittgenstein's ontology that the line of thought proceeds in the same manner in the *Ethics* and in the *Tractatus*. Both begin with a characterization of *deus-sive-natura,* or of that which is at the same time contingent creation considered as a whole (*natura naturata*/the totality of facts) and also the appropriate object of unqualified reverence (*natura naturans*/the mystical and inexpressible). Both also characterize the world (or God) in such a way as to make clear what the component parts are (finite modes/facts), and therefore how the world breaks down, so to speak, while still always remaining a unity or totality. It is worth noting that Spinoza and Wittgenstein, by proceeding in this manner, share a view of the relation of parts to wholes that is more characteristic of rationalism than of empiricism and of idealism than of materialism, and that is very different from the Russellian view about the relation of atomic propositions to complex propositions in the *Tractatus*. No doubt this view of the relation of parts to wholes, which is also evident in the relation of simples to facts and of names to propositions, is one thing that can lead commentators such as Stenius (1960) and Black (1964, 10) to characterize Wittgenstein as a rationalist or idealist of sorts.

Having characterized *deus-sive-natura* and its components, both Spinoza and Wittgenstein proceed to show how it is possible to come to comprehend the whole through knowing about or being able to speak about the components—though the comprehension of the whole is a different kind of knowledge and there is no guarantee that it will be achieved even through the best scientific knowledge of limited aspects of it. In both cases there are three sorts of knowledge, the first two comprising scientific knowledge. For Spinoza this involves distinguishing finite from infinite modes (roughly, things and events, or phenomena, from general laws and overriding features of the world like motion-and-rest) and then distinguishing the lowest sort of knowledge, empirical knowledge, as a simple awareness of finite modes, and rational or scientific knowledge as an understanding of the infinite modes and how the finite modes are related to and dependent on them. For Wittgenstein it involves distinctions among kinds of propositions. Atomic and (contingent) molecular propositions can be directly compared with facts and hence are empirical, whereas science, although it comprises all true propositions, seems to involve tautologies and generalizations and theories which cannot be compared directly with facts.

With respect to this last point, a further parallel between Spinoza and Wittgenstein lies in the puzzles that surround their discussions of generalizations. The status of scientific laws and theories, *vis à vis* propositions and tautologies, is one of the very hard questions about the *Tractatus,* as is made clear by Black (1964, 344ff.) and by Proctor (1959, 177–93). The status of the infinite (or eternal) modes is equally obscure in the metaphysics of Spinoza, as has been brought to our attention again by E. M. Curley in his seminal book, *Spinoza's Metaphysics.* Throughout his work, Curley uses logical atomism as a kind of baseline from which to approach Spinoza, and in the second chapter he presents, in terms very different from mine, a comparison of the metaphysics of Spinoza with that of the *Tractatus.* Particularly relevant to the present point is his identification of the infinite modes with "nomological facts"—a useful analogy, even though both concepts need further explication.

The advantage of surveying the broad structure is that we can see better that both the *Ethics* and the *Tractatus* end with a vision of salvation that depends on a third kind of knowledge that transcends empirical and rational knowledge. This is a kind of cognition that does not, so to speak, add any new information to what is already known, but serves instead to bring everything already known into a single perspective. For Spinoza this sort of apprehension is *"scientia intuitiva"* and results in an "intellectual love of God." For Wittgenstein it is "feeling the world as a limited whole" and results in clarification of the meaning (*Sinn*) of life, or of the world. Thus Wittgenstein writes in the *Notebooks* entries of 8.VII.16:

> To believe in a God means to see that the facts of the world are not the end of the matter. To believe in God means to see that life has a meaning.

For both Spinoza and Wittgenstein, happiness, or the highest good, consists in a sort of identification with God or the universe, which is to be achieved intellectually. In both cases, too, it is easier to see that this is the goal set out in the work prepared for publication by examining preliminary studies. Thus it is in his *Tractatus de Intellectus Emendatione* that Spinoza explains the nature of the highest good, "that it is the knowledge of the union that the mind has with the whole of Nature" (II/8/26–27), and indicates how learning is rightly directed toward that end. In the case of Wittgenstein we are even more dependent on the preliminary studies to see the goal of the published work; it becomes clear in the following passages from the *Notebooks,* which are neither repudiated nor recapitulated in the *Tractatus:*

> In order to live happily I must be in agreement with the world. And that is what "being happy" *means.*
>
> I am then, so to speak, in agreement with that alien will on which I appear dependent. That is to say: 'I am doing the will of God'. (8.VII.16)
>
> I cannot bend the happenings of the world to my will: I am completely powerless.
>
> I can only make myself independent of the world—and so in a certain sense master it—by renouncing any influence on happenings. (11.VI.16)
>
> How can man be happy, since he cannot ward off the misery of this world?

Through the life of knowledge.

A good conscience is the happiness that the life of knowledge preserves.

The life of knowledge is the life that is happy in spite of the misery of the world. (13.VIII.16)

As in Spinoza's work, the goal is salvation through acquiescence, to be achieved intellectually by knowing the world well enough to put oneself in agreement with it. The problem is to see how this goal, and the pantheism in which it is embedded, may have influenced the ontology of the *Tractatus*.

3. Ethics and Metaphysics

"It would be quite wrong," says Max Black (1964, 8), "to treat the metaphysics as a mere appendage: indeed it would be plausible to read the book as being primarily concerned with metaphysics." And yet the metaphysics remains obscure, and the parts of it that we can understand seem to lead to difficulties at a deeper level. Black (1964, 27) says that the ontology presented in the early installments was probably the last part of the book to be written. One bit of evidence for this, as well as one ground for the continuing obscurity of the passages, is that the metaphysical scheme of the *Tractatus* is largely absent from the *Notebooks*. It is true that the *Notebooks* contain many entries about simples and objects, but they do not clear up the metaphysical difficulties. One reason is that these remarks mostly have to do with the necessity that there be simples rather than with what simples are. Although a few of the entries are along the latter line, suggesting, for example, that simples can be points in the visual field (*NB* 6.VI.15) and that "relations and properties, etc. are *objects* too" (*NB* 16.V.15), Wittgenstein seems to have decided by the time he prepared the *Tractatus* for publication that all the problems of logic could be resolved without determining the nature of the simple objects that there must be—perhaps as an application of his dictum, "If logic can be completed without answering certain questions, then it *must* be completed *without* answering them" (*NB* 4.IX.14). It therefore remains unclear, though not uninteresting, whether the metaphysics of the *Tractatus* is realistic or nominalistic, about which there has been vigorous controversy involving Anscombe, Allaire, Copi, and others; but I shall have nothing to say about this difficulty, for I cannot see that Wittgenstein's being a pantheist throws any light on the problem.

The other reason the numerous remarks about simples do not ultimately help to understand the metaphysics of the *Tractatus* is that the ontology of simples is only one aspect of that metaphysics—very likely a secondary aspect at that. Wittgenstein gives primacy—the primacy of place at the very least—to facts rather than objects. This, as Black (1964, 27) has noted, is Wittgenstein's great innovation in metaphysics. It is true that Curley (1969) presents Spinoza's metaphysics as a metaphysics of facts rather than of things or events; but since Spinoza did not present it that way, and since Curley uses Wittgenstein's *Tractatus* as a model for understanding Spinoza, Curley's work only adds to the significance of Wittgenstein's innovation. It is a brilliant and awesome stroke that cannot fail to catch the attention of readers of the *Tractatus*. But it is puzzling because of the intrinsic difficulty of understanding what exactly an ontology of facts is, and also because of the uncertain metaphysical status the objects have if they must be thought of in relation to facts. It does not seem that objects and facts can be independent of one another, in separate realms, so to speak; for facts are concatenations or configurations of objects. But how are the two ontologies related to one another in the metaphysics of the *Tractatus?* On this question the *Notebooks* seem to give no help at all, because they contain no trace of the ontology of facts.

One might try to get some light on this metaphysical question by considering why there should be two ontologies at all. It seems reasonable to say that the dual metaphysics grew out of the problems about language that Wittgenstein was coping with. His account of language had to meet three requirements: (1) there must be a way to determine the meaning of propositions; (2) there must be a way to determine the truth or falsity of propositions; and (3) the criterion of meaning must be independent of the criterion of truth. So when Wittgenstein finally decided that language must be metaphysically grounded, it was clear that he would have to have two ontologies, one to provide determinateness of meaning and the other to provide the determination of truth and falsity. Unfortunately this line of thought, having got this far, runs afoul of our original question about the metaphysical priority of the two ontologies. Since knowing what a proposition means is prior, necessarily, to knowing whether it is true, one might expect that the metaphysical ground of meaning should have an analogous priority over the metaphysical ground for truth. But Wittgenstein seems to put things in just the opposite order at the beginning of the *Tractatus*. So this line of thought only deepens the mystery.

A second attempt to explain the primacy Wittgenstein gives to facts might begin by focusing on the famous dictum he adopted from Frege: "Only propositions have sense; only in the nexus of a proposition does a name have meaning" (*TLP* 3.3). One consequence of this dictum is that propositions are prior to names at the level of semantics. Sentences are, to be sure, composed of names; therefore, in a certain sense, there could not be sentences if there were not names. But when we come to consider how it is that these two sorts of linguistic expressions are understood, then, according to Wittgenstein, propositions are the primary units into which language breaks down, names being intelligible (having meaning, or reference) only if the sentences in which they occur are intelligible (have sense). This line of thought proves, then, to be more rewarding than the first, for it seems only fitting, in view of the semantic priority of propositions over names, that the metaphysical correlates of propositions should have analogous priority over the metaphysical correlates of names.

This is helpful, but two problems remain. One is that this position is difficult to reconcile with the familiar fact that we understand "new" sentences on the basis of the meaning of familiar component words (= names?), and with Wittgenstein's view that the sense of propositions, as distinct from their truth value, is ultimately determined by the correlation of names with objects. I can make no comment on this dilemma here. But even if it could be resolved, there would remain the question why metaphysical priority should be determined by the semantic priority of propositions over names, rather than by the epistemological priority of meaning over truth. Wittgenstein's ontology of facts is, after all, unconventional and at least initially implausible, and it is difficult to see why he should adopt it if he had an equally good reason, or perhaps even a better one, for having the world break down, more plausibly, into simple objects.

Wittgenstein's pantheism supplies the explanation that these other lines of thought cannot provide. If God is identified with the world, and if the idea of God is to continue to play the role it does for Wittgenstein in the *Notebooks,* then the world must be composed of facts rather than of objects. The reason for this is that pantheism implies a certain piety, a striving to live in accord with God-or-nature. Facts are the hard, unalterable data we must accept and come to terms with in our lives. It is true that objects are, in a certain sense, unalterable. (See *TLP* 2.012n, 2.203.) But what is unalterable about objects is their form, the possibilities they comprise, whereas the hard data we have to accept and cope with are never mere possibilities but actualities. Since the actualities, reality, must be determined by what facts there are rather than by what objects there are (*TLP* 2.06), the world must be composed of facts rather than of objects (*TLP* 2.03–2.063), if the *Tractatus* is to be compatible with the pantheism of the *Notebooks* and with the ethical insights on which the pantheism is founded.

Among the entries for 11.VI.16, Wittgenstein speaks of God as the meaning of the world. Here is one powerful religious idea which must be preserved in the metaphysics of the *Tractatus,* if the pantheism and piety of 1916 carry over into the book. Could God be thought of as the meaning of the world if the world were an aggregate of objects? Only by making a mockery of the idea and robbing it of the religious depth expressed in Wittgenstein's *Notebooks.* "Objects contain the possibility of *all* situations" (*TLP* 2.014; italics added), and hence they cannot convey to us the why and the wherefore of our *actual* situation. Objects constitute a form which our world must have in common with any other imaginable world (*TLP* 2.022–2.023), so the totality of objects cannot help us to understand the meaning of this particular world—which is what we need to know, since it is with this particular world rather than with other possible ones that we must, through our apprehension of God, reconcile ourselves. To say in response that we must also reconcile ourselves to what possibilities there are would perhaps be true, but it would betray a failure to comprehend the existential situation in which it is important to see God as the meaning of the world. For it is the world with its actual miseries, not the world with its possible glories, that we must come to understand and to reconcile ourselves with. It is the world of facts, not objects.

Another theme of Wittgenstein's pantheism is the ethic of acquiescence. Consider how the following passage from the *Notebook* entries for 8.VII.16 shows a line of thought that leads to the identification of God and the world:

> The world is *given* me, i.e., my will enters into the world completely from outside as into something that is already there. . . .
>
> That is why we have the feeling of being dependent on an alien will.

However this may be, at any rate we *are* in a certain sense dependent, and what we are dependent on we call God.

In this sense God would simply be fate, or, what is the same thing: The world—which is independent of our will.

I can make myself independent of fate.

There are two godheads: the world and my independent I [*mein unabhängiges Ich*].[. . .]

In order to live happily I must be in agreement with the world. And that is what 'being happy' *means*.

I am then, so to speak, in agreement with the alien will on which I appear dependent. That is to say: 'I am doing the will of God'.

This passage has its difficulties. Perhaps the greatest difficulty is that individual happenings in the world, or facts, seem at least as much a matter of fate as the world as a whole; so that if God is fate, it would seem that God would be revealed *in* the world, contrary to *Tractatus* 6.432. Perhaps an answer to this difficulty might be that whereas a fact can be a fact independent of everything else, it cannot be understood as fate, or as an aspect of fate, unless it is seen to be part of a whole universe of fate. I cannot pursue this interesting thought here. A second difficulty resides in the dualism between oneself and the world, for the sharp dichotomy seems to require either denying that one's body is in the world or (Wittgenstein's apparent choice) denying responsibility for one's body. Both these difficulties are too profound to be resolved here.

There are also certain ambiguities, some lines of the passage being compatible with the world being composed of objects (possibilities) rather than of facts. Both possibilities and facts, for example, are already there, given to me, and are independent of my will. But the main line of thought in the passage resolves these ambiguities decisively through its reference to fate. Fate cannot be understood just in terms of possibilities, just in terms of the form of the world. It has to do instead with what actually happens, with which of the possibilities happened to be actualized. What one has to learn to be in agreement with, according to the highly Spinozistic lines at the end of the passage, is not what possibilities there are, for one could hardly fail to be in agreement with that. It is the world as it actually is that one must strive religiously to be in agreement with. In spite of difficulties in the above passage, therefore, it is clear that the main thrust of it requires that the world have facts rather than objects as component parts.

That the pantheism of the *Notebooks* succeeds in providing an explanation for one of the prominent puzzles about the metaphysics of the *Tractatus* is a powerful consideration, in the absence of contrary evidence, in support of the view that Wittgenstein, although unwilling to allow it in print, continued to hold to that pantheism and to the ethical views associated with it. Such a view is attractive on other grounds. If it contains a full-blown Spinozistic ethic, the metaphysical setting for the logical doctrines certainly proves to be far less skimpy than it originally appeared. Ultimately the *Tractatus* may well be unacceptable because of its commitment to the ontology of simples and its rejection of intentional contexts. It would nonetheless be extremely interesting to work from the other direction, from the problem of reconciling Spinoza's noble ethic with the indeterminacy of modern physics, to see whether Wittgenstein's identification of God with fate, and his further identification of both with the universe conceived as an aggregate of facts, might provide a way of bringing Spinoza's ethico-religious philosophy into harmony with twentieth-century views about science and nature. For the present, however, it is enough simply to see how the recognition of Wittgenstein's pantheism helps to reveal the coherence of the *Tractatus*.

PART THREE

WITTGENSTEIN'S LATER WORK

9

Science and Natural History

1. The Dichotomy between Science and Philosophy

When Wittgenstein speaks of science, it is often to distinguish philosophy from science. This is certainly the case in the passages which occur in the middle of the *Tractatus:*

> The totality of true propositions is the whole of natural science (or the whole corpus of the natural sciences).
>
> Philosophy is not one of the natural sciences.
>
> (The word 'philosophy' must mean something whose place is above or below the natural sciences, not beside them.) [. . .]
>
> Psychology is no more closely related to philosophy than any other natural science. [. . .]
>
> Darwin's theory has no more to do with philosophy than any other hypothesis in natural science. (4.11–4.1122)

These remarks are aimed first and foremost to establish a general distinction between philosophy and science, a distinction on which Wittgenstein continued to insist throughout his philosophical career, and the examination of which will be the principal focus of this chapter. But they are also aimed more specifically at rejecting the special ties which in the nineteenth century were alleged to hold between philosophy and psychology and between philosophy and evolution.

The connection between philosophy and psychology originated from the central, even constitutive, role that has been assigned to the theory of knowledge in modern philosophy, by both Rationalists and Empiricists. If the first questions in philosophy are what one can know and how one can know anything at all, then there is no way of escaping beginning with psychology in some guise or other, whether it be under that name or as "phenomenology," or "cognitive science," or "laws of thought," or "philosophy of mind," or whatever. Knowledge must be in the mind: "What I know, I believe" (*OC* 177). Both Rationalism and

Empiricism have generally required that if anything is to be known, it must also be known to be known. That is to say, they seem to make knowledge into a particular state of mind, immediately accessible to the knower, and only to the knower. Putting these requirements first and foremost gives philosophy the appearance of being psychological.

At the time these philosophical theories were proposed, there was no science of psychology. As psychology became a separate and experimental discipline in the nineteenth century, the idea grew that philosophy is or should be properly subordinate to experimental psychology. While the view was first put forward by Alexander Bain, its most important expression in the last century was in the works of J. S. Mill. His earliest presentation was in his *Examination of the Philosophy of Sir William Hamilton;* but the most influential version by far was in his *System of Logic,* one of the best philosophical works of the century as well as an all-time best-seller. Mill maintained that even the propositions of logic and mathematics are essentially empirical, and that anything empirical is governed not [wholly] by the natural world but [in part] by principles for organizing the contents of our minds. The contemporary heirs of Bain and Mill are threefold: certain phenomenologists such as Köhler, pragmatists such as Quine, and cognitive scientists such as Fodor.

The connection between evolution and philosophy arose later, after the publication of Darwin's great work in 1859, and was especially promoted by T. H. Huxley. Its most famous manifestation is the rather brutish social philosophy known as Social Darwinism. Beyond this specialized application, the wider implication of evolution for philosophy is that philosophy and science, since they are simply evolutionary aspects of an evolved species, should simply be described in their biological setting rather than given an honorific status or an epistemic value.

Wittgenstein's rejection of these two special connections between philosophy and science is perfunctory, in large part because it derives from his more general stance. To understand his general insistence that philosophy is absolutely and decisively different from science, we must ask how Wittgenstein construes science and philosophy. What is there in his conceptions that leads him to this sharp distinction? It turns out that this is a more difficult question than it first appears; for although Wittgenstein continues to hold fast to the distinction, the underlying conceptions undergo radical revisions.

In the ellipsis in the passage from the *Tractatus* quoted earlier, Wittgenstein gives a brief characterization of philosophy:

Philosophy aims at the logical clarification of thoughts.
Philosophy is not a body of doctrine but an activity.
A philosophical work consists essentially of elucidations.
Philosophy does not result in 'philosophical propositions', but rather in the clarification of propositions.
Without philosophy thoughts are, as it were, cloudy and indistinct: its task is to make them clear and to give them sharp boundaries. (4.112)

From these passages we can begin to reconstruct how Wittgenstein conceived of philosophy and of science, but the terms of the distinction remain obscure, and Wittgenstein himself did not stick by them. The plan of the chapter will be to proceed chronologically, noting the changes in the way Wittgenstein conceives of philosophy and of science. The later conceptions will prove distinctly superior, being both more subtle and more realistic, but they entail (or are based on) a dichotomy between natural history and natural science that comes as rather a shock and that will need to be closely examined. Wittgenstein's final position is a sort of naturalism that differs as sharply from more conventional naturalism (such as Quine's) as it does from the nonnaturalism that is central to the *Tractatus* view, to which we now turn.

2. Science in the *Tractatus*

On the face of it Wittgenstein is saying that while science consists of propositions, and its domain is all that can be said, philosophy consists only of activity, more specifically the activity of clarifying propositions. One difficulty is that there is really no dichotomy between activities and propositions. Wittgenstein has earlier (2.1) said that we picture facts to ourselves, and since such picturing is nothing other than making propositions (3.11), Wittgenstein conceived of science as an activity too. Insisting that philosophy is an activity is insufficient to distinguish philosophy from science.

Nor is it sufficient to say that philosophical activity consists in clarification and elucidation of thoughts. Consider, for example, how greatly Kepler clarified our thoughts about the movement of the planets by discovering that they conform to three simple laws, or how much Newton elucidated our thoughts about motion through his scientific achievements, or how Pasteur's work in the laboratory cast new light on thoughts about fermentation. Scientific work can clarify and elucidate our thoughts quite as much as philosophy.

In 4.113 Wittgenstein says, "Philosophy sets limits to the much disputed sphere of natural science." The first thing to be noticed is that this remark has nothing to do with distinctions among the sciences but rather with the domain of natural science as a whole. About this latter domain he has already said (4.11) that it is the totality of true propositions. One might think that there are really no serious limits here at all—that all that is excluded is *false* propositions, and such an exclusion is no limit at all to the domain of science. This would be wrong, because Tractarian propositions make up only one kind of expression, namely those that are purely factual, and therefore much ordinary scientific work seems excluded. To appreciate this matter we need to look closely at the famous distinction between *showing* and *saying*.

In 4.113 Wittgenstein begins a series of remarks which culminate in the sharp distinction between *showing* and *saying*: "What *can* be shown, *cannot* be said" (4.1212). Many commentators have called attention to this dichotomy as one of the crucial features of the *Tractatus,* especially of its theory of symbolism. The main purpose of symbols, and of language in particular, is to state (or picture, or represent) facts, an achievement whose possibility is explained by the picture theory of meaning. According to the picture theory, every ordinary (factual) proposition presents us with a picture of what obtains in the real world, and we can ascertain the truth or falsity of the proposition by "laying it against" the world to see if the picture matches reality. A picture may be either simple or complex. If it is simple, the comparison is easy and direct. If it is complex, the complexity must be strictly truth-functional: "A proposition is a truth-function of elementary propositions. (An elementary proposition is a truth-function of itself.)" (*TLP* 5)

In this context it is clear that the limit on natural science is that it is confined to *saying what is the case,* and excluded from "saying" anything about possibility or necessity or value or meaning or sense or logical form, all of which can be "shown." Of these qualities, necessity and impossibility are most often associated with science, so let us look more closely at modalities. In the *Tractatus* Wittgenstein says that the modality of a thought is shown by the logical status of the sentence or proposition that represents it. It is possible if the proposition is contingent (can be either true or false); it is necessary if the proposition is a tautology; and it is impossible if the proposition is a contradiction. The consequence of this treatment of modality is summarized in his famous remark, "Just as the only necessity that exists is *logical* necessity, so too the only impossibility that exists is *logical* impossibility" (*TLP* 6.375). All modality is therefore extensional or truth-functional. Every elementary proposition represents a possibility, and a complex proposition represents a necessity (or impossibility) if and only if it is a tautology (or contradiction). This posture eliminates all *scientific* necessities and impossibilities, both the causal ones involved in engineering and the relational or proportional ones such as those of Boyle's Law. One reason for the elimination is that such necessities or impossibilities are not purely logical. But even if they were, they still could not be expressed in the propositions that can be *said,* for Wittgenstein does not allow that the modal status of a proposition can ever be *stated:* instead it *shows* itself.

Even if we give up the modal and stick to the simply assertoric, we find upon closer inspection that Wittgenstein's formula severely restricts the domain of science because of problems about limits and totalities. In 4.12 Wittgenstein says that "propositions can represent (*darstellen*) the whole of reality," but there is an implicit limitation. For although science includes each of the propositions in the totality that constitutes a picture of the world (3.01), one cannot *say* that they are *all* of the true propositions, because a "proposition" about a totality could never be a *picture* (*Bild*), as the propositions of natural science must be. Wittgenstein seems aware of this problem when he says that the generality sign is a "logical prototype (*Urbild*)" (5.522), and he says the following in this connection:

> Empirical reality is limited by the totality of objects. The limit also makes itself manifest in the totality of elementary propositions. (5.5561)

If the limit "makes itself manifest," it is an instance of what *can* be shown and hence *cannot* be said. So although natural science can describe the whole of reality, it cannot include as part of its description that this is the whole of reality—nor that some description is not the whole of reality. Wholes, parts, and limits are so important in modern science that this restriction results in a highly skewed domain from the point of view of ordinary science.

3. The Mature Dichotomy

When he returned to philosophy after a ten-year absence, Wittgenstein continued to speak disparagingly about science, especially in the *Re-*

marks on Frazer's "Golden Bough" and in the *Lectures and Conversations,* though the animus seems mostly focused on the conception of science as a model for philosophy. In any case his later conception of science took a radical turn. He held firmly to there being a sharp distinction between philosophy and science, but he substantially modified his description of each member of the opposition, as well as of the difference between them. The revisions give us a very different picture both of philosophy and of science, and there is no doubt that the new picture of science is far more satisfactory.

The new conception of philosophy has substantial continuities with the conception of the *Tractatus.* There is, for example, no reason to think that Wittgenstein would have to give up any of what is said in *TLP* 4.111–4.113. The change has to do with associating philosophy with *grammar* (in a broad sense) rather than with *logic* (in a strict sense), and with the use of natural history to describe uses of language. It is the latter that forces a sea-change in his conception of science.

Wittgenstein invokes natural history early on in the *Philosophical Investigations:*

> It is sometimes said that animals do not talk because they lack the mental capacity. And this means: "they do not think, and that is why they do not talk." But—they simply do not talk. Or to put it better: they do not use language—if we except the most primitive forms of language.— Commanding, questioning, recounting, chatting, are as much a part of our natural history as walking, eating, drinking, playing. (*PI* 25)

These sentences undoubtedly *say* something, even in the sense in which the *Tractatus* distinguishes saying from showing. The first sentence is a true description of what people sometimes say. The rebuttal begins with a description of animal behavior—somewhat problematic because humans are presumed not to be "animals," because of a vagueness about what it is to use language, and because the description is entirely negative. None of these problems, however, prevents us from seeing that the proposition is a factual one, and there seems little doubt that it truly describes a matter of fact. The rebuttal continues with another matter of fact, namely that certain uses of language are as characteristic of humans as are certain animal activities.[1]

---

1. Compare *On Certainty,* 358–59:

Now I would like to regard this certainty, not as something akin to hastiness or superficiality, but as a form of life. (That is very badly expressed and probably badly thought as well.)

The statements Wittgenstein here calls "natural history" would have to count as natural science in the terminology of the *Tractatus*. They are clearly meant to be true, and only contingently true, and are knowingly presented as belonging to a description of the world as it actually is—to be fact rather than possibility. That is to say, Wittgenstein is fully aware that he has made decisive use of contingent fact in a philosophical argument (or the statement of a philosophical position). He does not suppose that the facts are "natural necessities," nor that they are synthetic apriori, nor that they are not really crucial to the argument (or position). For such a remark to constitute a part of philosophy indicates a radical new conception of philosophy. Among other things, it means—given that he has not abandoned the dichotomy between philosophy and science—that Wittgenstein must now make a sharp distinction between natural history and natural science. This may initially seem implausible, but it in fact leads to a far more adequate conception of science.

Natural history has to do with the simple statement of plain facts, not necessarily esoteric ones but ones that escape notice because they are so very familiar:

> The aspects of things that are most important for us are hidden because of their simplicity and familiarity. (One is unable to notice something— because it is always before one's eyes.) The real foundations of his enquiry do not strike a man at all. Unless *that* fact has at some time struck him—And this means: we fail to be struck by what, once seen, is most striking and most powerful. (*PI* 129)
>
> What we are supplying are really remarks on the natural history of human beings; we are not contributing curiosities however, but observations which no one has doubted, but which have escaped remark only because they are always before our eyes. (*PI* 415)

The plain statements of fact envisaged here differ from science because they are purely descriptive: they avoid all necessity, all explanation, all hypothesis, and all proof.

Ironically, pure description of facts seemed the *central* characteristic of the propositions of natural science according to the *Tractatus*. Though there are some comments about laws at the end of the book (6.3n), the laws Wittgenstein discusses seem not to constitute a solid or indispensable part of science, since he says that ". . . all these are apriori

---

But that means I want to regard it as something that lies beyond being justified or unjustified; as it were, as something animal.

insights about the forms in which the propositions of science can be cast" (6.34). Of brilliant descriptive laws like those of Kepler or Huygens there is no mention, nor is there mention of brilliant explanations like those of Pasteur and Mendel. Nor of hypotheses, nor of experiments, nor of confirmation, nor of falsification. Though its propositions did involve the activity of picturing facts, natural science remained a pretty static affair in the *Tractatus*.

Here is how Wittgenstein comments in the *Investigations* on his earlier views:

> It was true to say that our considerations could not be scientific ones. It was not of any possible interest to us to find out empirically 'that, contrary to our preconceived ideas, it is possible to think such-and-such'—whatever that may mean. (The conception of thought as a gaseous medium.) And we may not advance any kind of theory. There must not be anything hypothetical in our considerations. We must do away with all *explanation*, and description alone must take its place. (*PI* 109)

The dichotomy with science now means, more concretely, eschewing statements about empirical possibility (or necessity, as other passages, e.g. *PI* 112, make clear), eschewing theory, and eschewing explanation. This last point clashes superficially with what Wittgenstein says elsewhere—not only in the *Tractatus*, where explanation (clarification and elucidation) is precisely what philosophy is about, but also in the *Investigations*, where explanations [*Erklärungen*, definitions] are often included within the domain of philosophy (3, 30, 43, 288, et al.). It is explanations of meaning that remain within the domain of philosophy —that is to say, explanations which merely clarify and do not justify, or which convey how certain things are rather than how they must be. It is explanations and predictions of fact which fall within the domain of science, since such explanations and predictions exhibit some fact or event as necessary relative to some law or theory. There are no doubt other sorts of explanations which are neither of meanings nor of facts, to be found, for example, in law, morals, and politics; but the distinction between these two sorts is what we need to understand Wittgenstein's flinty remarks in *PI* 107.

Other characteristics which Wittgenstein assigns to science and excludes from philosophy are doubt, evidence, confirmation and falsification, and experimenting. (See for example *PI* pp. 221, 232.) In these respects his continuing distinction between science and philosophy is absorbed into the wider distinction between certainty and knowledge on which he insisted so forcefully in *On Certainty:* " 'Knowledge' and 'certainty' belong to different *categories*" (*OC* 308). One main point here is that I can be *certain* of something without seeing it as necessary, but I cannot *know* something (in the sense of that expression for which science serves as a paradigm) without seeing it as necessary.[2] This later remark, in strikingly different terminology, therefore expresses solidarity with *Tractatus* 6.375: "Just as the only necessity that exists is logical necessity, so too the only impossibility that exists is logical impossibility." Science can offer explanations and make knowledge-claims because its theories are conditional in various ways and hence subject to change. A deep, pervasive, unchanging conviction of the radical contingency of the world underlies Wittgenstein's conception of science and his distinction between philosophy and science.

What Wittgenstein says or implies about science in the *Remarks on Frazer's "Golden Bough,"* the *Zettel,* and other writings fills out this picture somewhat but does not alter it. Overall this later characterization of the differentiation of philosophy from science is neither very subtle nor altogether adequate. There is, for example, nothing in it to distinguish history from natural science, and of course nothing to distinguish physics from geology. Nonetheless the mention of evidence, of experiment, of hypothesis, and of the explanation of facts comes far closer to characterizing science as we normally think of it than the simplistic formulation of the *Tractatus.*

What Wittgenstein has to say about natural science could be said both to have changed and not to have changed. His underlying metaphysical commitment is that there is only one reality, one world within which both scientific questions and philosophical questions (questions of meaning) arise and to which they have radically different relations. The *Tractatus* posited a *substance* of the world, thereby providing a niche for meaning, one that was safely isolated from science. In his later work he rejected any such transcendent substance, replacing it with the notion of a purely descriptive natural history, his version of natural history focusing not on curiosities but on facts that we do not notice because they are right in front of our noses. The main steady theme is that what constitutes our paradigm for knowledge and research cannot serve also as a paradigm for philosophy; but the way this point is

---

2. On this last point, recall Russell's inability to convince Wittgenstein that there was no rhinoceros in the room. See McGuinness (1988, 89).

formulated changed so dramatically that one might discern only the changes. In these circumstances it is absurd to argue simplistically that his ideas must either have changed or not changed. Rather one must look closely at just what happened, and note the felicitous maturing of his conceptions of both philosophy and science.

10
Neither Knowing nor Not Knowing

*The most important part of education
—to teach the meaning of* to know
(in the scientific sense).
—Simone Weil[1]

1. The Issue and Its Importance

Wittgenstein did not have a theory of knowledge. This is partly because he was more interested in problems of meaning than in problems of knowledge, and partly because he eschewed philosophical theories. But Wittgenstein does speak about knowledge and knowledge-claims, particularly in his later works, and his remarks certainly have relevance not only to the claims of various theories of knowledge but also to the very enterprise of epistemologists. It is exceedingly difficult to say with confidence what is the final implication of his scattered remarks on causality being a superstition, on the parallels between science and art and between science and magic, on the necessity for justifications to come to an end, on criteria, and on the contrast between knowledge and certainty. Some commentators, such as Wolgast (1977), have seen these remarks to imply a devastating critique not only of theories of knowledge but of any coherent conception of knowledge as a body of truth or of knowing as a distinctive enterprise. There is philosophical substance as well as sound textual exegesis in this line of commentary, and I do not wish to impugn its value. The problem is not that it is wrong, but that it represents only one side of a complex issue, and only one facet of a many-faceted philosopher.

I want to draw attention to some of the more conservative aspects of Wittgenstein's remarks about knowing: that public certification is more

---

1. These were the last words written in the notebook found after her death.

important to knowledge-claims than subjective certainty; that science remains the paradigm of knowledge; that the language-game we play with hypotheses and knowledge-claims is a social practice with distinctive features; and that its being a social practice or institution does not *ipso facto* impugn its objectivity. These insights are conservative in a broad cultural sense (see Nyiri 1992), not philosophically. That is to say, they accept as given our familiar practices of making and challenging knowledge-claims, including our respect for science as making more definitive claims, and therefore have at the same time the radical implication that philosophers need to discard the models of epistemology standard since Descartes and Hume, which all too easily lead to scepticism about these familiar practices, and even about science. The remark from Weil at the head of the chapter is one that I take to share this combination of being culturally conservative and philosophically radical. I will also argue that there are distinctly Kantian elements in Wittgenstein's posture with respect to justificatory regresses.

Rather than attempt a survey of the relevant remarks in Wittgenstein's constantly expanding corpus of posthumous publications, I shall focus on one of the most famous and most controversial:

> (A): It can't be said of me at all (except perhaps as a joke) that I *know* I am in pain. (*PI* 246)

I want first to make some comments, more sketchy than definitive, about the reading of that remark. I shall then say something about the language-game in question, that of claiming to know and of challenging, testing, doubting, and accepting or rejecting such claims. Finally, I shall identify and underscore the Kantian aspects of (A).

2. Explicating *PI* 246

I have been struck by frequent philosophical bewilderment as to why Wittgenstein should have asserted (A), and more generally as to why Wittgenstein should have said a number of things that he did say about knowledge or about the word 'know'. I take the bewilderment to be at least to some degree separate from, although perhaps coextensive with, doubts on the part of these philosophers about whether what he said was true. That is, these critics cannot see what difference it would make whether (A), and other remarks about the use of 'know' in English and of *wissen* in German, are true or false. On the other hand, Wolgast (1977), who develops some distinctly Wittgensteinian paradoxes about knowledge, does not discuss (A), and in particular does not consider how what Wittgenstein says here might bear on some of her general claims about our use of 'know'. The question of the critics about rational motivation, about the point of the remark, is just the right question to ask. (A) is typical of remarks in both the *Investigations* and *On Certainty* that ordinary literate people and native speakers find startling. Why did someone whose avowed philosophical method was to remind us of what is plainly true say things about 'know' which, he must have known, others (including G. E. Moore) would regard as plainly false? That is the question we have to face.

(A) is difficult to read not because of its vocabulary and syntax but because (1) it is not easy to be sure what *kind* of statement it is, and (2) it is not obvious what it implies about uses of the first-person statement (F)

(F): I know I am in pain

or of the third-person statement (T)

(T): He knows he is in pain.

These two matters are related; and perhaps when all the details are worked out they can be seen as two approaches to the same issue. So although I shall take up the first question first, I shall generally consider the two questions together.

One way to understand (A), and perhaps the simplest way, is to take it as a generalization in empirical linguistics. Such a generalization might say, among other things, that (F) and (T) do not occur, or occur only deviantly. I must have interpreted (A) this way on my first reading of the *Investigations,* because I wrote indignantly in the margin "But it is said!" Since I evidently supposed that it could be empirically refuted, I must have supposed (A) to be an empirical claim, and probably (I no longer remember) a claim about occurrences of (F) and (T). Morick must also read (A) as an empirical generalization, for he says that "there is evidence, *viz.* the intuitions of native speakers" for the invalidity of (A) (1978). Morick does not actually present the evidence; I take him to mean that native speakers would *not* regard all occurrences of (F) and (T) as deviant, and that such evidence would refute (A). If this is roughly the sort of evidence he had in mind, his argument presupposes (A) to be an empirical linguistic generalization.

This will not do. Such a reading is marked by superficiality as well as simplicity, and can be rejected by looking at either the statement itself or its immediate context. If one reads the statement itself carefully, one is struck by how elaborately (A) is constructed so as to avoid both mention of (F) or (T) (or any other explicit form of words) and even any clear reference to them. It would be simpler and more obvious, if one meant to comment on the use of (F), to say (B) or (C) or (D):

(B): I cannot say that I *know* I am in pain.

(C): You cannot say you *know* you are in pain.

(D): One cannot say one *knows* one is in pain.

These statements, while they do not mention (F) or (T), would readily be understood to refer to them. And, furthermore, they would be readily refuted by empirical evidence just because they so obviously refer (indirectly) to the occurrence of certain forms of words. Since Wittgenstein avoids these more obvious statements, the statement he does make, (A), should be seen as a circumlocution to avoid the cruder statements. This reading is confirmed by the immediate context, for Wittgenstein himself documents the occurrence of forms of words similar to (F) and (T). In the next section (*PI* 247) he considers the second-person sentence (S):

(S): Only you can know if you had that intention.

He comments that one might rightly say this when explaining the meaning of the word 'intention' to someone. So (S) is explicitly given a place in the language, and (F) and (T) must (at a minimum) have an analogous place. Wittgenstein also gives a gloss of the meaning of the word in this case: "And here 'know' means that the expression of uncertainty is senseless." So (A) cannot possibly be construed as excluding or prohibiting (F) and/or (T). So far as it applies to (F) and (T), it states instead that no occurrence of (F) or (T) can possibly be an instance of "saying of me that I *know* I am in pain."

A more promising contribution to understanding (A) is Ayer's remark that (F) is very like what Wittgenstein called a tautology in the *Tractatus* (Ayer 1982). Ayer's remark is true not in the technical sense in which tautologies are defined as formal logical truth-functions of a certain sort, but in a sense which is closer to the nontechnical sense of a tautology as a pointless repetition or redundancy of what has already been communicated. Ayer pointed out that I learn nothing more about a person from hearing that person say "I *know* I am in pain" than from hearing him say "I am in pain"; for although an animal or a very young child could be in pain without knowing it, that could not be the case with a person who has learned to speak. So the utterance of (F) is tautologous. (A) might then be construed as saying (rightly) that, because they are tautologies, (F) and (T) and similar expressions cannot be used to make reports or claims about the condition or state of persons. This is helpful.

But what are we to say about tautologies? And what is the status of (A), given that we accept Ayer's comment about (F)? We cannot simply assume that we still understand what tautologies are, with respect to either their identification or their use. In the *Tractatus* tautologies are explained in terms of truth-tables and the theory of truth-functions, and we need a new explanation if we are to understand (F) as tautology. And even then we need to ask what kind of statement (A) is if it says about (F) and (T) what Ayer implies that it does.

Fischer (1982) has made some contributions which promise help in answering these questions. In a recent paper he has pointed out that in Wittgenstein's later texts a number of comparable and equally tautologous expressions are called 'grammatical propositions,' and contends that we should therefore consider (F) and (A) as grammatical propositions. They are comparable to "Only you can know if you had that intention" (*PI* 247), to "One plays patience by oneself" (*PI* 248), and to "Every rod has a length" (*PI* 251). In these passages, all of which immediately follow the presentation of (A) and continue the discussion launched in *PI* 246, Wittgenstein mentions two characteristics of grammatical propositions. The first is that to the extent that we can form a picture corresponding to the grammatical proposition at all, we are quite unable to form a picture of its opposite (*PI* 251). The second is that grammatical propositions are appropriate in circumstances in which we mean to be talking about language rather than about the rest of the world: "One might tell someone this when one was explaining the meaning of the word . . ." (*PI* 247). Fischer adds, again usefully, that these propositions can be seen as *sinnlos* but not *unsinnig*, thereby evoking further continuity with the perspective of the *Tractatus*.

As helpful as Fischer's comments are in answering the two questions we have posed, they also have limitations. They omit reference to language-games, they borrow uncritically from the earlier work, and their treatment of the first-person statement (F) is faulty.[2] I shall take up these points by considering the two questions posed earlier about the *kind* of statement (A) is and about its relation to (F) and (T).

With respect to the first question, we may take it that to say that (A) is a grammatical proposition does say what kind of statement it is. But it does not say enough. Fischer's therapeutical account treats grammatical propositions as mistakes of a sort (as pretenses for, for example, empirical propositions); this account makes no reference to language-games, and hence making grammatical propositions is not seen as a distinctive language-game. (Fischer refers to language-games in connection with cultural "forms of life" rather than with elementary questions of meaning, which is a quite different fault and not relevant here.) Canfield (1981, 201) seems more perceptive on this point: "There is in natural language a language-game for making grammatical remarks." In the *Tractatus* there was only one language-game, "making pictures for ourselves of facts" (*TLP* 2.1); and a sign was said to "have sense" if it had a role in that game, to be "senseless" (*sinnlos*) if it had a role in logic but not in that game, and to be "nonsense" (*unsinnig*) otherwise. A major change in the later work is that "countless" language-games are recognized, "countless different kinds of use of what we call 'symbols,' 'words,' 'sentences'" (*PI* 23). Fischer notwithstanding, making grammatical remarks presumably is one of them, and a grammatical proposition is to be understood either as a statement used to make a grammatical remark, or a statement or sentence which could only be used to make a grammatical remark. So Fischer's account needs to be supplemented by an account of making grammatical remarks as a

---

2. Fischer (1987, 292–93) has published a comment on these remarks, in which he notes in part that our positions are closer than might appear from my detailed criticisms and replies in part to these points. He is certainly right that we have a great deal in common in our reading of Wittgenstein on key issues, and I much admire his book *Sprache und Lebensform,* even where I do not agree with it. Much of the difference that remains focuses on two issues: whether *Lebensformen* are primarily cultural, as he believes, or primarily natural, as I argue later in chapter fifteen; and whether *grammar* and the use of grammatical propositions constitutes a distinct language-game. The first issue is discussed in chapter fifteen. About making grammatical propositions he says, "Wittgenstein discussed no single language-game with grammatical propositions, but only language-games in which grammatical propositions are misunderstood for moves in the game. . . . Their being marked as 'grammatical propositions' therefore fits into Wittgenstein's program of philosophical therapy [entspricht deshalb Wittgensteins philosophietherapeutische Intention]" (292). The question is not whether there is a *single* language-game of making grammatical remarks, but whether there is a distinct one. Fischer's remark continues to make me think he is giving the wrong answer to this question by substituting a kind of Freudian therapy for the method based on language-games and uses of languages that Wittgenstein develops in the opening sections of the *Philosophical Investigations.*

naturally occurring language-game, as well as with a fresh account of what is *sinnlos* and what is *unsinnig*.

How is it that language-games are to be described or identified? It is clear from the first sections of the *Investigations* that the first requirement is to show how the use of language serves as a part of our activities, integral to them rather than a mere adornment. To do this one must show how and when it makes a difference to say something of a particular sort; or in Austin's terminology, how words become deeds. Perhaps to do this effectively one would need the outline or framework for a catalog of all our activities, but one can begin more modestly by specifying (1) the circumstances in which a certain sort of utterance is appropriate and (2) the words and deeds which are typically appropriate as a response to that sort of utterance.

(1) Grammatical remarks are appropriate when someone is confused about the use of some word or sentence. The remark in *PI* 248, "One plays patience by oneself," would be appropriate to make in response to the confusion my nephew displays, after a game of rummy, by asking that we play a game of patience together. Other examples are even more humdrum, bearing on questions of vocabulary and syntax. Wittgenstein, on the other hand, moves into less familiar territory, since the confusions to which his grammatical remarks pertain generally have to do with uses of words or sentences which can occur equally in English or German or any other language. This is true even of the use of (S) to explain the use of the word 'intention', since it is not just the word's dictionary definition as a lexical item in English that is at issue, but its role in language-games which transcend linguistic boundaries. So ordinary considerations of vocabulary and syntax are not the point of Wittgenstein's grammatical propositions. Grammatical remarks are appropriate in philosophy because philosophy speaks to (and sometimes contributes to) confusions about uses of words and sentences.[3] This at least is what Wittgenstein thinks, and what he thinks in particular about the issue of whether one *knows* what one is thinking. I can *know* what someone else is thinking, not what I am thinking:

> "It is correct to say, 'I know what you are thinking', and wrong to say 'I know what I am thinking'. (A whole cloud of philosophy condensed into a drop of grammar.)" (*PI* p. 222)

---

3. Fischer's therapeutical perspective is right in that Wittgenstein aims at confronting and correcting confusion; but the perspicuity and complete clarity at which Wittgenstein aims is more than simple therapy.

So the circumstances appropriate for making grammatical remarks are in a sense the same for philosophers and for schoolteachers, namely, ignorance or confusion about some use of language.

As for (2), the most important thing to say about the responses appropriate to grammatical remarks is negative, that it is not appropriate to argue whether they are true or false. This does not mean that it is morally wrong to do so, but simply that there is no room for it in the language-game. If my nephew were to object that my remark about patience is false, he would *thereby* be rejecting my remark as a grammatical remark. He would implicitly be claiming that he knows full well how to use the word 'patience', and that it designates a range of card games which include some for two players. He would be challenging me all right; but by the very challenge he turns my remark from (as I thought) a grammatical remark into an empirical remark. Whether a given remark is (can be, must be) grammatical or empirical is often a difficult or controversial question. The same sentence can often be used in different ways, and it may then be uncertain which language-game is being played or could be being played (which may itself be a grammatical question). The important point is that *if* a remark is grammatical, its truth cannot be challenged. This is perhaps part of the reason Wittgenstein says, in *PI* 128, that it would never be possible to debate philosophical theses.

With respect to the second question, about the relation of (A) to (F) and (T), it is clear that by saying that (F) and (A) are both grammatical propositions Fischer does not explain the relation between them. In particular there is no account of why what (F) expresses, or seems to express, is something that cannot be said of me. It seems very strange that (F) should have to be a grammatical proposition for (A) to be a grammatical proposition. So even if (F) is a grammatical proposition, the relations of (T) to (F) and to (A) are left unsettled. But it further remains unclear that (F) is a grammatical proposition, or at any rate that it always serves as a grammatical proposition. It would seem that (F) can be used, and often is used, for emphatic avowal, to protest against meddling interference, and in other ways.[4] Explaining why (F) and (T) seem to express something which cannot be said of anybody may require taking notice of these other uses.

The suggestions of Ayer and Fischer have enabled us to make some

---

4. Wolgast (1977, 67–74) describes five ways. Malcolm (1986, 211–12) also describes various ways in which "I know . . ." is used.

progress. (A) is a grammatical proposition which says, among other things, that what (F) and (T) seem to express cannot be predicated of anybody. This is still somewhat paradoxical. If I can say (F), why cannot what (F) says be said of me? Indeed, why is not my saying (F) an instance of predicting what (F) says of myself? The answer must depend on the nature of the language-game of which (A) is a partial description. To explicate (A) as a grammatical proposition will therefore require saying more about the language-game in question.

3. The Language-Game about Knowing and Not Knowing

So far as it applies to them at all, (A) says that (F) and (T) cannot be used to make knowledge-claims. Since (A) is a grammatical proposition, it says this to delineate, in part, a language-game, namely that very language-game for which (F) and (T) are not appropriate. This language-game involves knowledge-claims. I take it to involve making them, challenging them, doubting them, validating them, accepting them, and so on—a complex bundle of activities. (I fail to see how any one of these activities could make sense except as part of a large activity, or practice, in which they complement another. Here one can see vividly what Wittgenstein means by saying that there are countless uses of language, for one would not know whether to count challenging a knowledge-claim as a separate item from the comprehensive practice of which it is a part.) It is the comprehensive activity, for which we have no convenient name, which is delineated by saying that (F) and (T) cannot be used to make knowledge-claims.

The language-game in question concerns certifying something as known. Only certain things can be known; others cannot be. What can be known must be able to be justified or certified. This requirement imposes a limit because justification and certification are public, inter-personal processes, or the results of such processes. Therefore whatever can be said to be known must not only be something which can be said or predicated, but also something for the saying or predicating of which one must have what Wittgenstein called a 'criterion'. This applies directly to the case we are considering. The reason what (F) seems to express cannot be said of me is that my saying that I know I am in pain says no more than my saying I am in pain—and my saying I am in pain neither requires nor admits a criterion. My saying "I know I am in pain" is different from my saying of a certain person (whether myself or someone else) "I know that that person is in pain," for I do need a criterion for saying that there is some person in pain. Criteria, therefore, go hand in hand with the possibility of knowledge. One of the reasons (A) is so controversial is that correctly understanding it requires understanding criteria and the role they play in the language-game we are describing.

I discuss criteria in detail in the next chapter, but a preview of the main points is in order here. Criteria are part of grammar, as Canfield (1981, ix) rightly insists, in the sense that every proposition which states or explains a criterion for saying something is a grammatical proposition. Criteria govern knowledge-claims but not other uses of language. They are necessarily public rather than private; that is, other people must have equal access to them for my criteria to provide the justifications they are meant to provide. They are, however, not fixed and rigid things, and criteria themselves cannot be scientifically or empirically certified. Cavell, who apart from perhaps Canfield has made the most significant contribution to understanding Wittgensteinian criteria in the past two decades, says of them that "the philosophical search for our criteria is a search for community" (1979, 20). This is, I think, just the right thing to say, keeping their public nature and their elusive quality together in the same focus. It is important to stress, too, as Cavell does against Malcolm and Albritton, that "criteria do not determine the certainty of statements, but the application of concepts employed in statements" (1979, 45). This is simply the other side of the fact that the propositions which state or explain criteria are always grammatical propositions rather than empirical. As we saw in chapter three, a criterion determines the application of a concept in much the same way a schema does so for Kant, that is, by determining which phenomena can serve as evidence for or against a statement in which the concept is the predicate.

Criteria thus serve as the objective handles by means of which we can evaluate empirical statements. In this capacity they also make possible both doubting and learning. From there being a criterion for saying X, it follows that one can learn of X and that one can doubt X; from there being no criterion for saying X, it follows that one cannot learn of X or doubt X.

Of course, I cannot doubt or learn of my own pains or intentions—not the way that I can and often do doubt or learn of the pains or intentions of others, or they doubt and learn of mine. This goes hand in hand with the fact that I cannot be said to *know* of my own pains and intentions in the sense that I can know of the pains or intentions of others. It also means—and I take it Wittgenstein deems this too obvious to need stating in this context, though he does say it explicitly in *PI* 408—that it cannot be said of me either that I *don't* know I am in pain. If something cannot be said of me, neither can it be denied of me. Noting that these statements don't fit into it helps to delineate the practice of which doubting, learning, and claiming to know are constituent parts. The point is that what can enter into *this* game are statements for which there is a criterion. Because a criterion is something public, something to which everyone has in principle equal and common access, the certification of something through this language-game is appropriate for constraining the belief of others, as well as for attaining subjective assurance; though by its very nature, as Cavell argues persuasively, it cannot provide "absolute" certainty. Science, in the way it demolishes fixed ideas, holds theories open to challenge and correction, and insists on the reproducibility of experiments, constitutes a paradigm for the practice of this activity, as well as serving as an example of the sort of knowledge which properly constrains our belief and opinions.

Of what use is this knowledge, this certification? How does it enter into my life that I *know* something and do not merely believe it?

In some ways it makes very little difference. For me, as I formulate plans and take action to execute them, it matters not a whit whether the conception I have of the relevant facts is known or merely believed. Suppose that someone has taken an action which excludes me from a long-standing privilege. In considering various responses, I wonder whether (P) the action had another motive, its impact on me being inadvertent, or (Q) the action was meant to injure me. Suppose further that I am convinced that (P), that the effect on my ancient privilege was inadvertent, and that I believe this firmly and unquestioningly. This belief will shape my response. So will its certainty; if I were doubtful or unsure, rather than firmly convinced, the doubt might affect my response substantially. It would, however, make no difference in how I respond if I were to come to *know* that (P) instead of just feeling sure of it—say by a report (imagine it as reliable as you like) of the meeting at which the action was decided. Knowing would make a difference if it removed a doubt, but by hypothesis there is no doubt here. There is no reason why confirmation of an already fixed belief should lead me to alter, reconsider, or intensify my intended response. It is the degree of belief, not the degree of confirmation, that shapes action.

Where knowing would make a difference is in the justification of the action I take. Not, of course, "justification before myself." Before myself there is hardly a question of justification; or else I am "justified" by my belief and by my action's being reasonable in the light of my belief. Ordinary justification takes place in a public forum—this language-game, we might say, *is played*. Even where there is no formal forum such as a court of law, we often fend off criticism and solicit the good opinion of others by justifying our actions to them. Another person will naturally have two sorts of questions about my reasons for my action: whether my beliefs are warranted, and whether my action is reasonable in the light of, or relative to, my beliefs. Suppose now that others generally accept my action as reasonable relative to my beliefs: they will then regard my action as justified if they share my beliefs. But why should they share my beliefs? In general there is no reason for them to do so. Beliefs are varied, changing, disputed, and often idiosyncratic. Justification would be whimsical and illusory if it were always relative to beliefs; that is to say, there would then be no genuine justification of actions, such as ordinarily takes place every day. This is because it is part of the language-game of justification, as opposed to seeming justification, that what is justified for one person is justified for all. What I need to have good reasons for others to share my beliefs is knowledge rather than mere belief. Knowledge, if it is really knowledge, is fixed and universal. If I *know* that (P) is the case, others (assuming they do not challenge my knowledge) have no rational option other than to share my belief. *Knowing,* because it is justified belief, constrains others to share beliefs and thus furnishes justifications for actions reasonably based on those beliefs.

It is not misleading, though it still needs careful qualification, to say that whereas belief is a psychological concept, knowledge is a social concept. That is, believing is largely intelligible in the case of a solitary person, or in the case of a person apart from his relations to others, whereas knowing refers implicitly to other persons and to group process. Because it gives rise to rational constraint of belief, knowledge also makes possible a certain noncoercive (or rationally coercive[5]) uniformity of belief, without dogma or ideology. Such rational uniformity is itself a

---

5. Is being forced by good solid reason and evidence to believe something a case of coercion? There is an inclination to say that it is not, on the grounds that it is a paradigm of freedom and autonomy to be rational. But one should bear in mind Rousseau's *Social Contract* on forcing people to be free. On second thought I am inclined to say that rational coercion is a form of coercion, though a benign form.

kind of social cohesiveness, and unlike dogma or ideology it can contribute to stable social cohesiveness in a broader sense. Knowing thus entails a significant social ideal as well as a social process.

For the process to work and the ideal to be possible, knowledge can never rest on simple personal authority. Another way to put this point would be to say that knowledge is *justified* true belief, and therefore the constitutive rules of justification are also constitutive rules of knowing. The point is to achieve a certain noncoercive, or rationally coercive, convergence of belief, which is a narrower and rarer sort of community than that determined by shared criteria. For this to be possible at all, one must in principle be able to assure oneself of knowledge-claims another person makes. Therefore, "How do you know?" is always an appropriate response to a knowledge-claim. To continue playing the game (otherwise the claim, according to the rules, becomes void), the one who claims to know must give an account of the evidence—and perhaps also of the criteria according to which these phenomena count as evidence for his claim. I cannot, if I wish to stay in this game, brush aside the query with the rejoinder that I "just know," or that it is "obvious," or that it is something that "every right-thinking person knows," or that the evidence is secret (Senator McCarthy) or confidential (the bureaucrat's files) or private (the empiricist's sense-data). Such rejoinders betray and abuse the process—or perhaps better, withdraw from it—by attempting to reimpose dogma or personal authority at the expense of rational constraint. Of course we sometimes live with such imperfections; but toleration does not transform a shortcoming into a virtue.

At the other extreme from these authoritarian departures from the practice of distinguishing knowledge from mere belief, and also outside the practice, is the pretended certification of the indubitable. If I claim to know X, where X is a tautology, the opposite of which "cannot be imagined" or which dissolves into contradiction, then my knowledge-claim is mere pretense. What I say can never be a regular part of the practice of constraining rational convergence of belief if the opposite of what I say is impossible to conceive. It is in this sense that there is merit in Fischer's suggestion that grammatical propositions, like the tautologies of the *Tractatus,* are *sinnlos* but not *unsinnig.*

I conclude that a conception of knowledge which conforms to the rules of "know" presented by (A) and related texts, and whose purpose or integrity would be compromised by altering those rules, is central to a significant social process which embraces the development of science. It

is true that knowledge, as Wittgenstein conceives it, can never completely overcome scepticism,[6] since whatever can be known can also be
doubted. But this should be of scant comfort to traditional sceptics
(those who hold that we cannot know anything), since the only sort of
scepticism possible is one that is compatible with objective knowledge.
Far from inaugurating the scepticism its critics have charged it with
fostering—by denying that one can be said to know what one is most
certain of—the controversial remark in *PI* 246 does just the opposite: it
strengthens the defenses of objective knowledge against wholesale
scepticism. No doubt this is what Simone Weil had in mind in the
remark quoted at the head of the chapter. I have not attempted to show
that there can be no other sense of 'know'; nor have I claimed to have
shown all of Wittgenstein's actual reasons for saying some apparently
paradoxical things about knowledge and certainty, though I am confident I have given some of them. The main point, Wittgenstein apart, is
that the ideal of rational convergence of belief is important enough to
justify preserving the concept which makes it possible.

4.   The Antinomy of Pure Knowledge

So far I have attempted to explicate what Wittgenstein did say in one
controversial passage, and to articulate one good reason a person might
have for saying it. Some philosophers may now object that, however
beneficial its practice may be, the outcome of this social process is not
genuine knowledge. For a proposition to be known, the objection
continues, it is not sufficient to rest satisfied after carrying the justification just one or two steps so that there is a rationalization of the
immediate belief in question. It is also necessary that the justification be
justified, that is to say, that it be validly based on what is known rather
than merely believed. Knowledge, to be a rational constraint, must be
objective; and if it rests on what is subjective, even if it is subjectively
certain, it cannot transcend the subjectivity of its origin. According to
the exegesis given in this paper, Wittgenstein insists that justification
must depend on agreement about "what can't be said to be known."

---

6. This is a main theme of Cavell's *Claim of Reason*, a claim he discusses in connection
with morality as well as with epistemology. There remains a difficult question about just what
philosophical scepticism is. I think Cavell, though he generally endorses scepticism, would
agree that there is a traditional wholesale scepticism which, although not explicitly refuted,
does not survive Wittgenstein's investigations.

Such "justifications" are relativistic and rationally incomplete—the complaint continues—and therefore they cannot yield genuine knowledge.

These critics do not misrepresent Wittgenstein. Wittgenstein's frequent and repeated remarks about justification coming to an end and about the dependent status of foundations confirm that such critics have correctly characterized his position. The question is where the illusion lies, whether in Wittgenstein's view that genuine knowledge rests on certainties which cannot be said to be known, or in the critics' assumption that complete knowledge is at least in principle possible. I shall, by showing a parallel between Wittgenstein and Kant, show that the criticism is based on illusion, and that Wittgenstein has brought the concept of knowledge back down to reality. More specifically, Wittgenstein exposes the epistemological illusions of these critics through considerations very like those through which Kant exposes transcendental illusions in the *Critique of Pure Reason,* especially the arguments against cosmological illusions in the chapter entitled "The Antinomy of Pure Reason." Central to these epistemological illusions is the idea that I must either *know* or *not know* that I am in pain when I am indeed in pain. It is this underlying assumption that Wittgenstein denies. His point, to which the remarks in *PI* 246 contribute substantially, is that I neither *know* nor *don't know* that I am in pain. That is to say, it can be said of me *neither* that I know I am in pain *nor* that I don't know I am in pain. This is parallel to Kant's demonstration that one can neither assert nor deny that the world had a beginning in time, and so forth.

What Kant calls the antinomy of pure reason arises when Reason insists on conceiving the absolute totality (or completeness) of a series through which the Understanding (namely, a person using the rules and categories of the Understanding, through their respective schemata) makes phenomena intelligible. For example, through the rules of Understanding, a person conceives of events as ordered in time in such a way that given any moment of time we can always ask about its temporal condition and its temporal outcome, that is to say, about the moments of time immediately preceding and following it. Thus through the Understanding a person conceives of time as an infinitely extensible series of moments; or perhaps as two series, a regressive series infinitely extended into the past and a progressive series infinitely extensible into the future. Reason goes further. Reason holds that since the regressive series is complete up to the present moment (for any present moment) we can think about its totality and ask about its beginning. A similar pattern of argument is evident with respect to causation: since we must understand any and every event as caused, and each cause as itself caused, Reason proposes to think of the regressive series of causes as a complete or absolute totality and to ask about its beginning.

Each ordinary member of such a regressive series is conditioned by other members, and the general concepts acquire their capacity for application to phenomena through a schematism which, like Wittgenstein's criteria, restricts their application to data of experience. No antinomy results from considering a regressive series under these conditions, but only an expansion of our knowledge of phenomena. Reason, however, is not satisfied, and in thinking of the series as an absolute totality it is aiming at the unconditioned. That is to say, Reason seeks an unschematized use of the categories of the Understanding. This unconditioned, Kant points out, can be thought of in either of two ways: "It may be viewed as consisting of the entire series in which all the members without exception are conditioned and only the totality of them is absolutely unconditioned. . . . Or alternatively, the absolutely unconditioned is only a part of the series—a part to which the other members are subordinated, and which does not itself stand under any other condition" (*KdrV* A417=B445). The second of these alternatives gives us the general form of the thesis in each of the four manifestations of the antinomy, and the first alternative furnishes the general form of the antithesis.

Knowing is, or is part of, a language-game easily conceived as involving a regressive series which Reason would insist must be complete. The rule which might generate such a series and give rise to the insistence is the rule that one always has the right to know *how* something is known. The insistence on completeness entails that every proposition referred to in the justification of a knowledge-claim must itself be either known or not known. The thesis of the antinomy thus generated is that there are basic bits of knowledge, that is, knowledge that is not known through anything else but through itself alone. Ayer calls them 'primary recognitions' in the paper cited earlier in this chapter. Descartes held such a view, as do both phenomenologists and Empiricists. The argument for this thesis, as for the thesis in Kant's antinomy, takes the form of a *reductio ad absurdum:* Unless there is some knowledge that is self-evident, no justification can ever be completed and there can be no knowledge at all; and if the only absolute knowledge were the system as a whole, we could not know anything until we knew everything. Since we do have knowledge, it follows that there must be basic propositions, however difficult they are to agree about. The antithesis of the antinomy is the idealist view, found in Hegel, Bradley, Royce, and Quine, that the chain of epistemological justifications forms a single coherent absolute totality, none of whose parts has any privilege or priority. Again the argument takes the forms of a *reductio:* If there were nothing unconditioned, then there could be no knowledge; and if there were any unconditioned bits of knowledge, they could never be justified and therefore could not be known. Put another way, any basic proposition would have to be independent of every other basic proposition, and therefore could not be part of our system of knowledge. It follows that there can be only *one* unconditioned in the domain of knowledge, and this must not be part of the system but the whole system itself—the Absolute Idea.

These arguments are not found in just this form in Wittgenstein's work, and the details of the arguments for the thesis and antithesis would certainly have to be worked out differently for different philosophers: differently for Moore and Husserl on the one hand, differently for Bradley and Quine on the other. It seems likely that Wittgenstein, however, might accept both the argument for the thesis and the argument for the antithesis, so far as they are distinct and different and are negative in their thrust. That is to say, he might well agree that we could not now have any knowledge if we needed first knowledge of the whole system as a prerequisite; and he might agree that we could not know anything if we first had to have some basic knowledge, because what is basic cannot be justified and therefore cannot be known. So he might agree with both of the parties on the points on which they differ. On the other hand he clearly disagrees with them on the point on which they agree, namely, that we could know nothing if there were no self-evident or unconditioned knowledge. That disagreement is a central point of *PI* 246, for he says that others can know of my pains, whereas I cannot be said to *know* them. He disagrees with them, that is to say, by holding that the agreements at which our justificatory regresses come to rest are about matters which cannot be said to be either known or not known. This is the move which allows him to accept the substance of each of the opposed reductions and still avoid the antimony.

In the diagnosis of the antimony there are further parallels between Kant and Wittgenstein. Wittgenstein does not share Kant's faculty psychology, but the point seems very much the same when he puts the blame for philosophical errors on our craving for generality (*BB* 17, *PI* 104). Ultimately the fault lies, in Kant's words, with Reason's insistence on completeness and totality. More specifically the source of the trouble is located in the constitutive use of regulative ideas. That is, instead of simply using the categories of the Understanding as *rules* for processing our data and for making an intelligible synthesis out of what we see and hear, we try to use these rules (or categories) to create or constitute or prove the existence of realities of which we have no experience. The parallel idea in Wittgenstein is that the trouble arises through the empirical use of grammatical propositions. A grammatical proposition is again a rule for processing data—more precisely, for processing words and sentences which, among other things, refer to data of experience— and to make empirical use of a grammatical proposition is to try to employ it instead as a description of our data, or of our world. That is to say, claiming to *know* a grammatical proposition involves constitutive use of a regulative idea.

The analogy is not perfect. Because knowing is a social rather than a cosmological concept, it is not a rule of Understanding that it be applied to every item within its domain, that is, to every belief. But the analogy is nonetheless strong, and we have seen in earlier chapters how much Wittgenstein knew and respected Kant's critical philosophy. We may therefore suppose that the insight it gives us into the problem is not altogether alien to Wittgenstein's reasons for saying what he says about knowing in *PI* 246. The illusion is that whatever can be stated, particularly if it is something certain, can also be known. Or perhaps better: that whenever I state something, it must be either *known* to me or else *unknown* to me. Wittgenstein brings us down to earth: " 'Knowledge' and 'certainty' belong to different *categories*" (*OC* 308). This reminds us that knowing is part of a language-game, a different one from that of certainty and one according to which we say that a person knows something only on the basis of a social process involving criteria. There are other uses of "I know. . . .", but this language-game determines the conditions for saying of someone that he knows something. And it is a simple consequence of the conditions and rules of this game we play that I can't be said either to know or not to know that I am in pain— notwithstanding that it is permissible to say, "I know I am in pain." This much seems right, and a reasonable thing to say.

11

Criteria

1. Grammar and Criteria

The concept 'criterion' is almost as important in Wittgenstein's later philosophy as 'grammar', and equally bewildering. It is introduced in the *Blue Book* (pp. 24–25) with a flourish of qualification that invites exegesis, and it occurs prominently in many arguments. In attempting to explain what Wittgenstein means by 'criterion' I shall be assuming that the concepts of 'criterion' and 'grammar' are intimately connected, and that together these concepts are at the core of Wittgenstein's later logical theory.[1] That 'criterion' is a concept whose primary use is in the criticism of thoughts or arguments—in other words, is logical—is apparent at every occurrence of the term 'criterion'. That it is intimately connected with 'grammar' is equally certain, and can be supported both by textual citations and by considering the logical theory implicit in the *Philosophical Investigations*.

In the *Blue Book,* just prior to his rough explanation of the term 'criterion', Wittgenstein says, ". . . to explain my criterion for another person's having toothache is to give a grammatical explanation about the word 'toothache', and, in this sense, an explanation concerning the meaning of the word 'toothache'" (p. 24). Here we find 'criterion', 'grammar', and 'meaning' all together, and their juxtaposition presents at a glance a characteristic feature of Wittgenstein's later approach to logical theory. A close association between these concepts is reiterated in

---

1. By 'logical theory' I mean a set of general principles governing meaning (sense and nonsense as well as reference) and inference; or in the case of Wittgenstein, the ultimate arbiter of the propriety or impropriety of utterances and inferences. When I read an earlier version of this essay at the Oberlin Colloquium in 1962, Paul Ziff objected to the use of this term in connection with Wittgenstein, saying that Wittgenstein has no logical theory. Ziff was mostly right, and I now wish I had cut the expression from the essay. Theory in philosophy was anathema to Wittgenstein, and it misrepresents him to use the word to characterize his views, although he certainly did not shy away from saying things about sense and nonsense and inference, sometimes even in the form of principles, nor from trying to make what he had to say about these matters into a coherent account. I have left the essay in its original form because the term 'logical theory' is too deeply woven into the text to be easily removed.

his remark about the discontent of "the metaphysician" with our "grammar" and with "the common criteria—the criteria, i.e., which give our words their common meanings" (pp. 56–57) and again when he discusses the ordinary prerequisites for understanding the sentence "I am pointing to my eye" (pp. 63–64).

Wittgenstein's continuing intention that these concepts should be understood together is apparent at several places in the *Investigations*. When, for example, he discusses "the grammar of 'to fit', 'to be able', and 'to understand'," he says:

> The criteria which we accept for 'fitting', 'being able to', 'understanding', are much more complicated than might appear at first sight. That is, the game with these words, their employment in the linguistic intercourse that is carried on by their means, is more involved—the role of these words in our language other—than we are tempted to think. (*PI* 182)

Here the criteria for certain terms are presented as determining, or prominently influencing—very nearly as being identical with—the "grammar" of those terms. (See also *PI* p. 185.) In the remarks on various sorts of states, we find the following:

> But in order to understand the grammar of these states it is necessary to ask: 'What counts as a criterion for anyone's being in such a state?' (*PI* 572)

The powerful remark, *"Essence* is expressed by grammar" (*PI* 371), may also be cited; for although it does not explicitly mention criteria, the *least* we must know if we understand the essence of something is the criterion or criteria for it. There is, then, strong textual support for regarding *grammar* and *criterion* as companion concepts in Wittgenstein's later philosophy.

Further exegetical consideration reinforces this view. The concept 'grammar', supported by related concepts, is important in Wittgenstein's attack upon the claim of formal logic to be the sole arbiter of propriety in discourse and argument. The case against the view that logic, in this broad sense, must operate according to strict rules, with no vagueness or imprecision, is presented in a series of remarks in the *Investigations* (*PI* 65–108). In the place of the mathematical precision of formal logic Wittgenstein emphasizes "grammar," which rests upon an agreement in the way people act, upon a form of life. These remarks about logical theory are constantly presupposed and accented in the following discussions. Thus about certain propositions of which "I can't imagine the opposite" Wittgenstein does not, in the *Investigations,* say that they are "analytic" or "tautologous"—these terms being strongly identified with formal logic through Frege's *Grundlagen* and his own earlier *Tractatus*—but that they are "grammatical" (*PI* 251). The principal reason for examining 'criterion' in the light of Wittgenstein's conception of grammar is that sometimes we can also refer to criteria to decide about the propriety of an utterance or of an argument. Virtually every occurrence of the term 'criterion' in the later work is in connection with a question about the propriety of some utterance or about the circumstances in which some utterance is appropriate, and in some passages (e.g., *PI* 160, 625, 633, 692) the utterance in question would seem to express an inference. Thus the concept 'criterion' is a logical tool, used in connection with truth-claims and knowledge-claims (as we saw in the previous chapter), and as such must be part and parcel of the revised conception of logic in Wittgenstein's later philosophy.

Wittgenstein's use of the term 'grammar' has been subject to detailed exposition in previous chapters, so as to make clear its connections both with the mastery of a technique (*PI* 199) and with those matters of grammar (e.g., morphology and syntax) which are the concern of linguistics. Choosing the dependence of criteria on grammar, and more specifically on the grammar of knowledge-claims, as the perspective most likely to throw a nondistorting light on Wittgenstein's position is an approach I share with Canfield:

> Statements of criteria are themselves grammatical remarks, and part of understanding criteria is understanding the general nature and status of grammatical remarks. (1981, ix)
>
> Criteria govern judgments, assertions, propositions, those things that admit of being true or false. In a language that had *only* commands, criteria would not operate. (1981, 32)

2.   The Distinctive Features of Criteria

The distinctive features of Wittgensteinian criteria can be set out in a series of "grammatical propositions" (compare *PI* 251). Any of the thirteen italicized statements which follow might, in appropriate circumstances, be used as a grammatical explanation of 'criterion', in other words, to explain what criteria are.

1. *Criteria are human instruments.* A good way to begin is by identifying the genus, so to speak, to which criteria belong. If we are asked what *kind* of thing a criterion is, to say that it is an instrument of a certain sort would be as good an answer as any. The dictionary tells us that a criterion is a test or standard or canon of correctness, and I do not believe that Wittgenstein departed from this basic sense of the word. A standard is an instrument, although not the most common sort. The particular standard kilogram in Paris, for example, is an instrument of a certain sort, although not exactly the sort one uses ordinarily for taking measurements. Not all tests or standards are used in the same way as the standard kilogram, but it is not difficult to see them all as "instruments of a certain sort"—human contrivances with characteristic uses.

An instrument can be characterized in two different ways: we can speak either of its typical uses or of its typical shape, dimensions, and component materials. In the case of many tools both a functional characterization and a physical description seem important for understanding what such an instrument is. A scythe, for instance, is for mowing grasses and grains, and it has a certain curvature and size that distinguish it from other mowing tools; both aspects of what a scythe is are mentioned by the entry in the Merriam-Webster dictionary. In other cases, however, it is neither essential nor even useful to give a physical description in addition to a functional characterization in the course of explaining what a certain sort of tool or instrument is. A pump, for example, is "a device or machine that raises, transfers, or compresses fluids or that attenuates gases, esp. by suction or pressure, or both." In this case it appears that only the functional aspects are essential to something's being a pump, and that what physical characteristics a pump may have is, as it were, an incidental matter. It is not always easy to say what is essential (compare *PI* 62), and physical characteristics may assume a preeminent importance if the question is one of distinguishing two kinds of pumps, rather than of explaining what a pump is. Nevertheless, *some* functional characterization is always essential to an explanation of what some instrument is; where none can be given, as in the case of certain objects from anthropologists' diggings, it remains an open question whether the artifact is an instrument or an ornament.

It is important to realize that this initial characterization of criteria is only a very short step forward. Its import is mostly negative; it warns us against identifying criteria in every respect with the circumstances or phenomena out of which these instruments may be fashioned, and against divorcing them from their characteristic roles in human inter-course. We must also bear in mind that the variety of items which might fall under the label Tools and Instruments is very great, and criteria should not be too closely associated in our thoughts with any of the others. We still have to say much more to make clear what sort of instrument a criterion is.

2. *Criteria govern the use of certain linguistic expressions.* This second step is an attempt to answer the question "What are these instruments for?" At this point we begin to distinguish Wittgensteinian criteria from the rest.

At first it may seem that our answer to this question is at odds with the way Wittgenstein actually talks, for questions are raised in the *Investigations* about criteria for all sorts of different things—for a person's being of a certain opinion (*PI* 573), for someone's being in a state of expectation (*PI* 572), for a person's reading (*PI* 164), for "fitting," "being able to," and "understanding" (*PI* 182), for something's being a matter of course for me (*PI* 238), for the identity of sensations (*PI* 253, 288), for personal identity (*PI* 404), for visual experiences (*PI* p. 198), and so on. This is a varied list, and one in which linguistic expressions certainly do not predominate. If we think in terms of the criteria and standards to which we might refer in everyday affairs, it seems as though we would use the criteria to determine whether someone has a certain opinion, whether a person is in a state of expectation, and so on. Among the above examples it is only where Wittgenstein speaks of "the criteria for 'fitting', 'being able to', and 'understanding'" (*PI* 182) that criteria have the appearance of govern-ing linguistic expressions.

There are, indeed, other passages where Wittgenstein makes it appear that he takes criteria to govern, in some way, what is said. For example:

> The man who says "only my pain is real", doesn't mean to say that he has found out by the common criteria—the criteria, i.e., which give our words their common meanings—that the others who said they had pains were cheating. But what he rebels against is the use of *this* expression in connection with *these* criteria. (*BB* 57)
>
> Suppose I explain various methods of projection to someone so that he may go on to apply them; let us ask ourselves when we should say that *the* method that I intend comes before his mind.
>
> Now clearly we accept two different kinds of criteria for this. . . . (*PI* 141)

But these examples remain a minority. The decisive weight in favor of this second point is exegetical. Assuming that Wittgenstein's use of 'criterion' is distinctive, we must look to its relation to other prominent ideas in his later work for the key to its distinctive features; and the intimacy of the concepts of 'grammar' and 'criterion' requires that Wittgensteinian criteria characteristically have their application in connection with linguistic expression. When Wittgenstein speaks, for example, of the criteria for a person's reading, we must remember that this is a shorthand locution, that what the criteria govern is our use of such expressions as "*A* is reading." As Canfield says,

> [S]tatements of criterial rules may be thought of as setting up the language-game, as belonging to stage one, whereas statements of symptoms belong to the actual playing of the game. (1981, 34)

What criteria determine is not the empirical fact whether *A* is reading but the "meaning" of "*A* is reading." In this way they form part of the "grammar" of such expressions as "A is reading," or of *reading*.

This is the place to note an ambiguity in speaking of the criteria for someone's doing such-and-such. What is meant is not a test by which we might determine whether *X* does such-and-such (where it is assumed that the meaning of "*X* does such-and-such" is antecedently known); but rather the standard grammatical test according to which a sentence of the form "*X* does such-and-such" is used, when it is used in a normal or correct way. The manager of a supermarket might explain to a new employee that the way of telling that a flat of fruit from California contains tomatoes rather than peaches is that the cover-paper is light blue rather than dark blue, the labels being identical; but although such a "way of telling" might properly be regarded as a criterion, it would not be a Wittgensteinian criterion. This ambiguity is adequately resolved when the context of the passages is preserved and Wittgenstein's logical theory kept in mind; it need not obscure the focus of the concept of a criterion—as it might do for someone who has the supermarket criterion for tomatoes in mind when he reads Norman Malcolm's statement that a criterion is "something that settles a question with certainty" (1959, 60).

3. *The utterances for which there are criteria are those that make statements which the speaker has some way of knowing to be true or to be false, or which he might justify by reference to something other than what is stated in his utterance.* It is clear that 'criterion' is a narrower concept than 'grammar': not every linguistic expression has a criterion, though every

linguistic expression has a grammar. I cannot think, for example, what could be meant by "the criterion for 'Hello'"; and Wittgenstein explicitly says that there is no criterion of personal identity which makes it correct for me to say that "I" am in pain (*PI* 404), and again, that I do not identify my sensations by criteria (*PI* 290). It is therefore necessary to indicate *which* utterances have criteria—namely, those which have truth-conditions or make a knowledge-claim.

It might be noted in passing that we often speak of the criteria of such things as understanding or dreaming, where it is a phenomenon rather than a linguistic expression for which there is said to be a criterion. In such cases we must remember that *"Essence* is expressed by grammar" (*PI* 371). This rule works both ways. On the one hand, giving the grammar governing dream reports—the conditions in which they make sense and the sorts of discourse continuations they support—tells what dreams are, tells us the essence of dreaming. On the other hand, saying just what dreams are tells us the grammar of dream reports, the criteria for saying, for example, *"A* dreamed that."

4. *All utterances of this sort have criteria governing their use.* A criterion is a standard—that is, an objective reference for ascertaining or checking something; and the standard is, of course, public. Once we agree that criteria govern the use of certain linguistic expressions, it is reasonable to expect that they govern the use of all those utterances that make statements which the speaker can know, justify, or verify. This expectation is borne out by the texts. Albritton finds this feature of criteria prominent in Wittgenstein's discussion in the *Blue Book,* where a symptom is explained as a phenomenon which we find through experience to coincide with a symptom: "If there is *no* criterion by which I might judge that I myself have a toothache, for example, then it will follow that nothing can be a symptom for me of my having one" (1959, 849). So anything for which there are symptoms must have a criterion (or criteria). And since (*BB* 24–25) we can only answer the question "How do you know that so-and-so is the case?" by giving criteria (a grammatical explanation) or symptoms (an empirical justification), it follows that I must have some criterion for any statement which I can *know* or *justify.* In the later work, strong textual support for this point comes from the fact that Wittgenstein feels justified, whenever considering a dark or dubious assertion, in asking what the criterion for it would be; this is, indeed, the predominant use of 'criterion' in the *Philosophical Investigations.*

Canfield has spelled out a question about the universal applicability of criteria in the following terms:

> The question about scope can be set out as follows. First, we put aside statements without a truth value. Secondly, we exclude tautological statements, or necessary truths. Wittgenstein does not use the notion of a criterion in connection with these. Thirdly, there is the class of first-person statements like "I am in pain" or "I intend to leave." These statements are discussed below; it is clear that Wittgenstein thinks they are not governed by a criterion. The question then is this: Are all statements except those of the three types just mentioned governed by a criterion, according to Wittgenstein? We can also ask this as: Do criteria have universal scope? (1981, 130)

It is very helpful to specify in this manner the three classes of statements (declarative utterances) that need to be excluded from the range of the requirement that there be criteria. Canfield disagrees, for good reason, with the affirmative answer Hacker (1972, 258) gives. But what about the affirmative answer implied by what I have said? The answer is unclear. In particular it depends on whether all statements other than those in the three specified classes are ones that a person can know or justify; for it is only for statements that can be known or justified that criteria are needed. On the face of it it would seem that the statements of natural history are an exception, falling neither within any of the three specified types nor (as shown in chapter ten) among those statements which can be known or justified.

The last two points show an affinity between Wittgenstein's use of 'criterion' and the Verifiability Theory of Meaning. The similarity is that in both cases a statement is challenged or clarified by asking, in effect, what would show the statement to be true and what would show it to be false. This affinity finds its most open expression when Wittgenstein says, "Asking whether and how a proposition can be verified is only a particular way of asking 'How d'you mean?' The answer is a contribution to the grammar of the proposition" (*PI* 353). This congruity is worthy of note, for its historical as well as its philosophical interest; it brings out an important continuity between the earlier and the later Wittgenstein.

At the same time there are differences to be kept in mind. Most importantly, Wittgenstein appears to regard certain statements which are paradigms of verified utterances for the Verifiability Theory—basic or protocol sentences or avowals—as exempt from this logical test, as

Canfield notes in the passage just quoted. Such statements have been said in the past to be the only ones fully verified. That these have no criteria, according to Wittgenstein, comes out most clearly in his discussion of pain. No one would argue that I must have a criterion whenever I cry out in pain; when Wittgenstein says that "the verbal expression of pain replaces crying" (*PI* 244), the inference suggests itself that "I am in pain" and "My foot is sore" do not have criteria either. As Malcolm has pointed out (1958, 978), this comparison is surprising since no one would say that a cry of pain has a truth-value or a contradictory, whereas the *statement* that I am in pain has both. Wittgenstein, however, is not drawing a circle around what can be true or false (as do Verifiability Theorists), but around what can be known or justified. "I am in pain" lies within the first circle but not the second: "It can't be said of me at all (except perhaps as a joke) that I *know* I am in pain. What is it supposed to mean—except perhaps that I *am* in pain?" (*PI* 246). And since the concept of a criterion applies to all that is within the known-or-justified circle, and to nothing outside it, my saying that I am in pain is exempt from such a standard (*PI* 290). Malcolm puts the point neatly: "One does not find out that one is in pain by employing a criterion. Indeed it makes no sense to speak of *finding out* that one is in pain, when this would imply that one was previously in pain but not aware of it. There is, however, a criterion for determining whether someone uses the sentence 'I am in pain' correctly—and this makes it an intelligible sentence" (1959, 15).

This is a point at which Wittgenstein differs sharply from the Logical Positivists, while not directly contradicting them. At first blush, the import of Wittgenstein's remarks for the Verifiability Theory might be best thought of not as a repudiation of that theory but as a restriction of its application to statements which the speaker can know or justify.

5. *Criteria are always the criteria of some person or group of persons.* This feature should be evident from the mere fact that criteria are human instruments, and it is worth stressing chiefly because of the misunderstanding it can forestall—in particular that of confusing criteria with necessary and sufficient conditions. It would be absurd to suppose that for *you* the necessary and sufficient conditions for an acorn's growing into an oak might be different from what they are for *me*. The necessary and sufficient conditions for something are in the world, not in language or human conventions. With criteria the case is different, and there may be a divergence between your criterion for something and mine.

Wittgenstein gives an instance of this when he considers what might be said if someone were to ask him whether he still knows what he was going to say when interrupted:

> If I do know now, and say it—does that mean that I had already thought it before, only not said it? No. Unless you take the certainty with which I continue the interrupted sentence as a criterion of the thought's already having been completed at that time. (*PI* 633)

I do not mean that whenever one talks about criteria one must *say* whose they are. It may sometimes prevent misunderstanding to use the personal possessive pronouns with 'criterion', but much of the time this is not necessary. When Malcolm speaks of "the criterion of dreaming," it is clear enough that he is referring to the criterion which speakers of the language have in common, and which they all learn to use when they learn to tell their dreams. What is important is not any form of words, but rather that the human ancestry of criteria not be betrayed in the course of analysis, exposition, or extrapolation of the concept—as it is when Michael Scriven, in what he takes to be the spirit of Wittgenstein, says that the criteria for something's being a lemon are certain *properties* of lemons, and speaks of them as being either "analytic" or "normic" (1959).

Stanley Cavell (1979, 20) says that the search for criteria is a search for community. That is a wonderful way to put this point. It stresses that criteria are the criteria of some group or other, and it stresses at the same time their tenuous and fragile status. They cannot be imposed, we have to search for them. And where they are in place, they represent a kind of achievement, the achievement of having arrived at the kind of agreement in judgment that constitutes the beginning of community.

6. *Criteria are arbitrary, in that there need be no justification for criteria being what they are.*[2] At one point Wittgenstein supposes that I have explained that my criterion for another person's having a toothache is that he holds his cheek in a certain way. He goes on:

> Now one may go on and ask: "How do you know that he has got toothache when he holds his cheek?" The answer to this might be, "I say, *he* has toothache when he holds his cheek because I hold my cheek when I have toothache." But what if we went on asking:—"And why do you

---

2. Roy Harris stresses the parallel between Saussure and Wittgenstein on the arbitrary character of linguistic rules, as well as other fascinating parallels, in his *Language, Saussure and Wittgenstein: How to Play Games with Words* (1988).

suppose that [his] toothache corresponds to his holding his cheek just because your toothache corresponds to your holding your cheek?" You will be at a loss to answer this question, and find that here we strike rock bottom, that is we have come down to conventions. (*BB* 24)

The whole point of criteria is that they determine what we say; and so the question why, when we have some criterion or other, we say what the criterion determines we should say—this is a question which soon loses all point. We can consider a criterion as giving us a rule which indicates what we are to say. We do not have *reasons* for following such a rule as we do; we are rather trained to follow it when we learn the language.

> Let me ask this: what has the expression of a rule—say a sign-post—got to do with my actions? What sort of connection is there here?—Well, perhaps this one: I have been trained to react to this sign in a particular way, and now I do so react to it. (*PI* 198)
> *We need have no reasons to follow the rule as we do.* The chain of reasons has an end. (*BB* 143)

I do not believe that Wittgenstein intends that we can never give reasons for having the criteria we do, but rather that we need not and ordinarily do not. In the special case of the technical language of the sciences, where theory plays a large role and precise neologisms are frequent, the justification of criteria is probably more common than in lay speech. A Wittgensteinian scientist of the seventeenth century might have said, "I know the word 'force' is not used with such narrow precision in ordinary parlance; but if we rigorously take only *ma* and not *mv* as our criterion for the force of an object, we can formulate a simpler and more coherent theory." The facilitation of theory has often served in the past, and can still serve today, as a kind of justification for the criteria of scientific expressions. Wittgenstein acknowledges as much when he says that "Such a reform for particular practical purposes, an improvement in our terminology designed to prevent misunderstandings in practice, is perfectly possible" (*PI* 132). Such justification occurs but rarely, however, with respect to the common language which we all learn as we grow up.

7. *To explain the criteria of* X *is to give a partial grammatical explanation of* 'X'. This statement generalizes a remark made by Wittgenstein (*BB* 24), and I have already argued for it. It is worth repeating here because the connection between criteria and grammar is at the root of the next few features which I shall have to state.

8. *There is no such thing as an inner or private criterion,* in the sense of a criterion which another person could not even be conceived to use. Albritton raises the question, "And is there no inner criterion for a toothache?" He apparently thinks it might be answered in the affirmative. I find this suggestion implausible in the extreme, and I take the fact that Albritton draws this possibility out of his reading of Wittgenstein's remarks as a sign that his account of Wittgenstein's use of 'criterion' is inaccurate. A criterion, *C*, governs the use of a linguistic expression, 'P'. This means that if I know how to use 'P'—in other words, if I know how to apply *C*—I must be able to distinguish between a correct use of 'P' and a misuse of 'P'. If I have such a measure of correctness, it must be an objective one—otherwise it would be no real measure at all—and therefore open to the view of anyone who cares to look and see. If my criterion for 'P' were a private one, completely inaccessible to anyone else, I could never, however strong my impression of being right, make any sense of a distinction between my *thinking* such-and-such a use of 'P' to be correct and that use's really *being* correct.

There are two texts that might be thought to support the possibility of a private criterion. One is the remark, "An 'inner process' stands in need of outward criteria" (*PI* 580), where the occurrence of the adjective 'outward' suggests that there might be a sort of criterion that is not outward. The other is his remark (*PI* 141) that one kind of criterion we clearly accept for saying that the method of projection I intend comes before another person's mind is "the picture (of whatever kind) that at some time or other comes before his mind." But if the picture coming before *his* mind is a criterion for us, it cannot be a *private* inner criterion; here we should remember that an inner process stands in need of outward criteria and cannot, under such circumstances, be regarded as private.

Wittgenstein has pointed out that where there is no distinction between being right and thinking one is right there is no being right either: "But in the present case I have no criterion of correctness. One would like to say: whatever is going to seem right to me is right. And that only means that here we can't talk about 'right'" (*PI* 258).

Without a distinction between a correct use and a misuse, the notion of a private criterion evaporates into absurdity. It is, indeed, subject to the full impact of Wittgenstein's argument against the possibility of private language (*PI* 243–80, especially 256–70).

9. *Criteria are often embedded in linguistic practice, and the people who use them may be quite unable to say what they are.* Even in lands where

children are taught to formulate the grammar of the language, this training does not generally extend to the "grammar" with which Wittgenstein is concerned. Long after schoolchildren can handle the relevant expressions with perfect aptness, they still do not have any explicit idea what the truth-conditions for "He has a toothache" are, nor that there are no criteria for my saying that I have one.

Although people do not ordinarily *know about* the criteria they use, they do *know how* to use them. Here we come upon the familiar and still dangerous fact that the sentence "*N* knows the criteria for *P*" is ambiguous, since 'know' can have the sense of either 'know how' or 'know that', as Gilbert Ryle has put it (1949, 27–32). That the latter sort of knowledge of our common criteria is rare should not blind us to the fact that people make propositions at apt junctures, recognize good and bad evidence for them, teach their children to use the relevant sentence, and in general give every evidence of a sound practical knowledge of these criteria. Conversely the ubiquity of this practical knowledge should not lead us to expect to find any intellectual appreciation of the subtleties of criteria.

The fact that criteria are embedded in practice rather than in doctrine is an aspect of Wittgenstein's beginning with human activity rather than, as in the case of Descartes or Hume, with thought. As in the simple language-games at the beginning of the *Philosophical Investigations,* we do things; in the course of doing things we speak, and in the course of speaking criteria emerge. It is this insight about starting with activity rather than thought that explains Wittgenstein's fondness for Goethe's remark, "Im Anfang war die Tat."

10. *Criteria are generally rough and imprecise; it is regular use and acknowledgement, rather than precision, which makes them satisfactory.* They are, of course, as precise as they need be for human communication, but our requirements are a far cry from the "crystalline purity" which Wittgenstein, following Frege, once imagined to characterize our discourse.

There are two related ways in which this roughness of criteria shows itself. The first is that what the criteria for '*P*' determine is the *sort* of thing that would show '*P*' to be true or false; and to say whether some set of present circumstances are of this sort requires discrimination that is not determined by the criteria and cannot be prescribed, but can be learned only through practice. "I have further indicated that a person goes by a sign-post only in so far as there exists a regular use of sign-posts, a custom" (*PI* 198). *"We need have no reason to follow the rule as we do.* The chain of reasons has an end" (*BB* 143). Criteria are a part of the form of life which people have in common, and Wittgenstein offers little reason to believe that such a form of life might be precisely and exhaustively described.

The second way in which the roughness of criteria shows itself is in our inability to say exactly what the criteria are for even simple utterances. It is a noteworthy fact, apparent to anyone who reviews his use of 'criterion', that Wittgenstein never gives a detailed description of any criteria; he says, indeed, that "in most cases we aren't able to do so" (*BB* 25). An example may make it clear why this should be so, and why it is innocuous. A man puts a gun to his shoulder, a shot sounds, and a duck falls to the ground. We say that the man aimed at the duck and shot it. We may even say that *that* is just what we call 'aiming and shooting', and thereby indicate successfully the criterion for a man's aiming at and shooting something. But this does not mean that it is *certain* that the man did aim at the duck and shoot it. It may turn out that the man is blind, or that the gun was electronically rigged to aim itself, or that an accomplice did the shooting, or that there is no sign of a wound on the bird. If any of these further circumstances should obtain, the claim would have to be withdrawn or in some way qualified—although we might still correctly say that this is the sort of thing we ordinarily call 'aiming at and shooting a duck'. The number of possible exceptions to 'P' may be infinite, but my failure to specify them does not entail that I fail to indicate the criteria for 'P'.

11. *Criteria presuppose circumstances of application.* This feature is particularly apparent in cases where there are many different criteria for something, rather than one defining criterion. Albritton emphasizes this aspect of Wittgenstein's use of 'criterion', and it may be illustrated by the following passages:

> Now it cannot be doubted that we regard certain facial expressions, gestures, etc., as characteristic for the expression of belief. We speak of a 'tone of conviction'. And yet it is clear that this tone of conviction isn't always present whenever we rightly speak of conviction. "Just so," you might say, "this shows that there is something else, something behind these gestures etc. which is the real belief as opposed to mere expressions of belief."—"Not at all," I should say, "many different criteria distinguish, under different circumstances, cases of believing what you say from those of not believing what you say." (*BB* 144)
>
> And in different circumstances we apply different criteria for a person's reading. (*PI* 164)

In these cases we might say that the criteria are complementary, in the sense in which the different phonetic criteria of the English phoneme /p/ are complementary.

The vast majority of common concepts have several complementary criteria rather than a single defining criterion. There are exceptions among scientific concepts; it may even be an ideal of science that each of its concepts should have only a single defining criterion, and to the extent that scientific theory aims at enunciating propositions that are true in *all* circumstances, this ideal is readily understandable. But even in science the concepts with a single defining criterion are by and large limited to sections of scientific thought where there is a single universally recognized theory, and if one examines concepts in the vanguard of scientific advance—the concept of force in the sixteenth and seventeenth centuries or that of a chemical element in the nineteenth—one sees different criteria competing against or complementing one another. Whatever the case may be with science, ordinary assertions have a more limited use, bounded by the circumstances in which they are made; and their criteria need not be identical with the criteria of the same utterances in different circumstances.

12. *There may be a fluctuation between the criteria of something and the symptoms of it.* In *PI* 79 Wittgenstein takes note of this fluctuation in the case of scientific definitions: "what today counts as an observed concomitant of a phenomenon will tomorrow be used to define it"; and in *PI* 354 he says that "the fluctuation in grammar between criteria and symptoms makes it look as if there were nothing at all but symptoms." The supposition that in such cases there are only symptoms must certainly be illusory, for it is incompatible with the requirement that I must have a criterion for every statement which I can justify or know to be true. The fluctuation is real enough, however. The previous point has prepared us for finding different criteria for something in different circumstances; but we might have thought that what counted as criterion in one context could not count as symptom in another, and *vice versa.* Taking note of the fluctuation between criteria and symptoms makes it clear that the variation can be of the latter sort as well.

It is not hard to point to examples of this sort of fluctuation, and Wittgenstein has not been the only one to observe it. It is common for criteria and symptoms of something's having the temperature 0° C to be interchanged. On one occasion I may explain that thermometers are designed to indicate the temperature at which pure water freezes under a certain atmospheric pressure; here I take the change of state of pure water as my criterion for the temperature being $0°C$, and the behavior of thermometers as a symptom, that is, "a phenomenon of which experience has taught us that it coincided, in some way or other, with the phenomenon which is our defining criterion" (*BB* 25). On another occasion I may regard thermometers as having unquestioned authority, and state that the change of state of pure water at sea level is correlated (as a symptom) with the temperature being $0°C$; and here the former symptom is my criterion, and my former criterion a symptom. This sort of fluctuation also occurs with the term 'force': either the formula $F = k \Delta l$ or the formula $F = ma$ can be taken as expressing the criterion of force; whichever formula is taken as giving the criterion, the other will in that context express the correlation of a certain phenomenon with this criterion. Two points about such fluctuation deserve to be noticed. First, it might also be described as a fluctuation between the "grammatical" and the "empirical" use of the same expression (*PI* 251). The sentence "Water freezes at $0°C$" and the formula $F = ma$ have a "grammatical" use when they express the speaker's criteria; otherwise they have an "empirical" use. Secondly, such fluctuation occurs only where there is a reliable correlation between phenomena, such as obtains in scientific matters or between the visual and the kinesthetic criteria for touching my nose. Such fluctuation is common in scientific discourse because of what Feigl calls "the essentially network-like character of scientific theories."

The fluctuation between criteria and symptoms is conditioned by the contextual character of criteria. A conversation ordinarily has a certain aim and certain presuppositions, and the criteria must be among the presuppositions. They may be explained in grammatical propositions; but these explanations do not in themselves constitute progress toward the aim of the conversation—they make for progress only in the sense in which putting an edge on a scythe helps to mow grass, and thus, in Kant's terms, they are explicative rather than ampliative. Not all conversations have the same presuppositions or the same aim, and the same sentence which expresses a grammatical explanation in one context may express an empirical proposition in another—that is, the criteria may become symptoms. What cannot be permitted, by Wittgenstein or anyone else, is that phenomena should *in the same context* count as both criteria and symptoms, or that a proposition should be *simultaneously* both explicative and ampliative. But when we take cognizance of the fact that criteria are contextually conditioned, and do not attach irrevocably to terms or concepts, then we can see how the same concept may have sometimes one and sometimes another criterion. Since different criteria may be criteria for the same concept, a fluctuation between criteria and symptoms is not necessarily a sign of ambiguity, and does not "destroy logic"—as it would do if it meant that there were only symptoms.

13. *Criteria can "coincide" or "conflict."* We may begin by noting that the cases where one speaks of the coincidence or conflict of criteria are ones in which two or more sorts of phenomena regularly occur together: Wittgenstein speaks, for example, of the coincidence of the "many different criteria" (he mentions four) that a man may have for his pointing to his own eye (*BB* 63–64). It is in the light of this fact that we can see most easily what is meant by saying that criteria coincide. The criteria which a man may have for pointing to his eye, according to Wittgenstein's account, include (1) the kinesthetic experience of raising his arm to his eyes, (2) the tactile sensation of his finger touching his eye, (3) the visual experience of his finger appearing before his eye, and (4) the visual experience of seeing (in a mirror or a TV screen) his finger in the appropriate relation to his eye. He then says, "If these criteria, as they usually do, coincide, I may use them alternately and in different circumstances. . . ." I take it, then, that what it means to say that the criteria for 'P' coincide, is simply that the various phenomena, each of which is commonly (or sometimes) used as a criterion for 'P' in particular circumstances, are invariably associated (or very nearly so).

A "conflict" of criteria is more difficult to understand. The sense in which Wittgenstein's remarks about the concept of a man pointing to his eye seem to leave room for a conflict of criteria is that the criteria need not coincide—that is, the phenomena which are commonly regarded as criteria, and which as a matter of fact are invariably associated (or nearly so), might *conceivably not* occur in such regular conjunction with one another. If this explanation is correct, it gives a sense to the expression "possible conflict of criteria." But could there be in some sense an *actual* conflict among the various criteria of the *same* concept? To answer this question we shall have to examine what would happen if the various phenomena which we find in conjunction should cease to occur together.

In discussing another example Wittgenstein says:

> For the *ordinary* use of the word 'person' is what one might call a composite use suitable under the ordinary circumstances. If I assume, as I do, that these circumstances are changed, the application of the term

'person' or 'personality' has thereby changed; and if I wish to preserve this term and give it a use analogous to its former use, I am at liberty to choose between many uses, that is, between many different kinds of analogy. One might say in such a case that the term 'personality' hasn't got one legitimate heir only. (*BB* 62)

If our criteria cease to coincide, the concept as we know it breaks apart, and the expression in question no longer has *any* clear use. Consequently it is very difficult to see what sense there would be in continuing to give the name 'criteria' to those phenomena which used to count as criteria; and without criteria there could, of course, be no conflict of criteria.

We arrive, then, at the seemingly paradoxical position that criteria which in fact coincide might possibly conflict, but that there could not be an actual conflict among the various criteria of a single concept. There is, of course, no inconsistency in this position, and I think it sheds a useful light on Wittgenstein's use of 'criterion'. The apparent paradox disappears when we bear in mind that criteria are human instruments with characteristic uses, that their application presupposes circumstances which do more or less frequently obtain, and that where these circumstances do not obtain our criteria do not apply and thus, for all practical purposes, cease to exist.

3.   Albritton and Malcolm on Criteria

I have so far tried to be straightforwardly exegetical in my examination of the concept of a criterion. In conclusion I wish to be somewhat more polemical, and to make clear that I regard some of the important things Albritton and Malcolm have said about criteria as incompatible with the exegesis I have set forth.

Albritton and I differ in viewpoint. Rather than approach the exegesis of the concept 'criterion' on the basis of its affinity with the concept 'grammar', he begins by considering the expression 'defining criterion', which he takes to denote some sort of necessary and sufficient condition. Thus a criterion of X is some sort of a condition for X's being so, and Albritton's exegetical problem is to determine *what sort* of condition. But to begin in this manner is to set off in the wrong direction. The terminology is alien and inimical to Wittgenstein's thought, for the concept of a criterion was introduced by Wittgenstein precisely to avoid speaking of necessary and sufficient conditions with respect to those logical relations where such a formal notion does not apply. Criteria are human instruments, whereas conditions are natural phenomena; criteria are used or applied, whereas conditions obtain; criteria are arbitrary or conventional, and when we reach them "the chain of reasons has an end," whereas statements about necessary and sufficient conditions are justified by something else, generally by scientific laws; conditions are conceptually independent of what they are conditions for, whereas criteria (in Wittgenstein's sense) are not; and so on. Only confusion and perplexity can result from amalgamating two such diverse concepts; and although Albritton's paper has substantial merits, I cannot help but conclude that he goes astray at the very beginning by viewing Wittgenstein's logical theory from the wrong perspective.

Malcolm, if my exegesis has been sound, departs from Wittgenstein in two important respects. The first is his blurring of the distinction between criteria and evidence. He says that a criterion "settles a question with certainty" (1959, 60), and that "the application of a criterion must be able to yield either an affirmative or a negative result" (1959, 24). At another point he says: "If he [Mill] had a criterion he could apply it, establishing with certainty that this or that human figure does or does not have feeling . . ." (1958, 970). I take it that Malcolm's remarks apply to questions about how it is with the world, not just to questions about how a linguistic expression is to be used. To answer questions of this sort Wittgenstein insists that we must refer to "symptoms" or evidence; in maintaining that we can answer such questions "with certainty" by reference to criteria, Malcolm erases the distinction (which Wittgenstein was careful to preserve) between the truth-conditions and the truth-value of a proposition, between meaning and truth—and thus he threatens (as Wittgenstein did not) the foundations of logic.

Malcolm's second departure from Wittgenstein occurs in his implicit denial of "the fluctuation of scientific definitions" (*PI* 79) which occurs when scientists elaborate new criteria to coincide with the original ones. The whole burden of his attack on Dement and Kleitman (1959, ch. 13) rests upon his charge that they adopt physiological phenomena (REM periods and EEG patterns) as a criterion of dreaming, and the principal "error" with which he taxes them is that of not "holding firmly to waking testimony as the sole criterion of dreaming" (1959, 81). Finding a new coinciding criterion for a phenomenon under investigation is one of the legitimate and useful aims of a scientist, and to go along with Malcolm's second departure from Wittgenstein would be to take up a form of linguistic Romanticism and to place an unwarranted shackle on scientific progress. Malcolm appears, therefore, to have erred twice in the details of Wittgenstein's logical theory, and to have slipped into logical confusion which Wittgenstein himself avoided.

12
Meaning That Is Not Use

1. The Puzzling Qualification in *PI* 43

Wittgenstein is known for having defined meaning as use. This formula has no doubt several plausible applications. Most prominently, we are bound to get a very different result if we apply the formula "Meaning is use" to sentences rather than to words. The "meaning" (*Sinn*) of the sentence is, or is determined by, its use (*Verwendung, Anwendung*) in the course of some activity; that is, what difference it makes to the activity. The Verifiability Theory of meaning—that the meaning of a sentence is its method of verification—arises as a special variation of applying the formula "Meaning is use" to sentences, which Wittgenstein endorsed in his conversations with Schlick and Waismann (*WVC* 47) and in his philosophical *Nachlass* from 1929 to 1930 (*PR* 66, 77, 174, 200). Malcolm (1986, 133–35, 148) gives a good account of how the *Sinn* of sentences depends on our ways of applying them. The comparison of Wittgenstein's language-games with Aristotle's categories in chapter four could be considered another specialized account of applying the formula to sentences, since the discourse conditions referred to there are rules of when to use various types of sentences, and the discourse continuations are rules for ways of using them. As I pointed out in chapters six and seven, however, *Sinn* and *Anwendung* make up only one side of a radical duality about meaning which Wittgenstein carried over from the *Tractatus* (or from Frege) into his later work and which, as we saw in chapter three, involves deep philosophical puzzles akin to those about Kant's schemata. Applying the formula to words rather than sentences, neither of these two German words appears. The meaning (*Bedeutung*) of a word is its use in the language (*Gebrauch in der Sprache*). Here is the most famous passage on this subject in the *Philosophical Investigations*:

> For a *large* class of cases—though not for all—in which we employ the word 'meaning' it can be defined thus: the meaning of a word is its use in the language. (*PI* 43)

Here he is concerned only with *Bedeutung* (rather than *Sinn*), only with words (rather than sentences), and only with *Gebrauch* (rather than *Verwendung* or *Anwendung*). Rather than examine this formula directly, I propose in this chapter to examine its more neglected preamble, "For a *large* class of cases—though not for all. . . ." What are the other cases Wittgenstein had in mind, and what is the significance of this reservation about the basic formula?

2.   Proper Names and Sentences

Are proper names meant to be exempted from Wittgenstein's definition? That proper names are different from general names (and of course from verbs), in particular in their not having a "meaning" in the ordinary sense of that word, has long been a commonplace of philosophy. The distinction is prominent in Mill's *Logic,* but its importance for both Frege and Russell is more likely to have had a decisive influence on Wittgenstein. For Frege, since proper names refer to objects and are "saturated" expressions with (in the normal case) both sense and reference, they can be explicated directly by indicating the referent, whereas other expressions are "function names": they are "unsaturated," they signify operations on (functions of) objects, and their meaning can only be explained with the help of proper names and sentences. These unsaturated expressions are often predicative, and from Frege's point of view it would make sense to say that their meaning (*Sinn*) must be explicated as their general use (or function) in the language—that is, as how they serve in general to transform a name into a more complex expression. Frege might therefore have held that the definition of 'meaning' in *PI* 43 should apply only to these expressions and not to proper names. Russell probably would allow an even narrower role of the definition of meaning as use. The underlying reason is that thinking of meaning as determined by use is an alternative to thinking of meaning as determined by direct acquaintance. Since Russell held that we are acquainted with universals, he would no doubt exempt both universals and proper names, reserving the definition of meaning as use for what he called incomplete symbols, which do not have real meaning on their own (Russell 1956, 182).

In Wittgenstein's *Investigations,* however, proper names must certainly fall under the formula. Indeed the definition of *Bedeutung* as *Gebrauch in der Sprache* seems designed specifically to deal with certain questions about names. The previous sections (37–42) have all discussed proper names, including such specific ones as 'Mr. N. N.', "the tool with the name 'N', " and 'Excalibur'. *PI* 43, moreover, seems an answer to the question posed at the beginning of *PI* 37: "What is the relation between name and thing named?" In *PI* 43, as part of the answer to that question, Wittgenstein first gives the definition of 'meaning', and then goes on to say, in an often overlooked sentence: "And the *meaning* of a name is sometimes explained by pointing to its *bearer.*" This series of sections is too tightly woven together to allow us to suppose that proper names are to be exempted from the definition. Wittgenstein must rather be read as presenting a criticism of Frege and Russell, and perhaps of his own early views as well.

Names are the only class of words which might plausibly be thought to be exempted from the definition, since it applies easily to verbs, adjectives, and particles—that is, to the expressions that Frege considered unsaturated and ones that Russell called incomplete symbols. I conclude, therefore, that the definition is meant to apply to all instances of 'meaning' in which we speak of the meaning of a word.

As for sentences, the definition obviously does not work for them, and it is equally obvious that it is not the meaning of sentences that Wittgenstein had in mind when he allowed for exceptions to his definition.

It is true, as Hamlet said, that sentences are nothing but words, words, words. Nonetheless the definition of 'meaning' is stated in terms of the meaning of "a word," in the *singular,* and allows only of distributive rather than collective generalization. There is no way to apply the definition to the kind of *collection* of words that constitutes a sentence in such a way as to have a single meaning for the collection. A further consideration is that a sentence does not have a "use in the language" in the way a word does. A word occurs over and over again, and its repeated and infinitely repeatable occurrence is an essential feature of its having a use in the language. A sentence, on the other hand, may occur only once; indeed the reoccurrence of a sentence is such an improbability that the *New Yorker* makes a game out of hunting for such events, and reports its findings with a mischievous glee which implies that the reoccurrence cannot be a mere coincidence.[1] Because sentences

---

1. I am not sure that the *New Yorker* still does this. For years the magazine would occasionally print, as filler at the bottom of a column of text and with the heading "Department of Strange Coincidence," passages from two entirely different and supposedly

are normally a one-time thing, the definition of *PI* 43 cannot apply to them. One of the main problems one must face in reading Wittgenstein, as also in semantic theory, is the problem of saying how the meaning of words is related to the meaning of sentences. Certainly Wittgenstein's definition of meaning in *PI* 43 only makes us aware of this problem and does not take us any closer to a resolution of it.

In spite of the fact that the definition cannot apply to the meaning of sentences, this cannot be an exception that Wittgenstein had in mind. On the contrary, the "meaning" of a sentence is such a very different thing from the "meaning" of a word that Wittgenstein does not use the same word for the two sorts of meaning: a word has (or lacks) *Bedeutung,* a sentence has (or lacks) *Sinn.* Hallett argues convincingly in his *Companion* (1977) that this terminological distinction is carried over from the *Tractatus* into the *Investigations;* and, of course, uses of the word '*Sinn*' cannot be what Wittgenstein had in mind as other uses of the word '*Bedeutung*'.

3. Meaning as Feeling or Point

In *PI* 543–45 Wittgenstein notes several uses of the word 'meaning' which do not fit the definition of *PI* 43. These cases must have been among those which Wittgenstein had in mind when he wrote *PI* 43.

> Can I not say: a cry, a laugh, are full of meaning? And that means, roughly: much can be gathered from them. (*PI* 543)

It seems clear that it is the cry or laugh on a particular occasion that is said to be "full of meaning," rather than any cry or laugh whatever, and therefore that the "meaning" (what can be gathered from it) must depend on particular circumstances rather than on the "general use" of laughing or crying. A very different concept from that defined in *PI* 43 seems to be at work.

In *PI* 545 another recalcitrant employment of the word 'meaning' is set forth—again in a question:

> But when one says "I *hope* he'll come"—doesn't the feeling give the word "hope" its meaning?

---

original texts in each of which the same identical sentences appeared. Such research was not, of course, much appreciated by the author of the later text.

Wittgenstein remains aloof and noncommittal, and his comment is conditional:

> If the feeling gives the word its meaning, then here "meaning" means *point*.

"Point" is presumably to be distinguished from "use in the language," the latter but not the former being capable of being represented by rules (*PI* 564), and the former but not the latter depending on the special circumstances.

In *PI* 544 the feeling is said to give meaning not just to *one* word in an expression but to the words collectively:

> When longing makes me cry "Oh, if only he would come!" the feeling gives the words 'meaning'.

Here Wittgenstein puts the word 'meaning' in quotes—shudder quotes—presumably to note that this is a different concept of meaning. It is different, for one thing, in that it applies to the words collectively rather than individually, as Wittgenstein notes immediately with a rhetorical question: "But does it give the individual words their meanings?" It also differs, he suggests, in that in this case "one could also say that the feeling gave the words *truth*," so that "you can see how the concepts merge here."

All three of these instances of plausible uses of the word 'meaning' are ones for which the definition of *PI* 43 does not hold. It seems reasonable to regard all three under a single alternative rubric, but that does not matter, since the conclusion in any case is that the word 'meaning' occurs with at least one other meaning besides that defined in *PI* 43.

At first glance—we will take a second look in the next section—this conclusion seems to have very little significance. Many words have more than one meaning—'bank', 'use', 'is', and 'know' are examples. In these cases we may have to use two or more different expressions when translating into another language ('know' means either *wissen* or *kennen*, either *savoir* or *connaître),* and we may give a separate definition for each meaning. Superficially this other meaning of 'meaning', as illustrated in the three examples from *PI* 543–45, seems no more problematic than in the case of other words, and seems to throw no new light on the problems of meaning that Wittgenstein means to discuss. Certainly Wittgenstein seems to have carefully described these examples so that, even where this other sort of meaning applies to words, it is not the meaning of individual words that is at stake. Thus the soundness of *PI* 43 is underlined rather than challenged by these examples. But we should nevertheless not take comfort too quickly. If *Bedeutung* is sometimes associated with *feeling* (as in these examples) rather than with *use*, why could it not always be so associated? Even though Wittgenstein seems to settle this question in *PI* 43, it was a question that kept coming back to haunt him, and the inability to suppress the question may well be one of the reasons that he left room in *PI* 43 for another sort of meaning. (I owe this last point to Norman Malcolm.)

4.   Words with Two Meanings

We come finally to consider the case of those words which, like the word 'meaning' itself, have two or more meanings. This topic is more difficult in two ways. On the one hand, Wittgenstein's remarks are guarded, and it is not easy to determine whether he believed that words with two meanings are exceptions to the definition of *PI* 43, or whether they really are so. On the other hand, the phenomenon of words with two meanings must in any case lead to second thoughts about the definition, the final import of which is difficult to formulate.

Wittgenstein presents the problem and some comments in *PI* 558–68. He starts (*PI* 558) with the familiar insistence of Frege and Russell that 'is' has different meanings in the sentences "The rose is red" and "Twice two is four," signifying predication in the first and identity (*Gleichheit*) in the second. It might seem plausible to try to fend off the problem—for example, by arguing that there are really two uses or two words, or that both sentences involve predication—but Wittgenstein does not take that approach. He appears to accept the results of Frege and Russell and to acknowledge the challenge posed for his definition of 'meaning': ". . . I say that 'is' is used with two different meanings (as the copula and as the sign of equality), and should not care to say that its meaning is its use; its use, that is, as copula and sign of equality" (*PI* 561).[2] The problem for the definition of *PI* 43 remains tough no matter how we answer the question whether the one word really does have the two meanings, for even to *understand* the question we must separate meaning from use. "Now isn't it queer (*merkwürdig*)?" asks Wittgen-

---

2. The problem seems the same one as that which Mason (1978) develops by considering a passage from *On Certainty*. It remains unresolved here, as in chapter three and in Mason.

stein (thinking no doubt of *PI* 43), that we can insert this wedge between the meaning and the use of a word? "Queer" in a way in which the examples of *PI* 543–46 were not, since here we do not have another meaning of 'meaning' but the very same one (apparently) that was meant to be defined in *PI* 43. So it is as if the one word 'is' serves as the visible surface of two different bodies of meaning (*Bedeutungskörper*), just as a certain plane quadrilateral surface may be the visible surface of either a prism or pyramid (*PG* 53–54).

The problem here is not the old problem of the *Tractatus* (see 3.34–3.341) about how to describe the wedge between a word and its meaning, whereby the word is superficial, accidental, whereas the meaning is "substantial," essential. Wittgenstein's original treatment of this problem (*TLP* 3.3–3.5) is exceedingly complex, especially because of the difficulty of seeing exactly how the rules of logical syntax are supposed to work together with the meanings of signs (3.33) and their logico-syntactical employment (3.327) to determine what it is in a symbol that signifies (3.344). No doubt the whole thrust of Wittgenstein's later philosophy served to make him suspicious of speaking of a "body of meaning," or of what is "substantial" rather than superficial ("essential" rather than accidental) about a word and its use; but the definition of *PI* 43 can be read as identifying substance and essence with use, and agreeing with one central theme of the *Tractatus* solution to this old problem. The *new* problem, which seems unnoticed in both the *Tractatus* and in the early sections of the *Investigations,* is the apparent wedge between meaning and use, that is, between what is essential and accidental not in the *word* but in the use itself.

To distinguish between what is essential and what is accidental or superficial about a word, Wittgenstein turns to its use:

> What I want to say is that to be a sign a thing must be dynamic, not static. (*PG* 55)

To what can we turn to distinguish what is essential from what is inessential about a *use*? In *PI* 564–66 Wittgenstein suggests that we might turn to the point (*Witz*) or purpose (*Zweck*) of the use in question or of the activity within which it occurs: "The game, one would like to say, has not only rules but also a *point*" (*PI* 564). This suggestion, however, is presented for criticism and analysis rather than as Wittgenstein's solution to the problem. One indication of his reservation is the phrase "one would like to say," which suggests a temptation from which he will have to rescue his interlocutor rather than his final view of the matter. Indeed if one succumbed to the temptation, one would soon have to confront a distinction between essential and frivolous points and/or purposes. Wittgenstein further expresses his reservations (*PI* 566–67), and in *PI* 568 he proposes that the distinction might turn on understanding aright (*Verstehen*), or on a kind of seeing:

> If I understand the character of the game aright—I might say—then this isn't an essential part of it.
>   ((Meaning is a physiognomy.))

Here we have no solution of the problem but rather a restatement in terms that are taken up again in part 2 (pp. 181, 218). It seems that the question of what is essential about the use of a word won't go away—but cannot be resolved either; for to defer the question to the domain of physiognomies and of "seeing as" is to give up on attempts at analysis and/or explanation.

I conclude that the examples from both *PI* 543–45 and 558–68 are cases in which we use the word 'meaning' in such a way that it cannot be defined as in *PI* 43. The first set of examples is of secondary importance, for the existence of a second meaning of 'meaning' does not in and of itself challenge the definition of *PI* 43. The second set of examples, however, drives a wedge between the very same meaning and use which *PI* 43 means to bind firmly in place. The problem has to do with what is "essential," and leads on into the discussion of part 2 of the *Investigations*. No solution is in sight. These examples constitute a serious challenge to the definition of *PI* 43, therefore, and discussion of them will at the very least require us to revise our understanding of *PI* 43.

13
Private Language

1. "Sensations Are Private"

Professor Anscombe, in her lectures at Oxford in Hilary Term of 1954, just following the first publication of Wittgenstein's *Philosophical Investigations,* said of paragraph 258 that if the argument were wrong at that point, then the whole book would have no point philosophically. Some scholars may choose to locate the crux of the matter at another point, but there can be no question that the argument against the possibility of private language, and of private ostensive definitions in particular, is one of the most original, powerful, and dramatic themes of the *Investigations.* Unfortunately the importance of the argument is matched by its difficulty and obscurity—a fact which provides the aim of this chapter, namely, to try to clarify a part of the argument (*PI* 243–70).

The relatively direct and continuous discussion of the question of private language is to be found in paragraphs 243–317 of the *Investigations,* but there are many other sections which either lead up to that discussion or refer to it. The remarks on the nature of ostensive definition (27–38) are important, because without this prior clarification we might give a wrong answer, or too superficial an answer, to the question whether one could establish the name of a sensation for oneself by a "private" ostensive definition. In a similar way the analysis of what it is to understand and to obey rules and of the importance of rules in language-games (137–242) is necessary to understand why there cannot be a private language; at one point, indeed, Wittgenstein directly ties what he has been saying about rules to his thesis about private language:

> And hence 'obeying a rule' is a practice. And to *think* that one is obeying a rule is not to obey a rule. Hence it is not possible to obey a rule 'privately': otherwise thinking one was obeying a rule would be the same thing as obeying it. (202)

Also in the paragraphs which deal with the nature of thinking and personal identity (316–427) and the ones concerned with meaning (at the end of part 1), Wittgenstein makes many remarks that have a bearing—often a direct bearing—on the question of private language; for example, in 384: "You learned the *concept* 'pain' when you learned the language." Nevertheless sections 243–317 present the problem most clearly and argue for a certain solution to it most coherently.

It is necessary at the outset to have the precise problem clearly in mind. Wittgenstein sets the problem in 243 by asking, "Could we also imagine a language in which a person could write down or give vocal expression to his inner experiences—his feelings, moods, and the rest—for his private use?" The question as stated is liable to misinterpretation, and it is crucial for understanding what follows not to confuse this problem about the possibility of private language with either (1) the question whether I can, for my private use, keep a diary in ordinary English to record my pains, moods, and so on; or (2) the question whether there could be a language *in fact* used by only one person but *capable* of being understood by any explorer clever enough to see the connection between certain sounds (or marks) and certain circumstances. The answer to question (1) is clearly affirmative, and no one will mistake it for the question Wittgenstein raises. But a discussion between A. J. Ayer (1954) and Rush Rhees (1954) indicates that question (2) is more difficult and that it may become confused with Wittgenstein's problem. It will be useful, therefore, to see what question they discuss and how it differs from the question Wittgenstein discusses. Both Ayer and Rhees show a correct verbal understanding of Wittgenstein's contention, but their arguments are directed to a different contention.

Ayer formulates the thesis he is attacking as the assumption "that for a person to be able to attach meaning to a sign it is necessary that other people should be capable of understanding it too" (69–70). And Wittgenstein certainly does maintain such a thesis, although not as an assumption. Ayer then proceeds to his attack, which consists in the meager description of the case of a Robinson Crusoe, abandoned by humans and nurtured by kind animals, who invents words to describe the flora and fauna and also words to describe his sensations. This "language" is presumably private in the sense that no one else in fact understands the words that Crusoe has invented. Man Friday, however, then enters the picture, and Ayer carefully explains (72–74) that he might understand the words for sensations as well as the words for physical objects (though, Ayer says, he couldn't be taught the two sorts of words "in the same way," whatever that means). The most that Ayer has done (assuming that there are no other mistakes in his argument) is to give what seems to me a correct answer to question (2). He has shown that there can be a system of private signs which no one else understands, but which could be understood by another person (in this case by Man Friday).

Rhees correctly describes Wittgenstein's problem when he says that the main question "is a question of whether I can have a private understanding; whether I can understand something which *could* not be said in a language which anyone else could understand" (83). Appearances notwithstanding, however, the point of contention between them is question (2) rather than that of *PI* 243. Ayer's argument shows that there might be a Robinson Crusoe with a language which no one else understands, but which could be understood by another person (say, by a Man Friday). Rhees's main concern is to reject this argument, on the grounds that a language must consist of rules, and there could be nothing to show that a Crusoe was following rules rather than simply behaving (as ants do) with regularity. It appears to me that Rhees is wrong in this contention against Ayer. But at any rate this controversy should be distinguished from the question they formulated—namely, the question raised by Wittgenstein about private language.

The next two sections of this chapter will be devoted to an exegesis of the first two steps in Wittgenstein's presentation, the exposé of certain considerations which lend plausibility to the notion of a private language (244–54), and a *reductio ad absurdum* of the notion of private language or private understanding (256–70).

2. The Grammatical Character of the Remark

Sections 244–54 can best be understood against the background of the following argument *P:*

(1) Sensations are private; no one else can have my pains.
(2) I commonly use words to refer to my sensations.
(3) In any category the meaning of (at least some of) the words I use to refer to things are the things to which these words refer.

Therefore,

(4) the meanings which I have for the words which I use to refer to my sensations *cannot* be grasped by another person; I have a private

understanding of words, and so (by analogy) does every other person when he uses such words.

Each of the steps in *P* has a considerable plausibility, and the argument itself, although not strictly deductive, has a great deal of force. Even without (3), which is the only premise that can be flatly rejected, one is strongly tempted to agree to the conclusion on the basis of (1) and (2). And yet the conclusion is unacceptable, because all the evidence (apart from this philosophical argument) supports the proposition that other people *do* understand me when I refer to my pains, itches, and so on. The first problem for Wittgenstein is to remove this puzzle by bringing out the real import of (1) and (2) and by showing the impossibility of the conclusion—a problem which he says "is like the treatment of an illness" (*PI* 255). It is difficult to describe the form of Wittgenstein's argument in a completely satisfactory way, but I think it will be more helpful than not to think of 244–54 as remarks about (1) and (2) designed to show us that *P* is not a sound argument, and of 256–70 as a *reductio ad absurdum* argument against (4). Before we go on to support this interpretation of the passage, we should say a word about (3), which, if true, adds greatly to the persuasiveness of *P*.

Premise (3) is, as it were, held up to ridicule in section 264: "'Once you know *what* the word stands for, you understand it, you know its whole use.'" This quoted sentence is an echo of Mill (1865, 33–38) and Russell (1956, 189–202) and also of Wittgenstein's own early work (*TLP* 3.203). A reader who turns only to the passages in the *Investigations* directly concerned with private language may well be surprised that such a powerful and seductive notion is merely recorded as a misconception to be avoided. Actually the rejection of this idea is not at all arbitrary; it is one of Wittgenstein's most carefully considered revisions of his earlier philosophical views. His later view, which I have discussed at length in other chapters, is perhaps epitomized in section 43 of the *Investigations:* "For a *large* class of cases—though not for all—in which we employ the word 'meaning' it can be defined thus: the meaning of a word is its use in the language." By the "use" of a word Wittgenstein means the usual practice of speakers of the language with the word, the regular connection between the word and certain linguistic and nonlinguistic circumstances. We find out what this practice is in any given case by learning the rules that govern it, just as we find out what sort of game Hex is by learning the rules according to which it is played. Hence understanding a word cannot consist simply in knowing to *what* the word refers; it consists rather in knowing how to follow and apply certain rules. The purpose of 264 is simply to remind us of this previous argument. In 257 Wittgenstein makes it clear that the formula "The meaning is the use" applies to names as well as to other sorts of words:

> When one says 'He gave a name to his sensation' one forgets that a great deal of stage-setting in the language is presupposed if the mere act of naming is to make sense. And when we speak of someone's having given a name to pain, what is presupposed is the existence of the grammar of the word 'pain'; it shows the post where the new word is stationed.

Therefore premise (3) must be emphatically rejected.

When Wittgenstein asks the question at the beginning of 244, "How do words *refer* to sensations?" he is not asking a question about private language but about our everyday language. And of course there is no problem about that, since we all know how to use words to refer to and talk about our sensations. If we then ask how the connection between the name and the thing named (the sensation) is established, what kind of answer do we expect? Wittgenstein reminds us that the only way to answer such a question is to see how a human being learns the meaning of names of sensations—of the word 'pain', for example. A child might be taught verbal expressions of pain (exclamations or sentences) in circumstances when adults see from his behavior, from his natural expressions of pain, that he is hurt. A foreigner might learn by our pricking him with a pin and saying, "See, that's pain!" or by our pretending to be in pain. Common to these and other learning situations are certain circumstances, which always include a particular sort of action or expression on the part of some living being (namely, pain-behavior); and what is learned is the regular connection between the word 'pain' and such circumstances. Therefore learning the meaning of 'pain' depends on there being natural expressions of pain. Wittgenstein generalizes this point in 281: "It comes to this: only of a living human being and what resembles (behaves like) a living human being can one say: it has sensations; it sees; is blind; hears; is deaf; is conscious or unconscious."

The point of these remarks is to show that our use of words for sensations is tied up with the natural expressions of sensation, which are publicly observable. Hence when we explain how it is that words refer to sensations we do not have to fall back on mysterious private experiences. If we understand this much about premise (2) of *P* we shall be less tempted to use it as a justification for asserting (4).

Wittgenstein's examination of premise (1) extends through paragraphs 246–54. His main point is that both parts of (1) are grammatical statements; that is to say, they might be used to teach a person how to use the words 'pain' or 'sensation', but could not be used for ordinary communication between persons already fully conversant with the language. In this respect these propositions differ sharply (in spite of a resemblance in the pattern of words) from "My headaches are severe" and "No one else can look at my diary." They are—like "You play solitaire by yourself" (248) and "Every rod has a length" (251)— propositions which are misleading because their form makes them look empirical, whereas they are really grammatical.

I have said a good deal about grammar and grammatical propositions in other chapters. The question here is what difference it makes if the propositions in (1) are grammatical. It will not do to say that it is because they are really about language that they cannot be used as support for (4), for (4) itself is about language. The fact that the propositions in (1) are grammatical bears on the issue at hand in two ways. First, the natural employment for a grammatical proposition is to teach someone about the use of a word, and *not* to support a metaphysical thesis. This fact gives us a good reason for maintaining that (1) is misused in *P*. In particular, "No one else can have my pains" cannot be used to support the contention that your pains must be different from mine; for if there is no criterion for my pain being identical with yours—and this is the grammatical point of the remark—it *makes no sense* to say that our pains are either identical or different ones. This is not to say that the sentence is utter nonsense (*unsinnig*), for it would make sense in another context; but that it has no sense (is *sinnlos*) in a context that calls for a factual or experiential premise. Making sense or not is a contextual or functional feature of expressions, not a syntactical one, in Wittgenstein's later work. Second, to say that a proposition is grammatical is to say that it expresses some feature of the language—in the case of "No one else can have my pains" that it ordinarily *makes no sense* to say of two people that they both have one and the same pain. This tells us something about the *use* of 'pain', about the common practice with the word. If there were no common practice with the word, there could be no grammatical propositions about it. If, therefore, the warrant for saying "No one else can have my pains" is the grammar of the word 'pain' (and it is), 'pain' must have a use, must have an ordinary meaning rather than a private and incommunicable one. Understood in this way (1) not only does not support (4) but is incompatible with it.

3. The Absurdity of the Putative Claim

By these remarks on the grammar of words for sensations as we ordinarily use them Wittgenstein has completely cut the ground from under argument *P*, and it is natural to ask why the problem should be further pursued. The reason is that *P* is only one of a number of arguments which have led people to accept (4) or some similar doctrine to the effect that some signs get their meaning solely from their relation to our inner (mental) experiences and must therefore be understood privately. Probably the most influential of the views which lead to an acceptance of such a doctrine is Cartesian dualism, which maintains that Mind has nothing to do with Matter—in other words, that there can be no causal or conceptual connections between "mental phenomena" (such as sensations) and material or physical phenomena (such as bodily movements or other behavior). An obvious consequence of this view is that the meaning of 'pain' and other sensation words *cannot*, since they refer to private mental experience, be tied up with natural expressions of pain and certain physical circumstances. It would seem that on this view we must be able to learn these words only by associating them (each one of us privately) with appropriate sensations.

In 256 Wittgenstein proposes a thoroughly Cartesian account of the matter:

> But suppose I didn't have my natural expression for the sensation, but had only the sensation? And now I simply *associate* names with sensations and use these names in descriptions.

In the following section, speaking for himself now, he makes two observations on this account. The first is that one could not make oneself understood when using these words, since another person could not know with what one associated them. The second is that we cannot say that these words are names of sensations, since to name sensations presupposes the *grammar* of sensation-words, and this grammar, as we have seen, depends on the natural expression of sensations, which is by hypothesis ruled out.

These comments are apparently accepted by Wittgenstein's Cartesian interlocutor, and the problem then remaining is the one which Rhees (1954, 83) rightly regards as central: might there not be a *private* understanding of such words, even though they could not be understood by other people? To proceed with his *reductio ad absurdum* argument against this proposal, Wittgenstein allows his interlocutor to propose the following case for consideration at the beginning of 258:

> Let us imagine the following case. I want to keep a diary about the recurrence of a certain sensation. To this end I associate it with the sign 'S' and write this sign in a calendar for every day on which I have the sensation.

Wittgenstein's examination of this case and its absurdity extends through paragraph 270.

To understand the case which is being examined it is important to realize that it is being proposed by the Cartesian interlocutor and not by either Wittgenstein or an ordinary man. It could not be seriously put forward by Wittgenstein because in his view the case is unintelligible (though not logically self-contradictory); for to say that 'S' is used to record the recurrence of some sensation implies that 'S' is in some sense a sign for a sensation, and this in turn presupposes that 'S' shares the ordinary grammar of sensation-words, which is precisely what the proposed case attempts to rule out. It also could not be an ordinary man who proposes this case; for I can write 'S' in a diary to keep track of the recurrence of a certain sensation (say, an ache in my left shoulder) and, because the grammar of the sensation-words is presupposed, many of the difficulties which Wittgenstein urges against the proposed case will not arise: I do make a note of something (compare 260), the sign 'S' can be defined (I can explain its use—compare 258), there is no doubt that 'S' is the sign for a sensation (compare 261), and so on. It is only when the case is proposed by a Cartesian, who rules out any conceptual connection between sensation-words and natural expressions of pain, that the case is philosophically interesting. Then, as Wittgenstein points out, 'S' cannot be defined in any ordinary way, and so there must be some other way to establish the connection between the sign and the sensation.

The only avenue open to the Cartesian seems to be to suggest that the connection is established by a kind of ostensive definition—not the ordinary sort, to be sure, since no one can point to a sensation, but a *private* ostensive definition: I concentrate inwardly on the sensation when I write the sign down. The whole idea of giving oneself a private definition is suspect from the start, because it is pointless—like my right hand's giving money to my left hand, no one would be any the richer for it (*PI* 268). But pointless or not, let us see if the idea might work. Wittgenstein presents three telling objections which show that it cannot.

1. If this private ostensive definition is to achieve anything it must enable you to get the connection *right* each time, but in the present case there is no criterion of correctness: because there could be no distinction between thinking you were right and being right we cannot speak of rightness here at all (*PI* 258). You cannot even *believe* you get the connection right (that that sensation is the same one again); for you can only believe what *can* be true or false, and that that sensation is the same one again could not be determined to be true or false; at best you may believe that you believe it (*PI* 260). Nor will it do for you to suggest that there might be some sort of "subjective justification" for your calling it the same sensation (a table in your imagination, for instance), for justification consists in appealing to something independent (*PI* 265). Since there is no criterion for saying that a sensation is that certain one again, you could not promise yourself, or privately undertake, always to use 'S' for that certain sensation: the undertaking would be empty because you could never know whether you had fulfilled it (*PI* 263). In all of these ways Wittgenstein shows us that the lack of any criterion of identity for the sensation makes a "private" definition impossible. Therefore there is no possible way, on the Cartesian view, that a connection could be established between a word and a sensation, and the mere fact that we do use words to refer to sensations is a refutation of dualism.

2. We naturally assume that when you write down 'S' in your diary you must be making a note of something, but Wittgenstein reminds us that the assumption is unjustified (*PI* 260). 'S' is an idle mark; it has no use, no function, no connection with anything. How *could* we make a record of anything with such an idle mark? Wittgenstein's point here is liable to misinterpretation because of the context in which it occurs. It is the idleness of 'S', the fact that it has no regular use, no regular connection with certain circumstances, that implies that when you write 'S' in your diary you are not really making a note; that it was a sensation rather than a physical object you were attending when you wrote 'S' has nothing to do with the matter, for you would no more have made a note if you had been staring at your cat. Wittgenstein's remark in 260[1] is a

---

1. Ayer apparently overlooked this section, or he missed the point of it. He says, "It is all very well for Wittgenstein to say that writing down the sign 'S', at the same time as I attend to the sensation, is an idle ceremony. How is it any more idle than writing down a sign, whether it be the conventionally correct sign or not, at the same time as I observe some 'public' object?" (1954, 68) The answer, of course, is that it is not, but Ayer's suggestion that Wittgenstein would make a different answer is absurd. The object of 260 is to bring out just this point.

remark on the grammar of making notes, not on the grammar of sensation.

3. Even assuming, *per impossible,* that a connection between 'S' and a certain sensation were to be established by means of a private ostensive definition, where would that get us? There would be a certain sign 'S' which you privately understand. Could we call it the name of a sensation? We would have no justification for doing so, for by calling some mark the name of a sensation we make it intelligible in the common language (or perhaps better: in calling it the name of a sensation, we presuppose it to be intelligible in the common language), whereas 'S' is intelligible to you alone (*PI* 261). Names of sensations have a certain grammar, and 'S' as yet has none.

These points constitute an effective *reductio ad absurdum* of the Cartesian's proposal: writing 'S' in the diary is a pointless act, a record of nothing whatever; 'S' itself is a meaningless mark, having no established connection with anything and no possible use.

We have now left to consider only the perplexing section in which Wittgenstein appears to make an about-face:

> Let us now imagine a use for the entry of the sign 'S' in my diary. I discover that whenever I have a particular sensation a manometer shows that my blood-pressure rises. So I shall be able to say that my blood-pressure is rising without using any apparatus. This is a useful result. (*PI* 270)

After what Wittgenstein has said about 'S', this turn strikes us as a bit surprising. A moment ago the entry of 'S' in the diary was "a note of nothing whatever," and now it leads to a useful result! There is a weird twist here: all of a sudden the whole case changes.

Note first that we can give a sort of definition of 'S' now: 'S' is the sign for the sensation you have when your blood pressure rises.[2] From this it follows (1) that when you write 'S' in your diary, you are really making a note of something, namely, of a sensation; and (2) that the sign 'S' can be explained to other people; it is no longer intelligible only to you. 'S' is presented to us in 270 as a sign for a sensation, and since it is no longer supposed that the whole significance of the sign comes from being associated with "something about which nothing can be said" (*PI* 304), we no longer have any ground for doubting that it really is just

---

2. Such a definition could be used to explain the use of 'S' to other people, but not to *you.* There can never be an occasion for defining for you words which you use to refer to your own sensations.

what it is presented as; and we have a further justification in calling 'S' the name of a sensation in the fact that 'S' has the grammar of a sensation-word, namely that only you can know when to write down 'S', and so on. Note second that the problem about the identity of the sensation which you record by the entry of 'S' in your diary has completely disappeared. A sense can now be given to saying that you identify or fail to identify the sensation in question. Suppose you say you have a certain sensation, that you say further, when I ask you what sensation it is, that it is the sensation you have when your blood pressure has risen, and that you then check your blood pressure with a manometer; in such a case, on the basis of the manometer reading, we will be able to say that you identified or failed to identify the sensation.[3] The important point is that, if your blood pressure has risen, it makes no difference at all whether, in the sense required by the Cartesian, the sensation was "really the same" or not. As Wittgenstein says,

> And now it seems quite indifferent whether I have recognized the sensation *right* or not. Let us suppose that I regularly identify it wrong, it does not matter in the least. And that alone shows that the hypothesis that I made a mistake is mere show. (*PI* 270)

Here the entry of 'S' in your diary can no longer be supposed to get its significance in the Cartesian manner outlined in 256; to give the sign a use we have to jettison all of the restrictions of the Cartesian proposal. In 256–69 Wittgenstein's purpose is to show that a sign which is supposed to be simply "associated" with a sensation cannot have a use; in 270 he wants to show the converse, namely that any sign which has a use cannot be supposed to be simply "associated" with a sensation. The utility of a sign and its intelligibility in the common language go hand in hand, and it is this point which Wittgenstein brings out in 270—another nail, as it were, in the coffin of the idea that there might be a private language.

---

3. But you, of course, could not use the manometer to check whether one of your sensations was really 'S'.

14

Grammar and Metaphysics

Es ist aber noch keine Folge, daß etwas, was wir notwendig denken müßen, auch wirklich so ist.
—G. F. Lichtenberg

Albert Schweitzer, in his *Philosophy of Civilization,* identified dogmatic philosophy as a main source of the cultural crisis of our times, and he proposed that a naturalistic philosophy, or philosophy of nature, would be needed to restore to us a viable *Weltanschauung.* Such a *Weltanschauung* must of course be comprehensive and universal, so a key to the crisis is to understand how a metaphysical perspective can be universal without being dogmatic. As a contribution to the problem I want to explore what Wittgenstein says about grammar and metaphysics.

1. Continuities in the Work of Wittgenstein

My topic in this chapter is certain continuities pertaining to the work of Wittgenstein. When I speak of "continuities" I mean to imply obvious differences interwoven with some unvarying aim or design, the constant feature giving us some understanding (when other factors are taken into account) of reasons for the variations. These continuities embrace not only the whole of his work from the "Notes on Logic" dictated for Russell in 1913 through his reflections on Moore's commonsense realism in *On Certainty,* but also the critical philosophy that makes Wittgenstein a fresh exponent of the legacy of Kant, and the naturalism that makes him a fresh exponent of the legacy of Aristotle (though it separates him from Kant). This is a large theme, and entails many problems. It is, furthermore, difficult to state the problems at the outset, since a part of what is at issue is the sense and range of such key terms as 'logic', 'grammar', 'metaphysics', 'natural', and 'transcendental'. Wittgenstein's 'grammar' is continuous with both linguistics and what he previously called 'logic'. The continuities with linguistics arise

because of indispensable structural features of the grammar; but herme-
neutical elements are equally indispensable to this grammar. Grammar
cannot be divorced from metaphysics because it is both naturalistic (thus
showing the continuities with Aristotle that are detailed in chapter four)
and transcendental (implying continuities with Kant). The relevance of
this grammar to traditional metaphysics lies partly (as with Kant) in
criticism of speculative and foundationalist metaphysics, partly (as with
Aristotle) in its constructive account of the essences of things, and partly
(as with both of them) in its presupposition of a prelinguistic world
common to all humanity. It must be acknowledged, however, that the
terms in which these points are stated are contested. Further discussion
of 'natural' and 'transcendental' will be reserved for chapter sixteen; here
I will explore, but not entirely remove, doubts whether there is finally a
clear sense to Wittgenstein's use of 'grammar'.

2.   Logic as the Basis of Metaphysics

In the "Notes on Logic" Wittgenstein says that "Philosophy consists of
logic and metaphysics: logic is its basis" (*NB* 106). This is a remarkable
statement. It is one of the few places in the corpus where Wittgenstein
speaks of metaphysics without disparagement, it offers a more positive
statement of the content (as opposed to the role or function) of
philosophy than we usually find in his writings, and it presents a
program that Wittgenstein carried out in the *Tractatus*.

It is important at the same time to recognize how difficult it is to
understand this tantalizing remark. All its key terms are problematic.
Consider what "logic" must be here. Certainly a central part of "logic"
is what is developed in Frege's *Grundgesetze* and Whitehead and
Russell's *Principia Mathematica* (*PM*); hence, a formal account of
truth-functions and of quantification. But there must be more to it than
that. The metaphysics of the *Tractatus* shows, as Stenius (1960) and
Pears (1986, 1987) have been especially convincing in pointing out,
how *Sätze* (sentences, propositions) are possible at all, and hence the
"logic" on which it is based must include an account of all sorts of
propositions. This is obviously presupposed in a famous passage from
the *Philosophical Investigations:*

> If language is to be a means of communication there must be agreement
> not only in definitions but also (queer as this may sound) in judgments.
> This seems to abolish logic, but does not do so. (*PI* 242)

Why does the need for "agreement in judgments" seem to threaten "logic"? It does not pose any problem at all for the logic of Frege or Russell, interpreted as formal accounts of truth-functions and quantification. Frege and Russell never doubted that the principles according to which singular propositions make sense are distinct from the principles of logic in the narrow (formal) sense. If we construe logic formally, the requirement that there be agreement in judgments for purposes of communication does not entail any such requirement for principles of logic. There seems, on this view, no threat to logic at all. So 'logic' here (in *PI* 242) must mean the principles which make propositions or judgments possible at all, rather than just principles of truth-operations and quantification. It is, one might say, closer to what Kant and Husserl called "transcendental logic" than to formal logic. What seems to be threatened is the very possibility of saying anything at all. If for P to make sense there must be agreement on $P\prime$, and for $P\prime$ to make sense there must be agreement on $P\prime\prime$, and so on, then it would seem that we could never get started with individual propositions. The threat referred to in *PI* 242 therefore seems an echo of that expressed in *TLP* 2.02n:

> If the world had no substance, then whether a proposition had sense would depend on whether another proposition was true.
>
> In that case we could not sketch any picture of the world (true or false).

It seems clear that in the remark of 1913, as in *PI* 242, Wittgenstein used 'logic' in a broad sense rather than one limited to formal logic.

What did Wittgenstein conceive to be the relation of the "logic" of elementary propositions—elaborated in his celebrated "picture theory" —to the "logic" of *PM?* For it seems both that "logic" must be primarily what is done in *PM,* if it is meant as a serious discipline, and also that it cannot be that, since *PM* has nothing to say about the elementary propositions on which the metaphysics of the *Tractatus* is primarily based. Until we can answer that question, we lack a clear understanding of what Wittgenstein meant by 'logic' in 1913—even without bringing in the puzzle about the status of the scientific propositions mentioned in 6.3n,[1] which are neither elementary proposi-

---

1. Fischer (1987, 63–72) has an extensive and interesting discussion of *TLP* 6.3–6.3n. He places emphasis on the metaphor of a scientific theory, such as Newton's mechanics, as a net for describing nature, which he treats as the primary precursor in the *Tractatus* for the grammatical net that dominates the later work.

tions nor truth-functions or generalizations (so it would seem) of elementary propositions.

There is a similar problem of scope, already discussed earlier in chapters five and six, with respect to the concept of metaphysics. On the face of it, the *Tractatus* characterizes three domains of metaphysics: (1) the world of *TLP* 1–1.21, which is composed of facts and presumably differs from any other possible world; (2) the substance of the world, described in *TLP* 2.01–2.03, which is invariant for any possible world; and (3) the limits and the waxing and waning dimensions of the world, as they are pertinent to moral and religious issues discussed in *TLP* 5.6–5.641 and *TLP* 6.4–6.45. Did Wittgenstein have all three domains in mind in 1913? One would think so, but it is difficult to say for sure. Malcolm (1986), for example, confines the "metaphysics" of the *Tractatus* to the second domain, and does not even discuss *TLP* 1 and 1.1. The Hintikkas similarly ignore the early paragraphs and reduce the first domain to the second: "These facts are in the last analysis combinations of (simple) *objects (Gegenstände)*" (1986, 30). Pears (1986, 46) restricts the domain of metaphysics in the *Tractatus* in the same way:

> The first thing to be noted is that Wittgenstein's ontological conclusion is recondite. His view about the structure of reality is that it was composed of simple objects, which he calls "objects" leaving the qualification to be understood, and that this structure is precisely mirrored in the structure of elementary propositions.

The advantage of this narrow focus is that it then appears that what Wittgenstein meant by 'metaphysics' in the early work is just what he criticizes trenchantly in the later work. Heroic as its picture of Wittgenstein's progress may be, this exegesis leaves out too much to be convincing. Black (1964, 27) is surely right in characterizing the view that the world is a totality of facts (not objects) as a great metaphysical innovation on Wittgenstein's part; yet this is precisely what is omitted from the account given by Pears. So there is a deep division as to what the metaphysics of the *Tractatus* includes. Even though these issues cannot be adequately explored here, it is apparent that the concept of 'metaphysics' is more controversial than many have thought.

The problem about "philosophy" is to understand the relation of this remark from the "Notes on Logic" to the remark of the *Tractatus* that "Philosophy is not a body of doctrine but an activity" (*TLP* 4.112). Since both occur within the body of Wittgenstein's early work, it is reasonable to view them as parts of the same conception. We must therefore understand either logic or metaphysics, or (more likely) both, as *activity* rather than as *doctrine*—a conception which promises a rich and illuminating continuity with Wittgenstein's later work. The activity is that of elucidation and clarification. It is rather easy to see logic as concerned to make clear to us the underlying order of things about which we are confused, and useful to think of doctrines within the three domains of metaphysics broached in the *Tractatus* as functioning in a similar way.

3. From Logic to Grammar

There is much to be said, whenever either makes sense, for taking the wider rather than the narrower sense of a word. Let us follow that strategy with respect to the senses of 'logic' and 'metaphysics' and see how far it takes us.

My first suggestion is that after 1930 Wittgenstein realized that the broad sense of 'logic' would not do; in any case he began using the term 'grammar' at those constructive junctures of his thought (as opposed to critical ones, as in *PI* 242) where, on the basis on his early work, one would have expected the term 'logic'. So one might say that the remark from the "Notes on Logic" is transformed after 1930 to read as follows:

Philosophy consists of grammar and metaphysics, the former its basis.

In this new formulation we see expressed both continuity and difference between the two main periods of Wittgenstein's activity.

Wittgenstein reports in the *Investigations* (*PI* 81) that Ramsey once called logic "a normative science." This may have been a factor in Wittgenstein's new insight. If "logic" is normative, it must be the logic of the picture theory and *PM,* which together represent a kind of ideal—at least for scientific discourse and perhaps for discourse in general. Russell, in his introduction to the *Tractatus,* took it that Wittgenstein was proposing such an ideal language (*TLP* ix), and members of the Vienna Circle followed him in this. An ideal, however, is not a proper starting point for a Kantian inquiry. Questions of the form "How is so-and-so possible at all?" are philosophically interesting only when so-and-so is *actual,* not merely ideal. To the extent that Wittgenstein's metaphysics has to do with the question "How are *Sätze* (e.g., battle reports, dream reports, pain reports, promises, metaphors, jokes, orders, etc.) possible at all?", the *Sätze* must be ones which actually occur rather than ones which ideally could (or should) occur. Ideals presuppose existing reality, and problems about how ideals are possible are problems about how one might modify or manipulate or reform or enhance existing reality. These problems are not uninteresting, but they are not metaphysical. They either presuppose or bypass an account of how reality is possible at all. So the *PM* component of "logic," together with the picture theory of elementary propositions, must be discarded. There remains just the description of actual *Sätze* — and such description is better conceived as "grammar" than as "logic."

But in what sense is it "grammar"? Moore never could understand. When he asked Wittgenstein in what sense he was using the expression 'rule of grammar', Wittgenstein replied that he was using it in its ordinary sense, although he was "making things belong to grammar which are not commonly supposed to belong to it" (*M* 276). That response is more paradoxical than enlightening, especially coming from a man who would a short time later write that, in many cases, the meaning of a word just *is* its use in the language (*PI* 43). It is nonetheless possible, by exhibiting continuities between Wittgenstein's work and linguistics, to do away with most of the air of paradox, so that this answer to Moore becomes useful.

Grammar has always been conceived as primarily descriptive, in spite of our familiarity with its normative application in grammar school. The main entry under "Grammar" in the *OED* runs for more than two-and-a-half columns. The first sense of the word is glossed (presumably by Henry Bradley, though no doubt under the eye of James Murray) as follows:

> That department of the study of a language which deals with its inflectional forms or other means of indicating the relations of words in the sentence, and with the rules for employing these in accordance with established usage; usually including also the department which deals with the phonetic system of the language and the principles of its representation in writing. Often preceded by an adj. designating the language referred to, as in *Latin, English, French* grammar.

This gloss is followed by three paragraphs of more general information about this sort of study of languages, in somewhat smaller print, which reads in part:

> In early Eng. use *grammar* meant only Latin grammar, as Latin was the only language that was taught grammatically. In the 16th c. there are

some traces that the word might have some extended applications to other languages . . . ; but it was not before the 17th c. that the term became so completely a generic term that there was any need to speak explicitly of *'Latin* grammar.'

. . .

Until a not very distant date, Grammar was divided by Eng. writers (following the precedent of Latin grammarians) into Orthography, Etymology, Syntax, and Prosody, to which Orthoepy was added by some authors. . . . The division now usual is that into Phonology, treating of the sounds used in the language, Accidence, of the inflectional forms or equivalent combinations, and Syntax, of the structure of sentences; the branch of grammar dealing with the function of the alphabetic letters is usually treated along with phonology.

A bit further on, after some illustrative citations from the fourteenth through the nineteenth centuries, there is the following addendum to the primary sense of the word:

b. *General Philosophical* or *Universal Grammar:* the science which analyses those distinctions in thought which it is the purpose of grammatical forms more or less completely to render in expression, and which aims to furnish a scheme of classification capable of including all the grammatical categories recognized in actual languages.

Three points should be noted about this entry in the *OED*. The first is that the primary sense does not seem to allow us to speak abstractly of grammar in general; there are many grammars (at least one for each language) but no generic grammar. This would seem to argue against Wittgenstein's claim to be using the word in its usual sense, since Wittgenstein's points do not require modification when translated from one language to another. This worry is, however, considerably lessened by the second point to note, namely that the addendum (b) gives the word generic uses, since what is called 'General Grammar' or 'Universal Grammar' is explicitly said to apply to all languages. In this connection we should also note that the generic sense of 'grammar' has both a philosophic and a scientific component. The scientific component, "Universal Grammar," is roughly what we would now call "linguistics," the word 'linguistics' being less used before the turn of the century. The third point is that grammars are first and foremost descriptive, in that the rules of a language which they express are those of "established usage." It is true that these same rules are used prescriptively in the education of the young, and further true that Philosophical Grammar and Universal Grammar (linguistics) might be construed to be normative in a different way (as setting ideals for descriptive grammars to aim at). It is nonetheless clear that the first criterion for judging grammars of individual languages is whether they accurately represent actual established usage.

It cannot be supposed that these dictionary definitions are without philosophical perplexities. It is exceedingly difficult to grasp how something can be essentially particular—there must be a different grammar for each language—and also universal. The point has been made forcefully by Benveniste: "We also see this other difference: that thought can claim to set up universal categories but that *linguistic categories are always categories of a particular language*" (1971, 56); but in fact, as we shall see, Benveniste's italicized claim is mistaken. Even if Wittgenstein's conception of grammar is no less confusing than these *OED* glosses, it will still fall considerably short of perspicuity. But if we press on from these gloomy abstractions, and look more closely at actual linguistic practice, some of the perplexity is likely to disappear.

4. The Genius of Linguistic Description

Modern linguistics is a science, and hence is normative as well as descriptive. It is the science of how to construct grammars (in the sense of systematic presentations of features and rules). A grammar is a description of a particular language. Languages are generally spoken, so the description ideally begins with the sounds and sound patterns distinctive to the language, and the description of sound patterns serves as a paradigm for grammatical description in general.

Describing the sounds and sound patterns is trickier than one might think. Anyone familiar with a second language knows that sounds differ from language to language, and that one cannot give a very good account in English of the sounds of French or German or Arabic or Chinese. Linguists who work in the field have developed an international phonetic script, which makes it possible to transcribe a very wide range of sounds without too much initial bias. The key to the sound patterns of a language, however, is given by phonemics rather than phonetics. While a phonetic transcription might reveal hundreds of distinguishable sounds (phones) occurring in the speech of a given language, every language has only twenty to fifty significant sounds (phonemes), with phonetically distinguishable phones clustering as "allophones" of the same phoneme. The discovery of how to describe phonemes was due to the Swiss linguist Ferdinand de Saussure (1959), and constitutes the basis for modern linguistics.

Some examples will help to understand. The English phoneme /p/ has distinctive phonetic values in 'pin', 'spin', 'skip', and 'skipper'. One differentiating feature is aspiration, which occurs with the /p/ in 'pin' and 'snap' but not with the /p/ in 'spin' and 'skipper'. This feature, although not normally noticed by speakers of English, can easily be confirmed by holding one's hand in front of one's mouth as one says each of the four words. Other differentiating features are not so easily brought to our attention. Most of them can be recognized by trained phonologists, whose tools often allow them to describe differences in individual speech as well as the systematic differences among the allophones that constitute a single phoneme. Because we generally attend only to phonemic differences—they are the only ones we need to speak the language—a phonologist who can recognize and reproduce phonetic variation often seems like a wizard. G. B. Shaw took advantage of this phenomenon in creating the figure of Professor Higgins in *Pygmalion*. Today, of course, machines are much more sensitive than the human ear, and a sound spectrograph can record and display phonetic differences that escape the best phonologists. What is remarkable about the sounds of human language is not their phonetic subtlety but, on the contrary, that they acquire significance (as phonemes) by ignoring phonetic differences.

Phonemic familiarity often becomes phonetic incompetence, even a kind of deafness. Most of us have experienced the effects of such acquired incompetence when trying to learn to speak a foreign language. I have had great difficulty, for example, in learning to pronounce the difference in the vowel in German between *die Nuß* (the nut) and *die Nüße* (the nuts), since there is no parallel distinction in English. I experienced a reverse instance while teaching English to a Palestinian student. His native language was Arabic, in which there is no contrast such as that between 'pin' and 'bin'. The sounds which we would identify as /p/ and /b/ both occur in Arabic—for example in 'biyipkiy' (s/he, it begins)—but they never contrast, for the phonetic sound [p] is an allophone of the Arabic phoneme /b/, which has a phonetic shape of [p] whenever it occurs with /s/, /t/, or /k/. My Palestinian student had assimilated Arabic phonemics so thoroughly that he was unable to *hear* any difference between 'pin' and 'bin'. I remember in particular trying without success to get him to say "Pepsi

Cola": it always came out "bepsi," and he was unable even to hear the difference between "pepsi" and "bepsi"! This deafness, though phenomenologically similar to the aspect-blindness Wittgenstein discusses (*PI* pp. 213–14), is in fact its opposite. It is of considerably less philosophical interest. In this deafness there is no inability to apprehend aspects (phonemic values of sounds), but only a constricted ability to make physical discriminations. Since some of us have always been worse than others at making such discriminations, and all of us are worse than machines, this phenomenon is easily assimilated to our wide experience of human finitude and variability. Aspect-blindness, if it were to occur, could not be so assimilated.

As these examples illustrate, there is nothing in the phones themselves which enables a linguist to predict which phonetic differences will be phonemically significant. That is to say, phonemics (a branch of linguistics) cannot be reduced to or replaced by phonetics (a branch of physics). This does not, of course, mean that there could be phonemes even if there were no phones. It does mean that a phonetic description of phones never suffices to identify phonemes. To identify phonemes, and in particular to count how many there are in a language, one must show how they contrast with one another within a system of phonemes. And since each language has its own system, phonemic analysis (unlike phonetic analysis) is always relative to some specific language or other. A phonemic analysis, furthermore, can only *describe* the sounds of a language, and has no basis for saying what the phonemes "should" be or "must" be.

Phonemics can be considered the first level of linguistic articulation. By means of a system of somewhat arbitrary contrasts, the infinite variation of physical sound becomes articulated—"jointed"—so as to consist of sequential segments, which are the basis of alphabetic transcription. With this practical dimension in mind, Kenneth Pike subtitled his book *Phonemics,* "A Technique for Reducing Language to Writing." In phonemics, therefore, we have not only, to borrow a phrase from Arthur Danto, a "transformation of the commonplace" which initiates the first level of linguistic significance and articulation, but also a practical technique which facilitates writing.

Linguists, including Benveniste, sometimes talk about "double articulation," usually having in mind that sentences are more than mere sequences of words, though they are at least that, just as words are more than mere sequences of phonemes. It is surely right to stress—as, indeed, Plato did in the *Sophist* (see Ryle 1971, 1:54–73)—that words and sentences are very different sorts of linguistic expressions, and that words (which one can look up in a dictionary) have a completely different sort of meaning or significance from that of sentences. But to say there are two levels of articulation omits a great deal. If phonemics constitutes the first level of articulation, there are at least three further levels: *phonemes* are distinct things, not just "sounds"; *words* are distinct things, not just clusters of phonemes; *sentences* are distinct expressions, not just random strings of words; and *speech-acts* are distinct sayings or doings, not just utterings of sentences. So language typically exhibits not just double but quadruple articulation. Since significance goes hand in hand with articulation, there are also at least four levels of linguistic significance.[2]

5. Wittgenstein's Grammar

It now is possible to see more clearly the truth of Wittgenstein's answer to Moore. Grammar describes language by showing how it is articulated. It shows this by describing both the construction of expressions (in terms of shapes, arrangements, distributions and contrasts, and transformations) and also their significance (in terms of contrasts and inclusions). That is what we *mean* by 'grammar'. The word is normally applied, however, to only two or three of the four levels of articulation, morphology (the construction and transformation of words) and syntax (the construction and transformation of phrases), with the recently more frequent extension to phonology. Wittgenstein's grammar concerns what is said or done through uttering words or sentences in various circumstances. Sayings and doings are described by contrasting them one from another in terms of both the circumstances in which they occur and the subsequent action or discourse which they initiate. There are, for example, various circumstances in which it makes sense to say, "It will rain tomorrow." But in answer to a question about what the stock market will do, it can only be metaphorical, and as a theorem in geometry it makes no sense at all. And in response to A's saying "It will rain tomorrow," it makes sense for B to respond, "I doubt it" or "What

---

2. This is a more conservative generalization than that of the great linguist Kenneth Pike. Pike (1967) abstracts the endings of the words 'phonetic' and 'phonemic' and speaks of the distinction between "the Etic" and "the Emic" as the most fundamental distinction in social science. Though they grew without, alas, being influenced by this work, we can see here the seeds of both structuralism and hermeneutics—as well as of their reconciliation.

makes you think so?"—as it would not, if *A* had said "Please go home" or "I sentence you to a year and a day in prison." When Wittgenstein writes,

> The proposition "Sensations are private" is comparable to "One plays patience [solitaire] by oneself" (*PI* 248),

he means that uttering the one would be the same kind of saying or doing as uttering the other, namely, a grammatical rather than an empirical or imperative remark.

Close attention to what linguists do when they set out to describe a language enables us to see that Wittgenstein really is using the word 'grammar' in its ordinary sense but applying it where it is not commonly applied. This insight helps us reconcile the particularism of ordinary grammar with the apparent universality of Wittgensteinian grammar, when taken together with a bit of natural history having to do with very general matters of fact. The fact is that, in spite of the variation in human actions and human customs, the same basic language-games, or uses of language, belong to "common human behavior" (*PI* 206). It is a simple fact that in all human groups there are distinctions between ordering, asking, urging, and praying; between describing the past and foretelling the future; and among all the activities enumerated in *PI* 23 and *PI* 25 as language-games or uses of language. Experience overwhelmingly shows that, except in the case of abnormalities (admitted or putative), this range of activities is both common to humans and unique to humans. Given this fact of our natural history as humans, rules of grammar pertaining to or constituting these uses of languages are, *pace* Benveniste, naturally valid with respect to every particular language.

Residual problems remain, to which I will return later. For now these two points are sufficient to dissolve Moore's doggedly commonsense puzzlement about Wittgenstein's 'rules of grammar'. That is to say, they dissolve the initial paradox enough to allow us to proceed, and to take Wittgenstein at his word.

6. From Grammar to Metaphysics

If this is what Wittgenstein means by grammar, it is related to traditional metaphysics in three constructive ways, in addition to its critical role in impugning speculative metaphysical theory.

Since grammar is descriptive, it presupposes something to describe.

At the very least it presupposes that there is a world of human beings who are doing things. "Im Anfang war die Tat," he says, quoting Goethe; and he makes several references to the natural history (*PI* 25, 415) or common human behavior (*PI* 206), as well as to forms of life as "what has to be accepted, the given" (*PI* p. 226; *OC* 358–59). The German *Tat* means deed or action, and the language-games which are (as Hintikka and Hintikka [1986] rightly insist) primary in Wittgenstein's later work are actions or patterns of activity:

> Here the term language-*game* is meant to bring into prominence the fact that the *speaking* of language is part of an activity, or of a form of life. (*PI* 23)

This robust naturalism underlies Wittgenstein's later work, and is continuous with his insistence on the "world" as the totality of facts at the outset of the *Tractatus*.

The second metaphysical thrust of grammar comes in answer to questions about the nature or essence of things:

> *Essence* is expressed by grammar. (*PI* 371)
> Grammar tells what kind of object anything is. (*PI* 373)

I have already given some examples of Wittgenstein's descriptive metaphysics, with respect to feelings and emotions, in chapter four. In line with this general principle, Wittgenstein takes 'pain' to be what is expressed by expressions of pain or described by descriptions of pain, 'dreams' to be what is presented in the telling of a dream, 'meaning' to be what is explained in explanations of meaning, and so on. I can understand what pain is only by showing how reports of pain compare and contrast with other sorts of reports. Metaphysical questions about essence, that is to say, can be given only grammatical answers.

There is a famous, but problematic, passage where Wittgenstein exults in the grammatical resolution of a metaphysical problem:

> I can know what someone else is thinking, not what I am thinking.
> It is correct to say "I know what you are thinking," and wrong to say "I know what I am thinking."
> (A whole cloud of philosophy condensed into a drop of grammar.)
> (*PI* p. 222)

The passage belongs to the unrevised portion of the text, and contains inaccuracies Wittgenstein might not have allowed to survive publication. At any rate they do not occur in the equally famous remark in the revised portion:

... It can't be said of me at all (except perhaps as a joke) that I *know* I am in pain. What is it supposed to mean—except perhaps that I *am* in pain?

The truth is [Das ist richtig]: it makes sense to say about other people that they doubt whether I am in pain; but not to say it about myself. (*PI* 246)

One difference is that the unrevised passage seems to regard rules of grammar as regulative rather than constitutive, for they determine what is "right" and "wrong" rather than what "makes sense." A second difference is that the unrevised passage speaks about sentences (the third level of linguistic articulation) rather than the use of sentences, which Wittgenstein means to speak about if my exposition has been sound. It is inaccurate to say that grammar forbids uttering a particular sentence, for uttering the sentence may have other uses than the "standard" one: uttering "I *know* I am in pain" may well have uses, as Wolgast (1977) has argued; Wittgenstein's point is just that it has no use as a knowledge-claim. This is not because of any regulative rules (prohibitions); it is because the language makes no provision for doubting or confirming what a person says when she says "I *know* I am in pain"; whereas doubting and confirming, as was made clear in chapter ten, are regular possibilities of the subsequent discourse that is initiated by knowledge-claims. So although she can say "I *know* I am in pain" (as a protest to a foolish doctor, or as a grammatical remark along lines given in *PI* 247), it makes no sense to *say of her* that she *knows* she is in pain. This is not a matter of something being prohibited, but rather of there being no such thing because our grammar has not provided for (constituted) it.

In this stance Wittgenstein's later work differs from the *Tractatus* just because and insofar as grammar (as descriptive) differs from logic (as normative). At the same time, however, as we saw in chapter four, it approaches more closely to Aristotle.

The third constructive import of grammar for metaphysics, which is discussed more fully in chapter sixteen, is that it provides a kind of Kantian transcendental. The Kantian problem is to find principles which show how something (knowledge, speech, meaning, etc.) is possible at all, in that these principles (1) are presupposed by anything in the domain, (2) expose speculative metaphysics as illegitimate or futile, and (3) belong to the domain they certify rather than the domain they condemn. The self-reference in the last point flies in the face of Bertrand Russell, who equated self-reference generally with the "vicious circle" fallacy; but Bubner (1974, 1975) has argued persuasively that it must be a distinguishing characteristic of any Kantian transcendental argument. The general reason is that since the principles of such an argument cannot be speculative or other-wordly (they would then cancel themselves, for they show such ideas to be illegitimate), and since they cannot be subject to infinite regress or merely arbitrary (they could then not serve as certifying or validating principles at all), they must therefore be self-referential in that they validate themselves (at least in general terms) as part of the domain they govern.

It is clear that the grammar of the *Philosophical Investigations* is self-referential in a way the logic of the *Tractatus* is not. The *Tractatus* declares itself, with admirable cogency and forthrightness, to be nonsense. The *Philosophical Investigations,* insofar as it consists of making grammatical remarks, shows that it itself makes sense. For making grammatical remarks (even at the fourth level) is an ordinary use of language, and to describe a certain proposition (e.g., "Sensations are private") as "a grammatical remark" is itself a grammatical remark. So long as we distinguish naturalism from empiricism, we can appreciate that Wittgenstein's later work is much more deeply Kantian than the *Tractatus.* It not only shows how *Sätze* are possible; it also shows, in the very process of showing how *Sätze* in general are possible, how its own inquiries and revelations are possible.

7. Three Problems

I hope now to have made plausible the claims which I presented at the outset. I want instead to close on a rather different note, calling attention to three especially refractory problems that pertain to Wittgenstein's conception of grammar and metaphysics, if I have succeeded in identifying the main lines of his thought. Two of them have to do with his naturalism, and the third with paradoxes about grammar in relation to rules and perceptions.

The most obvious problem, to which I shall return in chapter sixteen, is how something can be both natural and transcendental. Wittgenstein's master problem is how language (or meaning) is possible. The traditional sort of transcendental answer would identify the transcendental domain with necessary prerequisites or necessary features of language. That is to say, there would be a claim for the necessity of the necessary, as in Kant's insistence that there is nothing contingent about either the forms of intuition or the categories of understanding. Wittgenstein, on the other hand, insists time and again on the contingency of the necessary. Necessities (essences, for example) are expressed by rules of grammar; but the rules could be different. It is not just that rules often are different in other languages. Even in the case of linguistic universals, such as giving orders and making truth-claims, Wittgenstein insists that they are only contingently universal, in that we can "easily imagine" (*PI* 19) other languages and other forms of life in which these particular uses of language would be absent. "This complicated form of life" (*PI* p. 174), which is characterized by countless different language-games (*PI* 23), is itself not necessary; it is rather part of "what has to be accepted, the given" (*PI* p. 226). Grammar, therefore, seems to be both contingent and transcendental—and cannot dispense with either trait without threatening the whole of Wittgenstein's enterprise.

It helps to be reminded that the starting point of the *Tractatus* is the world, which is contingent. It helps, too, to recognize that what is transcended in this scheme is not the accidental or fateful but the empirical or experiential: Wittgenstein's transcendentalism implies a rejection of empiricism but not of existentialism. Still it remains mysterious and awesome that something—even such a thing as "grammar" or "form of life"—should be both contingent and transcendental. Awe and mystery should mark the beginning, not the end, of philosophical inquiry. But we sometimes cannot go much further.

The second and third problems concern the nature of rules. The puzzlement about rules and naturalism can be stated simply: How can a *rule* possibly be the sort of thing that is *found* in the natural world? On first blush it seems as though we must be dealing with totally different categories when we speak of what is found in the natural world and what is "rule-governed." The facts we come across, and the laws of nature which govern them, have to be accepted; we have to adjust to them. Rules, on the other hand, are human constructions. They not only can be changed without contravening laws of nature, but occur already in many variations. Rather than our having to adjust to rules, we can adjust the rules instead. We can adjust them whether they are constitutive or regulative; neither sort is fixed by laws of nature.

How, then, are we to reconcile the fact that language involves following rules with language also being a part of the natural history of mankind? Does it make a difference whether rules of grammar are conceived as constitutive rather than regulative? Does it make a difference that Wittgenstein never seems to recognize that distinction? Are we to think of "natural history" as not subject to laws of nature? What sort of conception of nature would that involve?—Without a firm conception of 'nature' and 'rules', both of which are exceedingly elusive, Wittgenstein's seminal and pivotal notion that grammar is part of nature, or of our "natural history," must itself escape our understanding.

There is finally a deep problem, or set of problems, about grammar. Even in its ordinary sense, and within its ordinary scope, it is far easier to give examples of rules of grammar, and to operate with them, than it is to grasp just what grammar is. A practice, an institution, is always antecedent to a grammar; and the practice provides truth-conditions by which to judge the accuracy or adequacy of the grammar. That is why the Hintikkas (1986, 181, 195–99) insist on the primacy of language-games over grammar and criteria in Wittgenstein's mature philosophy. A grammar, therefore, is genuinely descriptive. But at the same time a grammar is expressed in rules, and this gives rise to several problems. It remains, first, very difficult to understand how rules of any sort can be descriptive and subject to truth-conditions. Is it really the very same things which are followed or obeyed that are subject to truth-conditions? Ziff (1960, 34–38) thought that it is not possible and therefore concluded that the description of language involves only regularities rather than rules; but neither his problem nor his solution have been seriously considered.

In any case, secondly, grammar involves a puzzling interaction between rules and perceptions. We have seen in phonology, for example, how rules of contrast and inclusion define the phonemes and the phonemic structure of a language. A dominant element of structuralism is inevitable in grammar. But we have also noted how learning the sounds of a language involves perceptions. One has to learn to hear the various phonetic allophones of a phoneme as the very same sound; one needs to learn to hear one thing (a phone) as something else (a phoneme). From this perspective we might better say that phonemics involves a kind of phenomenology, or the hermeneutics of acoustical sound, than that it is simply a matter of rules and structure. Rush Rhees, sensitive to questions about *recognizing* moves in a language-game, where the language-game itself is a structure or set of rules, said in his introduction to the *Blue and Brown Books*, "One cannot do so much with language-games." This seems right. Its implication, however, is that all of the long section xi of part 2 of the *Philosophical Investigations,* which concerns "seeing as" and "aspects," must be part of "grammar," too. Nobody has yet made sense of this radical amalgamation of structuralism and hermeneutics.

A third aspect of the problem about grammar is the extent to which grammar may already incorporate metaphysics. The grammatical remarks Wittgenstein focuses on concern uses of language, and hence how human beings respond to one another and to the world around them. This sort of grammar presupposes a world, and makes reference to the world in ways in which morphology and syntax do not. *On Certainty* is full of remarks about the world which Wittgenstein suggests to belong to grammar. So the new scope Wittgenstein gives to the ordinary sense of 'grammar' raises questions whether his "grammar" is as innocent of metaphysical presuppositions as the grammar of the grammarians from which it was derived. Perhaps it need not be, in view of the inevitable self-referentiality of Kantian metaphysics. Nonetheless this aspect, too, of Wittgenstein's conception of grammar needs more thorough examination before we can fully understand, let alone accept, grammar being the discipline to supply answers, or solutions, to questions of metaphysics. Of course, it stands to reason that there must be presuppositions about reality built into our conception of grammar, if grammar is to resolve metaphysical issues. The question of who is guarding the guardians, the suspicion that the ideas of realities and modalities implicit in grammar already import uncritical metaphysics, is too deep and too far reaching to be dismissed so quickly and so easily.

These broad problems indicate further continuities, beyond those I have already sketched, pertaining to the philosophy of Wittgenstein— continuities with the tradition of philosophy and its perennial problems. We find in his conception of the relation of grammar to metaphysics the sort of naturalism Schweitzer called for, combined with the sort of Kantian self-referentiality that is essential for critical criteria that can combat the dogmatic philosophy of which he was suspicious. It is, whatever the residual problems, a tremendous achievement. In arguing for continuities with respect to Wittgenstein's philosophy—continuities in concepts and aims as well as in problems—I have no doubt implied that Wittgenstein was not so wholly unique or revolutionary as some have suggested. That is inevitable, if he proves to have made a contribution at all. As T. S. Eliot has said, "No poet, no artist of any art, has his complete meaning alone." Philosophers, as Murdoch (1992) makes clear, are artists too. If the framework of thought I have sketched as Wittgenstein's can, even though it finds its meaning within a tradition not of his making, contribute to resolving the crisis of our times by facilitating a comprehensive overview of our human world, that will compensate greatly for its not being wholly and utterly unique.

15
Form of Life

1. Introduction: The Meager Passages to Consider

There are just five explicit references to *Lebensform* (form of life) in Wittgenstein's *Philosophical Investigations,* all of them a bit cryptic; and no more than a handful in his other later writings, some of which add puzzles rather than clarity to the impression left by the original five. Black (1978) examines the corpus carefully and concludes that 'form of life' is a deliberately vague expression, which has no clear and firm implications and for which it would be a mistake to seek a clear and precise understanding. One might think, in view of the slim textual basis, that this cautious conclusion would be more or less universally accepted—or that, at the very least, a large number of philosophers would join Nestroy is mocking the very idea of a *Lebensform* or *Lebensbild.* That has not been the case. The idea of a form of life figures at crucial junctures in the *Investigations,* even if not frequently, and many readers seem more inclined to accept Malcolm's emphatic estimate without Black's caution: "One could," Malcolm wrote in his review of the *Philosophical Investigations,* "hardly place too much stress on this . . . notion in Wittgenstein's thought" (1966, 91). Malcolm's advice has

certainly been heeded, and more so than Black's. It may be that
Malcolm's advice was not altogether necessary. Philosophers ever since
Plato have been fascinated by the idea of *form* as that within which a
significant range of possibilities is contained. Wittgenstein wrote within
this tradition when he said, "Form is the possibility of structure" (*TLP*
2.033). Although I doubt very much that he had this dictum in mind
when he wrote of "forms of life," it is not unreasonable to think of a
form of life as containing the possible events and alterations that could
occur in that life, with the consequence that differences in form of life
would not be superficial or contingent differences but essential and
unbridgeable ones. I suspect that it is this idea that has contributed most
to the fascination of Wittgenstein's enigmatic use of this expression.
But, of course, even if we agree to gloss the term in this manner, such
agreement settles very little about how and where the expression is to be
applied. It is to that problem that I want to devote my attention.

Here are the five passages from the *Investigations:*

It is easy to imagine a language consisting only of orders and reports in
battle.—Or a language consisting only of questions and expressions for
answering yes and no. And innumerable others.——And to imagine a
language means to imagine a form of life. (*PI* 19)

But how many kinds of sentence are there? Say assertion, question,
command?—There are *countless* kinds: countless different kinds of use
of what we call "symbols", "words", "sentences". And this multiplicity
is not something fixed, given once for all; but new types of language,
new language-games, as we may say, come into existence, and others
become obsolete and get forgotten. (We can get a *rough picture* of this
from the changes in mathematics.)

Here the term language-*game* is meant to bring into prominence the
fact that the *speaking* of language is part of an activity, or of a form of life.
(*PI* 23)

It is what human beings *say* that is true and false; and they agree in
the *language* they use. That is not an agreement in opinions but in form
of life. (*PI* 241)

Can only those hope who can talk? Only those who have mastered the
use of a language. That is to say, the phenomena of hope are modes of
this complicated form of life. (*PI* p. 174)

It is no doubt true that you could not calculate with certain sorts of
paper and ink, if, that is, they were subject to certain sorts of queer
changes—but still the fact that they changed could in turn only be got
from memory and comparison with other means of calculation. And
how are these tested in their turn?

What has to be accepted, the given, is—so one could say—*forms of life.*

Does it make sense to say that people generally agree in their judgments of colour? What would it be like for them not to?—One man would say a flower was red which another called blue, and so on.—But what right should we have to call these people's words "red" and "blue" *our* 'colour-words'? (*PI* p. 226)

And here are four others, particularly problematic (even as to translation), in which *Lebensform* occurs:

The primitive form of the language-game is certainty, not uncertainty. For uncertainty could never lead to action. I want to say: it is characteristic of our language that the foundation on which it grows consists of steady ways of living (*feste Lebensformen*), regular ways of acting. (*C&E* 420)

But how then does the teacher interpret the rule for the pupil? (For he is certainly supposed to give it a particular interpretation.)—Well, how but by means of words and training?

And if the pupil reacts to it thus and thus; he possesses the rule inwardly.

But *this* is important, namely that this reaction, which is our guarantee of understanding, presupposes as a surrounding particular circumstances, particular forms of life and speech. (As there is no such thing as a facial expression without a face.)

(This is an important movement of thought.) (*RFM* VII:47)

Now I would like to regard this certainty, not as something akin to hastiness or superficiality, but as a form of life. (That is very badly expressed and probably badly thought as well.)

But that means I want to conceive it as something that lies beyond being justified or unjustified; as it were, as something animal. (*OC* 358–59)

Instead of the unanalysable, specific, indefinable: the fact that we act in such-and-such ways, e.g. *punish* certain actions, *establish* the state of affair (*Tatbestand*) thus and so, *give orders,* render accounts, describe colours, take an interest in others' feelings. What has to be accepted, the given—it might be said—are facts of living.* (compare *PI* p. 226d)

*"*Forms of life*" was a variant here. [Trans.] (*RPP* 1.630)

In the early parts of this chapter I review what has been said about Wittgenstein's "forms of life," paying close attention to the five passages in the text. Toward the end of the chapter I discuss the relevance of the concept of 'form of life' to the understanding both of certain other passages and of Wittgenstein's general approach to these matters. In this discussion much is left unexamined or unfinished. In view of Wittgenstein's remark that "to imagine a language means to imagine a form of life" (*PI* 19), I have used the word 'determines' to speak of the relation which then holds between a particular such language (language-game, activity) and a particular such form of life—without examining the nature of that relation or the problems it may entail. I also use the expression "form of life," without further precision, in whatever vague sense Wittgenstein used it; and I assume that other commentators, even where they have attempted a definition, have been governed by his use, too. Even at the end of the chapter, I attempt no definition or analysis either of what a form of life is in general or of our own form of life. It is likely, in the light of his use of the expression in lectures and notebooks, that Wittgenstein used 'form of life' to refer sometimes to culturally variant patterns of living rather than to biological forms and patterns. The most important conclusion is that there is no warrant for the widespread view that Wittgenstein implies or suggests a plurality of human *Lebensformen*, in the sense in which the expression is used in the *Philosophical Investigations*. The plurality of "forms of life" may include imaginary ones, such that of the builders (*PI* 2) or that of the woodsellers (*RFM* I.149); but first and foremost Wittgenstein's forms of life are those of natural history: bovine, piscine, canine, reptilian, human, feline, leonine, etc.

2. Sources and Shortcomings of the Standard Reading

There is a widespread view, approaching general consensus, that there exist a large variety of what Wittgenstein calls human *Lebensformen*. Thus Danford says that "we cannot make a list of all human forms of life" (1978, 117). Whittaker (1978, 44–45) claims that "the scope of what we call 'forms of life' will vary according to the discourse in question and the needs at hand," on the grounds, as he thinks, that Wittgenstein uses *Lebensform* "interchangeably" with *Sprachspiel* in *PI* 23. Whittaker's paper contains useful references to Nielsen, Winch, and Sherry, all of whom also understand Wittgenstein's talk of 'form of life' in the orthodox way. Stroud speaks of "our human practices or forms of life," (1966, 495) suggesting that practices and forms of life might be identical and in any case implying a plurality of human *Lebensformen*. Trigg (1973, 59) says that "Any religion, however bizarre, has to be accepted as a form of life"; and presumably, then, many things other than religions would be forms of life as well. Hilmy (1987, ch. 5, passim) gives elaborate argumentation and textual citation to support an extreme form of the received view, namely the identification of "form of life" with "language-game." Such examples could be multiplied *ad libidum*.

The only possible exceptions that have come to my attention (the literature is too vast for me to have canvassed it completely) are in essays by Kripke, Hunter, and Malcolm. Kripke refers to form of life in passing, and the implications for the issue at hand are unclear: "The set of responses on which we agree, and the way they interweave with our activities, is our *form of life* . . . No apriori paradigm of the way concepts ought to be applied governs all forms of life, or even our own form of life" (1982, 96, 105). Hunter (1968), on the other hand, focuses on forms of life and argues for an "organic account." He proposes "to see speaking or language-using, which is what Wittgenstein says is a form of life, as a biological or organic phenomenon" (p. 235). While not quite accurate, this ought to lead him in the right direction. In fact he never explicitly affirms or denies that there is just one human form of life, and it is this wary vagueness which makes his organic account the one possible exception. On the other hand, (1) he misses the connection between forms of life and natural history; (2) he explicitly rejects the connection between form of life and the common behavior of mankind (p. 242), for rather feeble reasons; and (3) he lapses once into a commitment to a plurality of human forms of life, through a misreading (discussed below) of *PI* 23 (p. 240). Malcolm writes:

> Another landmark of the second philosophy is the notion of '*a form of life*'. This expression is found in natural history, where different species are described in terms of posture, locomotion, habitat, feeding, breeding, social organization, the sounds they make, the way they play. . . . Wittgenstein says that what he is providing are 'really remarks on the natural history of human beings' (*PI* 415); that 'Ordering, questioning, recounting, chatting, are as much a part of our natural history as walking, eating, drinking, playing' (*PI* 25). (1986, 237–38)

This passage rightly stresses the naturalism but leaves open the relation of *Lebensform* to *Sprachspiel*. In another passage, however, he implies that there is just one human form of life:

> We go on, all agreeing, following rules and applying rules in new cases—without guidance. Other than the past training, there is no

explanation. It is an aspect of the form of life of human beings. It is our nature.[1] (1986, 181)

Some of the references to a plurality of human forms of life are casual or careless, rather than motivated by some interpretation of the text or some stance on philosophical questions. Cavell (1979, 30), for example, says that Wittgenstein "speaks of our ability to use language as depending upon agreement in 'forms of life' (*PI* 241)." Here the plural derives simply from careless citation, for *PI* 241 speaks instead of agreement in "form of life" in the singular. The same misquotation occurs in von Morstein (1980). Pitcher (1964, ch. 10) says that speaking a language presupposes "what Wittgenstein calls 'forms of life' (*PI* 19, 23, p. 226)," whereas Wittgenstein uses the plural in only one of the three passages, and in that passage the plural does not seem a necessary part of a presupposition for speaking a language. This slip leads Pitcher to a gratuitous plural in his otherwise sound comment that the reason we would not understand the talking lion (*PI* p. 223) is that "he doesn't share the necessary forms of life with us." Another example occurs in the essay by Black (1978). Black reviews the five passages and infers three principles:

(1) Mastery of a particular sub-language . . . entails having a particular form of life. . . . (2) 'Form of life' applies to an 'activity'. . . . (3) A language-game counts as a proper *part* of the corresponding form of life.

He immediately adds: "I believe that is all we can infer" (326–27). But he *also* says that hope, grief, joy, and fear are "aspects of forms of life that presuppose linguistic competence," tacitly inferring, contrary to his explicit caution, that more than one form of life presupposes linguistic competence.[2]

These latter examples, just because they are so casual, show how widespread this assumption or allegation is that Wittgenstein spoke

---

1. The first landmark of Wittgenstein's later philosophy that Malcolm notes is "the rejection of essentialism: the assumption that the concepts we employ are governed by necessary and sufficient conditions" (1986, 236). In discussion of this paper I have been criticized for betraying—or at least for not taking sufficient account of—Wittgenstein's substitution of "family resemblances" for "essences" (*PI* 65–68). Malcolm is exactly right in saying that the latter discussion has to do with whether natures can be *defined* rather than with whether things have them.

2. Black's second principle is unconvincing, and appears to derive from too casual a reading of *PI* 23. It also seems careless of him to have included fear and joy in the list of aspects of life that presuppose linguistic competence, since Wittgenstein says on the same page that dogs can be joyful and fearful.

about a plurality of human forms of life. The assumption is, however, unnecessary and misleading.

One apparent reason for imputing to Wittgenstein a plurality of human *Lebensformen* is the idea that he says, or as good as says, that each language-game (or perhaps each activity) determines a separate form of life distinct from that determined by any other language-game. This view was set forth prominently, albeit a bit casually and obscurely, by Malcolm in his review, when he wrote that the "notion ['form of life'] is intimately related to the notion 'language-game'. . . . Forms of life, embedded in language-games, teach us what justification is" (91–92). Attracted by this idea, I myself also identified forms of life with language-games in an earlier version of chapter fourteen. The same rather extreme form of this idea (i.e., *identification* of language-games and forms of life) is seen in the claim of Whittaker, cited earlier, that 'form of life' is used interchangeably with 'language-game' in *PI* 23. There are at least muted echoes of the same idea in the remarks of Trigg, Stroud, Pitcher, and Black, cited earlier.

The idea is based not only on *PI* 23 but also on *PI* 19, where Wittgenstein first introduces the term. These passages appear to give strong support to the correlation between language-games or activities and forms of life. As is common with Wittgenstein, however, the context of these passages makes them especially problematic. Wittgenstein has just said that one can "easily" imagine a language consisting only of orders and reports in battle, or another consisting only of questions and expressions for affirming and denying. That startling remark goes hand in hand with his earlier comment (*PI* 6) that we could imagine the "language" of the two builders in *PI* 2 as the *whole* language of those people, or even of a tribe. I have regularly stumbled over these passages because I am unable to imagine what Wittgenstein says one can "easily" imagine. In the language of questions and affirmation/denial, for instance, there could never be questions like "When are you coming?" or "How long will that job take?" or "Why did you do it?" since these questions cannot be answered with an affirmation or denial. For these matters we would have to continually play games of Twenty Questions, and I cannot imagine what would lead people to live like that. Nor would it be clear exactly what a *question* is; for in our language a question is distinguished from statements, imperatives, and interjections, and by hypothesis none of these contrasts occur in the language it is supposed to be easy to imagine. These difficulties could be multiplied indefinitely for this imagined language as well as for the others. So while

I understand abstractly the idea that to imagine a language means to imagine a form of life, I have a lot of trouble applying it to the examples Wittgenstein seems to have in mind—and just because, as Wittgenstein's remark would have it, I have trouble conceiving whether creatures whose use of language is so constrained would really be speaking a language, or would still be human beings.

This difficulty is, of course, not one which affects me alone. Here is Rhees's comment on the language of the builders:

> But I feel there is something wrong here. The trouble is not to imagine a people with a language of such limited vocabulary. The trouble is to imagine that they spoke the language only to give these special orders on this job and otherwise never spoke at all. I do not think it would be speaking a language. (1970, 76)

Rhees mentions three anomalies: that in the instruction of children the same expressions would be being used differently, namely for pedagogy rather than for building; that these people who use words in connection with their regular activity would have to remain speechless when they encounter an irregularity or try to work out a snag; and that "there would not be any distinction of sense and nonsense" (77–78). So Rhees doubts the builders can be said to be speaking a language: "Unless there were a difference between learning to move stones in the ways people do, and learning what makes sense, then I do not think we could say they were learning to speak" (77–78).[3] He does not explicitly mention 'form of life', but it is clear that one of the reasons he finds it difficult to conceive the verbal signals of the builders as a language is that he has difficulty imagining their form of life. On the one hand they seem to be human, since they are said to be builders and are said to be speaking a language; on the other hand they seem not to be human, since their "language" is crude and confined to just one rather narrow activity.

There would be similar difficulties in trying to conceive any other single activity or language-game as constituting a whole language or as determining a form of life. If that one activity were their only use of language, such creatures would not be recognizably human (see *PI* 25). That is to say, their form of life would differ from ours as much as that of dogs and lions. About these cases we have to say something similar to what Stroud (1965, 512) says about the woodsellers of *RFM* I.149:

---

3. Mosedale (1978) has made some interesting and thoughtful criticisms of Rhees's discussion of the builders, but his criticisms do not touch the point cited here.

Problems involved in understanding what it would be like to sell wood in this way can be multiplied indefinitely. . . . When we try to trace out the implications of behaving like that consistently and quite generally, our understanding of the alleged possibilities decreases.

Although there is some intimate relation between *Sprachspiel* and *Lebensform*, Wittgenstein cannot be thought to have identified the two in these passages, much less to have used the two terms interchangeably. What he does say is problematic in part because the key expressions are singular. The problem is to surmise how the plurals would go. In each case there are two principal possibilities:

19 plural A: To imagine various languages means to imagine various forms of life.

19 plural B: To imagine various languages means to imagine a form of life.

23 plural A: Utterances are parts of various activities, or of various forms of life.

23 plural B: Utterances are parts of various activities, or of a form of life.

The orthodox reading would pluralize both passages in the first way (*19A, 23A*), probably without considering the alternative. Is that the correct surmise? Is the correlation one to one, as in *A;* or many to one, as in *B?*

The first thing to say is that this orthodox idea is unnecessary. From the premise that when I imagine a language I imagine a form of life it does not follow that when I imagine two languages I imagine two forms of life. Logically speaking the assumption goes beyond what is in the text or entailed by it. And similarly it is unnecessary to assume that the second part of the phrase "part of an activity, or a form of life" is in apposition to the first part or that it designates the same sort of thing, rather than designating an *alternative* sort of thing. This elementary logical point is necessary to break the grip of the reading which leads Hunter to say that "the wording of *PI* 23 marks forms of life as *activities*" (1968, 240); a prerequisite not only to the correct reading, but even to an adequate overview of the alternatives.

One should next note the improbability of the idea thus interpreted —not only, as Rhees has shown, if "languages" are understood to be individual language-games, but also if they are taken to be ordinary languages. There is no interesting sense in which I must imagine different *forms* of life when I think of French and German. I don't even have to think of different customs, though I tend to. It is, on the other hand, very easy to imagine a whole series of families, each speaking a different language, in which the patterns of the lives of family members and their relations to one another and others in their society are barely distinguishable, no matter which language the family speaks; the similar life-style might be determined by, say, common socioeconomic conditions. So the plural forms *19A* and *23A* result in a weak and improbable doctrine in either case, whether "languages" are taken to be ordinary languages or individual language-games. Such an improbable thesis is not likely to have been what Wittgenstein had in mind.

Most importantly, this orthodox reading is misleading. This will become more obvious later, but it can be seen in relation to the immediate text, too. The point in *PI* 19 is that a language cannot be conceived just in terms of words and syntax but only as used; that is, as integrated into the activities of some sort of living being. I cannot understand the words without understanding the activity, I cannot understand the activity without seeing how it fits into the life of the speaker, and I cannot do that without knowing what general form the life of the speaker has. Now it is a very general fact that speakers all have the same form of life. They are all human. What determines this form of life is the capacity to use language. So it is the same form of life which I imagine no matter which linguistic activity or which language I think of. This form of life is presupposed by a language or a language-game, that is, by the speaking of a language, because it is presupposed by the activities of the speakers. To suppose that many forms and different sets of possibilities are involved obscures the point of these passages.

I conclude that the correlation between *Sprachspiel* and *Lebensform* is many to one rather than one to one. Each language-game does constitute or determine a special form, namely, a form of activity or of behavior, not a form of life. Along with the activity or behavior the language-game presupposes a form of life of which it is, as Black (1978) points out, a proper part—somewhat the same way a proposition presupposes the whole of logical space although determining only one point in it (*TLP* 3.42).[4] To imagine a language, or even a language-game, means to imagine a form of life. But so long as it is one of the natural languages or

---

4. Rather than identifying forms of life with language-games, it would be less misleading to think of 'form of life' as analogous to what Wittgenstein called 'the whole of logical space' in the *Tractatus*.

one of our familiar language-games (such as those mentioned in *PI* 23, 25), the form of life we imagine is always "this complicated form of life" of human beings.

Another common reason for saddling Wittgenstein with a plurality of human forms of life is based on Spranger's use of the expression in his book *Lebensformen* (1922), with which, as Janik and Toulmin have argued (1973, 230), Wittgenstein must have been familiar. Spranger's idea is that different human forms of life are determined by dominant commitments and activities, so that bankers, taxi drivers, farmers, and housewives all have different forms of life, as do Sunnis, Shiites, atheists, Jews, Catholics, and Protestants. Thus Janik and Toulmin speak of "all the alternative *Lebensformen*—all the possible human styles of thought, character, and language" (231). According to this view there seems no essential connection between language-games and forms of life, the latter being determined instead by ethnic, linguistic, and occupational identities.

It is difficult to see any basis in Wittgenstein's texts for this way of speaking about forms of life. Wittgenstein does sometimes imagine people who have a different form of life from ours—the builders (*PI* 2, 6), for example; or the person who counts by two, as he thinks, by counting by four after one thousand (*PI* 185ff.); or the woodsellers (*RFM* I.149), who sell their wood according to the area it covers rather than according to volume.[5] But these cases do not connote that there are differences among actual human forms of life. On the contrary. By their divergence from our common practices, they make evident how much *we* have in common. Wittgenstein also mentions some radical breakdowns in understanding among actual human beings. In *PI* 194 he suggests that because of their radical misunderstanding of how language works, philosophers "are like savages, primitive people, who hear the expressions of civilized men, put a false interpretation on them, and then draw the queerest conclusions from it." And on page 223 he notes that "one human being can be a complete enigma to another. We learn this when we come into a strange country with entirely strange traditions; and, what is more, even given a mastery of the country's language." There is no doubt that Wittgenstein was keenly aware of the estrangement and alienation from others which human beings (both singly and in groups) often feel. But the point here is that understanding

---

5. There is an excellent discussion of the weird woodsellers and the curious counters (a somewhat similar example found in *RFM*) in Stroud 1966.

depends on *"customs* (uses, institutions)" (*PI* 199). That is, in Wittgenstein's former terminology, it depends on both form and content. These breakdowns, however poignant they may be, are contingent and corrigible, since they result from not having learned the practices rather than from not having the capacity to learn them. Therefore they do not connote any difference in form of life.

There are certain advantages which this way of conceiving a multiplicity of human forms of life might have over the identification of forms of life with language-games. One advantage is that each human life may be conceived as a whole rather than as a composite of activities and capacities, that is, as a composite of forms. (Compare *TLP* 5.5421: "Indeed a composite soul would no longer be a soul.") Another possible virtue is that this view would make Wittgenstein's thought closer to the popular fascination with the contingent differences we confront in our daily lives. But neither of these putative virtues is very attractive when examined closely. The first would provide a Procrustean tabulation, chopping and stretching human beings who in actuality have crisscrossing commitments and complex sociological identities. The second turns what were supposed to be very general facts which we can barely imagine to be otherwise into trivial contingencies. Neither consideration is compelling in the absence of textual basis. What is at stake in the last three passages (*PI* 241, p. 174, p. 226), where agreement in form of life is invoked as a stopping point for inquiry, are such activities as naming colors, measuring, doing mathematics, hoping, and grieving. It is absurd to imagine that any of these characteristically human activities depend on having some particular life-style or "form of life" in the sense of Spranger. Although Wittgenstein may have borrowed the *word Lebensform,* he certainly made it refer to something entirely different from what Spranger discusses.

Although Winch (1958) was the first commentary to construe Wittgenstein's idea as a kind of cultural relativism, Fischer (1987) has taken up the cudgels with renewed vigor. The textual evidence on which he bases his interpretation of 'forms of life' as culturally divergent is of three sorts. One is the use of the German expression in this sense not only by Spranger but also by other well-known German scholars such as Wundt and Spengler (Fischer 1987, 33–36). The second sort of evidence is that Wittgenstein sanctioned (according to Rhees) the translation of *Lebensformen* as "ways of life" (1987, 40), and we surely must grant that ways of life are culturally variant. The third bit of evidence (1987, 277) is that Wittgenstein in the *Lectures and Conversa-*

tions on Aesthetics says, "Zu einem Sprachspiel gehört eine ganze Kultur." All of this evidence is worth taking seriously, but none of it is decisive. What needs to be acknowledged is that Wittgenstein seems to have used the expression to refer to different things—without needing to change the sense, I should think, since the sense is in any case so vague. It certainly remains the case that none of Wittgenstein's key language-games or examples depends on or even involves any significant cultural variation, and that the thrust of his *Philosophical Investigations* has to do with what is characteristic of humans in general. The fatal weakness of Fischer's argument is that he remains silent on this central point.

The interesting and creative side of Fischer's conception of *Lebensform* is that he applies it to psychiatric problems by considering mental illness as a divergent form of life. When we remember how Wittgenstein in *On Certainty* insists that some instances of false beliefs are crazy rather than merely mistaken, we can appreciate what a rich suggestion this is to explore. Fischer's work is most stimulating in this regard. Among other things, it reminds us that Wittgenstein's conception of form of life, as I have explicated it, contains an assumption of normality in those cases in which he supplies "remarks on the natural history of human beings" (*PI* 415).

Another reason for thinking that Wittgenstein implied a plurality of human forms of life, though one not common in the secondary literature, might be the idea that Wittgenstein meant by a "form of life" something like a very basic trait of character or temperament. Malcolm once suggested in private conversation (and one can find echoes in his article of 1982) that one might say that two persons have different forms of life if they have radically different attitudes toward the pains of others and toward any indication (verbal or otherwise) of what another is feeling. The one person might be always trusting and sympathetic, the other always sceptical and never sympathetic. Or perhaps better, since "the primitive form of the language-game is certainty, not uncertainty; for uncertainty could never lead to action" (*C&E* 416): the other always responds to expressions of feeling with manipulative behavior (oiling the squeaking hinge, so to speak) rather than with pity or sympathy. One can think of these as primitive, instinctive patterns of behavior, which are then refined and extended—but not essentially altered—by the use of language. If these two persons met and tried to converse, there would be little understanding between them: they would "talk past" one another. One might similarly think of an optimist and a pessimist, of a bellicose person and a conciliatory person, of a happy person and a miserable person, as having different forms of life.

Since Malcolm had many informal conversations with Wittgenstein, it is probable that the idea behind this way of conceiving of "forms of life" corresponds to ideas Wittgenstein expressed. It seems unlikely, however, that Wittgenstein himself used the expression this way. The published texts do not support such a reading; and although they do not refute it decisively, it seems farfetched to hold, say, that the optimist and the pessimist have different language-games, rather than that the language-game of speaking of the future allows all the possibilities of which they (differentially) make use. On the other hand, one might claim (though Malcolm did not) that a continuity with certain ideas of the *Tractatus* lends support to this reading. For example:

> If good or bad exercise of will does alter the world, it can alter only the limits of the world, not the facts—not what can be expressed by language.
>
> In short the effect must be that it becomes an altogether different world.
>
> The world of the happy man is a different one from that of the unhappy man. (*TLP* 6.43)

To say that a happy person and an unhappy person have different *Lebensformen* is less offensive to common sense than saying they have different worlds, yet it retains much of the dramatic impact of *TLP* 6.43.

One problem with this reading is that Wittgenstein seems not to have used 'form of life' to refer to this sort of difference, at least not in material so far published. Another problem is that the life of every actual person is a mixture of these opposed and differentiated qualities. One is sometimes happy and sometimes miserable, sometimes sympathetic and sometimes manipulative, sometimes hopeful and sometimes despairing. Such alterations seem a regular feature of our lives. It is only in a Pickwickian sense that there is a different "form of life" in such cases—just as it is only in a Pickwickian or prophetic sense that the world can be different when all the facts remain the same. One may perhaps imagine a person for whom sympathy, or manipulation, or pessimism, etc., is not even *possible,* and we might in that case speak of a different form of life, a different range of possibilities. But all the facts, all our experience, show a single range of possibilities which includes both pity and manipulation, both hope and despair, and so on. I should think, furthermore, that this conception of *Lebensformen* would also prove mischievous with respect to religious and moral questions where it might initially seem attractive. So one cannot rationalize a plurality of human *Lebensformen* along these lines either.

I have cited Cavell (1979), von Morstein (1980), and Pitcher (1964) as misquoting "forms of life" where the text has "form of life." They are not alone. Finch, for example, believes that forms of life are "patterns of action shared in by members of a group," such as shopping, building, fighting battles, and calculating (1977, 90). "The last two," he then asserts, "are specifically mentioned as forms of life"—which a quick inspection of the texts shows to be inaccurate. I have also heard a number of philosophers assert in discussion that Wittgenstein uses the term in the plural in key passages in the *Investigations*. In fact the key passages are all in the singular. The only passage in which the term is used in the plural is the passage on page 226: "What has to be accepted, the given, is—one could say—*forms of life.*" The passage is certainly a dramatic one, and certainly important for understanding the role which forms of life are meant to play. But it is full of problems. More than the others, this passage presupposes that we already know what a *Lebensform* is, which we do not. One should also note that Wittgenstein's wording suggests that he may be presenting the idea tentatively rather than with conviction—since he uses both the subjunctive mood (in the German) and also the qualifying phrase "one could say."

A rather different kind of problem arises from the publication of a passage which is nearly identical, except that Wittgenstein speaks of *facts* of life (or of living) rather than of *forms* of life, although 'forms' is given as a variant in the notes:

> Instead of the unanalysable, specific, indefinable: the fact that we act in such-and-such ways, e.g. *punish* certain actions, *establish* the state of affairs thus and so, *give orders,* render accounts, describe colours, take an interest in others' feelings. What has to be accepted, the given—it might be said—are facts of living (*Tatsachen des Lebens*). [variant: are *forms of life* (*Lebensformen*)] (*RPP* I.630)

The existence of this passage makes the fifth passage in the *Investigations* unique, since, to the best of my knowledge, none of the others has a twin in some other text where 'form' is transformed into 'fact'. I do not mean to suggest that 'form' must take on an entirely new meaning if a *Lebensform* is a kind of fact. On the contrary, I incline to the view that forms of life are normally found in the world, even though that cannot, of course, be the case for the imaginary forms of life. What it suggests instead is that Wittgenstein was less certain about the employment of the term in this passage than in the others, and on at least one occasion thought that another expression would serve better. This passage should, therefore, weigh less heavily than the others on matters where there are divergent indications about Wittgenstein's use of the term 'form of life'.

One further consideration is that the remark occurs in the context of observations about our agreeing on names of colors and about mathematicians not quarreling. This context exactly parallels that in *PI* 239–41. Since the earlier passage was revised for publication by Wittgenstein and the passage on page 226 was not, it is reasonable to conjecture that he finally found the singular form somehow preferable. So the passage on page 226, while important, is not a key passage for understanding the meaning of *Lebensform* in the *Investigations*.

3. ". . . this complicated form of life"

The fourth passage is a key passage for understanding Wittgenstein's concept. It provides the most detailed information about the relation of a language-game to a form of life, and it furnishes clear support for believing that Wittgenstein views human beings as having a common form of life. To be able to *hope,* he says, one must have "mastered the use of a language." And he continues right on: "That is to say, the phenomena of hope are modes of this complicated form of life." The expression, "this complicated form of life," is striking. What can Wittgenstein mean? Or as Finch puts it: "What is the form of life referred to in this passage?" (1977, 94) Finch himself gives without hesitation what seems the only answer available to a reader convinced that there are various human forms of life: "It is the activity of hoping . . . which Wittgenstein calls 'this complicated form of life'— various patterns of activity which might be called hoping behavior" (94). The first drawback of this reading is that hoping would not ordinarily seem to be an "activity"; but perhaps a little conceptual stretching could be tolerated in this regard. The second drawback is that a *form* is not an activity; that is to say, not something that is carried on or that takes place. Here there seems a basic confusion of categories that cannot so easily be tolerated. The third and decisive drawback of this reading is that it utterly trivializes Wittgenstein's remark. It entails that what Wittgenstein is saying is that phenomena of hoping are modes of hoping! Wittgenstein nowhere else says anything quite so silly, and there is no good reason he should bother saying it in this context. No wonder, then, that Finch finds this "the most difficult of these passages to understand" (94). His proposal is one of desperation, and thereby betrays the inadequacy of conceiving of forms of life as patterns of activity. It is quite hopeless, as Hunter (1968, 240) had earlier pointed out, to try to understand the passage this way.

There is only one alternative allowed by the text, that the form of life referred to is that of those who can talk. And then it can only mean *the* form of life determined by having mastered the use of a language. That is, Wittgenstein could not have expressed himself this way if he supposed, as Black does in the remark cited above, that there are various forms of life which presuppose linguistic competence. If mastery of the use of a language determines a form of life of which the phenomena of hope are modes (modifications, aspects; the German is *Modificationen*), then the phenomena of forecasting, regretting, counting, naming colors, giving orders, obeying them, and so on, are all also "modes of this complicated form of life."[6]

It is interesting not only that there is a single form of life determined by mastery of the use of a language, but also that it is complicated. Why "complicated"? It is true that there are many subtle nuances of hope, but they would seem to be a rather insubstantial basis for calling the form of life complicated. What complicates this form of life are all the other possibilities besides just the phenomena of hope. Here we have an echo of an earlier passage in which Wittgenstein spoke of form of life. That is, this form of life is complicated because it involves "countless different kinds of use of what we call 'symbols', 'words', and 'sentences' " (*PI* 23).

It might be useful to compare the fourth passage with what Wittgenstein said about modes of signifying in *TLP* 3.3421:

> A particular mode of signifying may be unimportant but it is always important that it is a *possible* mode of signifying. And that is generally so in philosophy: again and again the individual case turns out to be unimportant, but the possibility of each individual case discloses something about the essence of the world.

Wittgenstein might no longer use the word 'essence' in such a context, but he has retained and further refined the method here indicated—the method, that is, of calling attention to intrinsically insignificant particu-

---

6. On this point see Malcolm (1982). Although Malcolm is not explicitly discussing 'form of life', he has a useful discussion of how activities such as these come to be part of our lives.

lars to disclose more fully the nature or essence of something, by disclosing more fully the range of its possibilities. Such a range of possibilities is an important part of what Wittgenstein means by 'grammar'. The continuity of method, as well as the relevant relation of *PI* to *TLP,* may therefore be seen in the remark, *"Essence* is expressed by grammar" (*PI* 371). I have argued that the expression "form of life" refers to just such a complicated range of possible modes. Whether this is altogether right as an explanation of Wittgenstein's meaning, it would in any case be a mistake for a philosopher to think (as psychologists, sociologists, politicians inevitably must do) that the details of particular modes are what is important, even in philosophy, rather than the possibilities they disclose.

This understanding conforms nicely to the remark that to imagine a language means to imagine a form of life. It makes no difference whether I think of Tamil or Swahili instead of German or English: the same complicated form of life (differently worked out, to be sure) is associated with the mastery of the use of any one of them. This fact is somewhat obscured by Wittgenstein's bold, and I think indefensible, comment that "it is easy to imagine a language consisting only of orders and reports in battle" (*PI* 19). The reservations which Rhees has about the language of the builders apply equally to this "language." If we take the restriction seriously, it means that in this language no questions can be asked about the reports, nor about the sources of information, nor about how to execute the orders; nor can the language be used outside of battle, even for instructing people in the use of the language. And this is only to scratch the surface, for, as Rhees has shown, the difficulties in conceiving the details of this language and the lives of its users can be multiplied indefinitely. Such a "language" would be unlike any human language, and so the form of life of its speakers would be unlike ours, perhaps. But through the obscurity thus created, Wittgenstein's point still holds; for to imagine a language one must imagine how it is used; and that means to imagine not only how speech is integral to certain activities but also how these activities are integral to the lives of the speakers; and for this one must imagine the *form* of life of the speakers, which will comprise *all* that is or might be or might have been possible for them. And the very general fact that all actual speakers in fact have the same form of life also still holds. It is only imaginary languages that determine different forms of life; natural languages all determine the same one.

4.   Forms of Life as Bits of Natural History

Forms of life are neither transient nor variable. It might at first be thought surprising to find certainty and fixity in conjunction with vagueness, that is, where there are no precise criteria or definitions. First thoughts and really basic thoughts, however, are bound to be vague. Analysis, precision, and definition are scientific procedures, which make possible not only scientific knowledge but also the doubt and variability that is here excluded. It is because they are vague that forms of life can be accepted as fixed and invariant. That is, they are accepted as among the hinges on which our ordinary thought swings back and forth: "If I want the door to turn, the hinges must stay put" (*OC* 343). The metaphor is perhaps overly suggestive, since that the hinges stay put can easily—too easily, perhaps—be seen as a transcendental requirement; nevertheless, forms of life are first and foremost things found in the natural world.

Elsewhere Wittgenstein says in this connection: "My *life* consists in my being content to accept many things" (*OC* 344), and he refers to this absence of doubt—not absence of dubitability, but simple absence of doubt—as "*comfortable* certainty" (*OC* 357). I suppose, then, that two persons might have different lives in part by being content to accept divergent sets of things; which is, no doubt, contingently true for any two of us. On the other hand a person would have a different *form* of life from us only if never content to accept anything. Our comfortable certainty would then seem to be self-referential in the sense of Bubner (1975), and therefore transcendentally necessary. That is to say, one could hardly share this form of life (being content to accept many things) and yet deny being so content; nor, indeed, could one honestly deny it at all, for even our expressions of discontent rest on a basis of being content to accept many things. So, in a sense, one *must* be content to be content to accept many things.

But in spite of repeatedly suggesting necessities that face us in our daily living but that transcend what is given to us empirically—I will discuss the transcendental dimension of his thought in the next chapter—Wittgenstein avoids transcendental argumentation. What he says immediately after speaking of "*comfortable* certainty" is the following:

> Now I would like to regard this certainty, not as something akin to hastiness or superficiality, but as a form of life. (That is very badly expressed and probably badly thought as well.)

But that just means that I want to conceive it as something that lies
beyond being justified or unjustified; as it were, as something animal.
(*OC* 358–59)

On the one hand this passage lends support to Hunter's suggestion
(1968) that a form of life is something organic or biological, a
suggestion that has been strongly endorsed by Malcolm (1986, 237–
38). Hunter's interpretation has the merit of explaining Wittgenstein's
idea without depending on conceptual analysis or metaphysical abstraction, and is one of the few which fits with this passage from *OC* as well as
with those from *PI*. On the other hand, this comfortable certainty,
which "lies beyond being justified or unjustified," cannot belong to or
be derived from a critical and explanatory science like modern biology.
In fact, such fixed and determinate forms of life are given to us neither
by metaphysical abstraction nor by science. They are, on the contrary,
found in the natural world and given to us as facts of natural history.[7]

This mastery of the use of a language involves in turn the capacity to
enter into countless language-games. The particular activities Wittgenstein mentions in the context of the third passage and the fifth passage
are mathematics and the naming of colors. With respect to these
activities—surely also a part of our natural history, for "mathematics is
after all an anthropological phenomenon" (*RFM* V.26)—one might
indeed say, *"this language-game is played"* (*PI* 654). We must also
recognize, as a matter of natural history, that language-games have rules,
and that these rules are components or aspects of the natural history of
mankind, just as much as the activities themselves. We then can see more
clearly the point which Shwayder (1969) and Stroud (1966) have
elaborated, that there is no more explanation for logical necessity than
that it is an aspect or component of our complicated form of life.

None of these parts, these individual activities or individual components of our lives, is given separately. Nor is any of them to be accepted
separately. The capacity to do any one is intertwined with the capacity to
do the others. It *need* not be so intertwined, but it is. It is another fact of
natural history that all and only those who can name colors have the
capacity to do mathematics. So ultimately what is given, what has to be

---

7. Wolf children (humans who have survived in the wild without human parents)
therefore have a different form of life from ours. In the rare cases where wolf children are
found, they seem a different sort of animal rather than seeming really human. Reading
accounts of wolf children one is struck by the fact that no one knows how to treat them as
humans, even though some people may try to.

accepted, is, one could say, the whole vague fabric of "this complicated form of life."

There are, of course, some language-games which some people do not play. This is hardly surprising, since we are all limited in various ways. It would, however, be exceedingly difficult to demonstrate of any normal person that there is some language-game which that person could not participate in; that is, could not even learn to participate in. Part of the reason is connected with the uncountability of language-games, which Wittgenstein insists on in *PI* 23. The reason that there are "countless" language-games is not that there are so many that we could never finish counting them, but rather that they are so intertwined, that it is so unclear what is to count as *one* language-game, that we could never begin counting. The reason, in other words, is that language-games do not have definite limits. In addition there are no specifiable limits to what human practices a person *might* have learned if given the opportunity. Therefore no language-game can be shown to be absolutely alien to a person, even though some are in fact alien to each of us. The other part of the reason is subtly connected with the first. The interconnections among the activities which constitute "this complicated form of life" are such that once you have the capacity to make normal use of language at all, you have *ipso facto* the capacity to gain access to any language-game whatever. Of course, you may have to work very hard to gain such access, for the capacity to gain access does not alone guarantee access; and for each of us there will be many language-games to which we have not acquired access. But it is very difficult to see what considerations could serve as proof that access to some language-game could not in principle be acquired. It is worth remembering in this connection that even congenitally blind persons can learn to use color-words. In this sense the limits we are all subject to are contingent rather than necessary, whereas our form of life is, relatively, necessary rather than contingent. That is to say, our limits are a matter of biography rather than of natural history, pertaining to individual lives rather than to form of life.

That Wittgenstein thought of form of life together with natural history is confirmed by the remarks which immediately precede the reference to "this complicated form of life" on *PI* p. 174:

> One can imagine an animal angry, frightened, unhappy, happy, startled. But hopeful? And why not?
> A dog believes his master is at the door. But can he also believe his

master will come the day after tomorrow?—And *what* can he not do here?—How do I do it?—How am I supposed to answer this?

These are bits of natural history. Wittgenstein notes certain characteristics which distinguish dogs from humans. It seems, furthermore, that these differences can only be noted, not explained. Some of the teasing questions which Wittgenstein asks here, particularly the final one, seem designed to show how very difficult it would be to do anything more than simply note the differences. Wittgenstein's most decisive use of the term 'form of life' follows immediately after this bit of natural history:

> Can only those hope who can talk? Only those who have mastered the use of a language. That is to say, the phenomena of hope are modes of this complicated form of life. (If a concept refers to a character of human handwriting, it has no application to beings that do not write.)

It is clear from the sequence of these passages that Wittgenstein thought of forms of life in connection with facts of natural history, and that he meant to distinguish our form of life from the canine.

There are five other passages in which Wittgenstein takes note of facts of natural history to distinguish our form of life from that of animals. In *PI* 650 he makes a remark which has similarities to that quoted above. He notes that we can say of a dog that he is afraid that his master will beat him, but *not* that he is afraid that his master will beat him tomorrow. In *PI* 250 and again on p. 229 he notes that a dog cannot be a hypocrite—cannot really be faking pain, for instance—but cannot be sincere either. In *PI* 357 he compares the possibility of a human being talking to himself with the impossibility of supposing that a dog is talking to himself. Here he makes reference again to common patterns of behavior, that it makes sense for me to say that I am saying something to myself only because of my "behaving in such-and-such a way." He does not further describe what this behavior is, and therefore we must assume that the details do not matter so much as the general form. That is to say, it is because of the form of human life that it makes sense to say that a person is saying something to himself, and it is because of the form of canine life that it does not make sense to say this of a dog. Such a point also lies behind the famous remark on *PI* page 223: "If a lion could talk, we could not understand him."

If form of life is given as part of natural history, then the form of human life can be equated, as Haller (1988, 130) has noted, with the common behavior of mankind. For that reason my estrangement from a person who is a complete enigma to me (*PI* p. 223) is entirely different from my estrangement from the talking lion (*PI* p. 223), and perhaps Wittgenstein juxtaposed the two cases so that we would see the contrast. There are ways to overcome the enigmas of a foreign culture, which are only minimally present in the case of the builders (*PI* 2) and are completely absent in the case of the lion. The case of the explorer shows how understanding aliens presupposes common behavior, or a form of life:

> Suppose you came as an explorer into an unknown country with a language quite strange to you. In what circumstances would you say that the people there gave orders, understood them, obeyed them, rebelled against them, and so on? The common behavior of mankind is the system of reference by means of which we interpret an unknown language. (*PI* 206)

This explains why we could not understand the lion, since there is no common behavior of lions in which they use sentences at all.[8] The wording in the last sentence of the passage also further confirms the connection between natural history and form of life. Wittgenstein has earlier referred to giving orders as belonging to our natural history (*PI* 25), and there seems no difference between saying that I must imagine common behavior and saying that I must imagine a form of life, when I imagine a language-game such as giving orders.

So form of life is a matter of natural history, and thus not subject to controversy:

> What we are supplying are really remarks on the natural history of man: not curiosities however, but rather observations on facts which no one has doubted, and which have gone unremarked because they are always before our eyes. (*RFM* I. 14z; see also *PI* 415)

It is the differences between humans and animals which are always before our eyes and which no one has ever doubted. Human differences, on the other hand—those between Christians and Jews, for instance, or

---

8. Savigny (1991) understands *"die gemeinsame menschliche Handlungsweise"* as referring to the common behavior of the alien people, rather than to human behavior in general. This ingenious—and to my mind implausible—reading leads him to give a different explanation of why we could not understand the lion as well as to retain a thoroughgoing relativism. The greatest weakness of his reading, to my mind, is that it requires a hypothetical reconstruction of *what would happen if* (e.g., if we heard grammatical sentences, with good Oxford enunciation, coming from a lion), thus departing from Wittgenstein's reliance on what is before our eyes all the time.

between Israelis and Nazis—are always controversial. That there *seem* to be significant human differences is undeniable. But the apparent differences are denounced as illusions as vigorously as they are proclaimed as genuine. Sociologists rightly concern themselves with human differences, and may even believe that the common characteristics of men, their common differences to animals, are too much before our eyes to deserve attention. From the point of view of natural history, however, there is just one common form of life for all humans.

5. Evolution, Fantasy, and Natural History

In saying that forms of life are neither transient nor variable, I do not mean to deny evolution. The fixity of forms of life must be understood as compatible with the variation of biological forms through evolution. This seems paradoxical, but it is not really a contradiction. The reason these remarks on natural history do not conflict with the theory of evolution is that they are entirely different kinds of statements, in ways that were spelled out in more detail in chapter nine. We can therefore apply to this paradox the treatment which Wittgenstein recommended in another context:

> You need to call to mind the differences between the language-games. (*PI* 290)
>   The paradox disappears only if we make a radical break with the idea that language always functions in one way, always serves the same purpose: to convey thoughts—which may be about houses, pains, good and evil, or anything else you please. (*PI* 304)

According to the scientific theory of evolution, homo sapiens evolved from earlier primates. No one knows exactly how, nor when, nor why. It nevertheless seems most probable that during the times of transition there were forms of life intermediate between the human form as we know it today and that of the monkeys or apes. This conjecture, which I regard as almost certainly true, rests on theory and hypothesis, and the hypothesized intermediate forms are remote from our experience. They are vague, and we can imagine entirely different things about them. When we look at artifacts from our ancestors of one hundred thousand years ago, we don't know what to infer about their lives. Certain artifacts may signify religious practice; but they may have been used in cooking. The confidence we have in the theory of evolution applies to general principles and anatomical details, and especially to the general form of explanation for the variety of life-forms. But it does not apply to the details of behavior; and even where we are confident about details, we depend on hypothesis rather than acquaintance.

This is fertile ground for speculation, whether scientific or literary. Literary speculation has included works of Rousseau, Čapek, and Vercors. When Rousseau (1968) considered the form of life of primitive humans, he supposed that their lives were dominated by feeling rather than logical thought. Therefore he supposed that in the first language there were only vowels, that there were only expressions of feeling and metaphors, and that language was not used in connection with practical activities such as hunting. Exactly how do these emotive expressions fit together with the rest of the lives of these people? What role do the metaphors play? Since Rousseau was mainly interested in the development of language from this hypothetical beginning, details of this primitive way of life are omitted—and are not easy to fill in.

Far more detailed are the contrary hypotheses of Vercors in his novel *Les animaux dénaturés* and Karel Čapek in his novel *The War with the Newts*. Vercors supposes that some creatures who do not look human can understand and follow orders. After they are put to work in factories, a journalist, a priest, an attorney, a trade unionist, and various others worry about whether these creatures have souls, whether they have rights under industrial labor-relations laws, whether killing them is murder, and so on. This work comes to grips in a powerful way with some of the questions raised by the intermediate forms of life hypothesized by the theory of evolution. It seems to me that its effect is to confirm Wittgenstein's remark that the form of life is what is given and just has to be accepted. It does this by showing that we would not know what to say if things were radically different from what they are, so that we must just accept forms of life as given. Čapek imagines large pelagic salamanders, who live in the ocean and work on land. At first exploited by humans, they then multiply and undermine the coastlines where human cities have been built, to create new habitats for themselves. This novel, too, is a fine "object of comparison," helping to throw light on the human condition. In any case the works of Rousseau, Vercors, and Čapek show how much in the realm of conjecture and even fantasy, and how open to alternative conjectures, the theory of evolution leaves the details of primitive or protohuman forms of life.

Wittgenstein, too, is given to conjecture about forms of life. Consider the "primitive languages" which Wittgenstein invites us to imagine in *PI* 2–19. The idea of *PI* 19 is that we might imagine a "language" by imagining any one of the various language-games as the *whole* language of its speakers, or of a tribe. The "languages" thus imagined would be objects of comparison:

> Our clear and simple language-games are not preparatory studies for a future regularization of language—as it were first approximations, ignoring friction and air-resistance. The language-games are rather set up as *objects of comparison* which are meant to throw light on the facts of our language by way not only of similarities, but also of dissimilarities. (*PI* 130)

We must keep the dissimilarities in mind. *If* we can, for example, imagine people who use language only in connection with their building activity and who remain silent in all their other activities—which Black (1979, 346) says it is not easy to do—we must necessarily conceive of them as people whose whole life differs markedly from ours—and differs far more radically than the life of bedouins or Eskimos. With respect to each language-game, or speech activity, conceived in this way as a *whole* language, we can see that Wittgenstein's comment is right on the mark, for to imagine such a "language" is to imagine a form of life—and indeed a different form of life in each case.

The builder *A* and his helper *B* seem to be human, since they are said to be builders and are said to be speaking a language. On the other hand their "language" is cruder than that of most mammals; and since it is confined to one very narrow sort of activity, the vast majority of their lives must be not only nonverbal but also in every way independent of language. The "language" consisting of only battle orders and battle reports would pose similar problems. If it is to be the *whole* language, we must assume that the speakers remain silent while going about all their other activities. There would therefore arise the question of whether the lives of these creatures would be recognizably human. The "language" consisting of nothing but questions and expressions for affirmation and denial would, like the others, be difficult to imagine because the creatures speaking the "language" would be so very odd. How would they give orders? or make reports? If the "questions" they uttered were recognizably different in these cases, then, in a profound sense, they would no longer be *questions*. Perhaps we should imagine that all those ordinary activities which involve other forms of expression—praying, giving thanks, making requests or reports, expressing hopes and fears, confessing loves and hates, accusing, avowing, and so on—would be absent from their lives. In that case the form of life of the creatures who speak this "language" would differ markedly from any human life we know.

There is another imaginary example Wittgenstein introduces in *Z* 108, which has similarities to Čapek's fictional example:

> Suppose it were a question of buying and selling creatures (anthropoid brutes) which we use as slaves. They cannot learn to talk, but the cleverer among them can be taught to do quite complicated work; and some of these creatures work 'thinkingly', others quite mechanically. For a thinking one we pay more than for one that is merely mechanically clever.

In all these cases we are confronted with forms of life different from those we know. There is no such tribe of builders, no human being who speaks only in battle or only in "questions," none of the creatures imagined by Vercors or Čapek. In connection with a much less spectacular deviation from human life, Wittgenstein takes note of this absence:

> Suppose a human being never learnt the expression "I was on the point of . . ." or "I was just going to . . ." and could not learn their use? A man can after all think a good deal without thinking *that*. He can master a great field of language-games without mastering this one.
>
> But isn't it odd that among all the diversity of mankind we do not encounter defective humans of this sort? Or are such people just to be found among the feeble-minded, only it is not closely enough observed which uses of language such people are capable of and which not? (*Z* 43)

Perhaps, for some reason that is not clear, there could be no such (normal) human being. Probably some of the other fantasies don't really make sense. But fantasy need not make sense. Wittgenstein proposes imagining a "four-dimensional cube," and then remarks: "That one can 'imagine' something does not mean that it makes sense to say it" (*Z* 249–50). On this basis we can easily imagine different forms of life in all these fictional cases, and compare them with our form of life.

Our form of life is distinguished from the multitude of animal forms of life by mastery of the use of language, in which it is unique in the natural world. It is distinguished from the multitude of imaginary forms of life by its complexity and by being found in the natural world. In contrast to these two multitudes, there is in fact a single human form of life.

There is, by contrast, nothing hypothetical or conjectural about the forms of life of natural history, such as those Wittgenstein notes in *PI* 23 and 25. They are given to us in experience, and we experience them as part of what simply has to be accepted. Dogs, cats, and raccoons not only have different appearances but different forms of life. One small aspect is their different ways of moving. An experienced observer can tell from two or three steps the animal takes whether it is a dog or a cat or a raccoon. That is to say, details such as characteristic ways of moving and characteristic activities are given along with the form of life. And they are given as fixed, as Wittgenstein notes or implies in the final three of the seven passages quoted above—not given as necessarily so, as if they had to be the way they are, but as fixed. Except in fairy tales, where I deliberately dissociate my thoughts from my experience, I can no more conceive my dog suddenly behaving like a cat than I can conceive him discussing romantic poetry.

It is because they belong to an entirely different language-game that the certainties of natural history which contribute to the framework of our thought do not clash with the defeasible hypotheses of the theory of evolution.

6.   A Main Thrust of Wittgenstein's Work

It remains to consider why Wittgenstein speaks of 'form of life' to refer to what is *common* to human beings, and why he cannot mean, in accordance with the usage of Spranger and others, to be referring to human differences. The reason is that his concern, like Kant's, is how it is possible at all for us to have the sort of lives and experiences that are typical for us. Where he does discuss individual and cultural differences, as in *Vermischte Bemerkungen* and in his remarks on Frazer's *Golden Bough*, it is to plumb the full range of the possibilities of "this complicated form of life," rather than to draw any philosophical conclusions from the differences he notes. His discussions of language-games, of meaning, of hopes and fears, of science and mathematics, of religion, of knowledge and certainty, and so forth, all focus on what is distinctively human—and on how it is related to mind, to behavior, and to language. This is true even in his discussion of pain, a feeling we have in common with every sentient being: "the verbal expression of pain replaces crying and does not describe it" (*PI* 244); this, too, he might have said, is part of our natural history.

It is beyond all reasonable dispute that Wittgenstein is neither a mentalist nor a behaviorist, and that the distinctive phenomena he discusses depend on the use of language. Much of his discussion goes into intriguing subtleties of language and speech because these details are at the heart of the phenomena. That is to say, the details of the distinctive phenomena hang more closely together with the details of the uses of language than with independently certifiable details of mental processes or of overt behavior. So our form of life is determined by the capacity to use language. If a further "question" is asked about the status of language, Wittgenstein insists that neither science nor metaphysics can provide an answer. The only proper response to the question—and it would not be an answer, because it would be a descriptive rather than an explanatory response—would be by reference to the common behavior of mankind, that is, to our form of life.

Given the predominance of conceptual and metaphysical explanations in the history of Western philosophy, this is a brilliant innovation. The innovation is not entirely without precedent, given similar ideas of Ibn Khaldun, Condillac, Peirce, Dewey, and others—including even Kant. But the existence of precedents hardly impugns the brilliance and originality of Wittgenstein's work. It is evident in his development of language-games, at the beginning of the *Investigations,* as a tool for analysis, as well as in his insistence (*PI* 124, 126, 211, 217, 485, 654) that the uses of language which structure our lives can only be accepted, not justified or explained. It is no wonder, then, that natural history, the most purely descriptive of the sciences (if it is a science), should provide the very general facts which enable us to characterize forms of life. Within that perspective the forms of life which are given are canine, leonine, human, feline, etc.

One may, of course, use the expression "form of life" in the manner of Spranger, Winch, and Fischer rather than that of the *Philosophical Investigations.* One might even eliminate the concept by identifying *Lebensform* and *Sprachspiel* in the manner of Hilmy. No one can monopolize words, and Wittgenstein himself was particularly anxious to avoid jargon. But to suppose that Wittgenstein means to refer to those transient cultural variations that separate humans, rather than to those conditions common to us all, is more than a small error. It misrepresents the central thrust of Wittgenstein's work, which is to describe phenomena typical of the human world, as distinct from the canine world and from the worlds of imaginary humanoids. He was, of course, loath to generalize and acutely alert to differences—so much so that he once considered using as a motto for a book Shakespeare's line from *King Lear*, "I'll teach you differences." The differences which he discusses in his philosophical work, however, are not differences among individuals nor among nations and cultures. They are differences among human activities and uses of language. *These* differences do not divide humanity but are common to its diverse linguistic and cultural groups. They do not signify diverse forms of life, but rather they constitute an important aspect of "this complicated form of life" which is common to us all and which distinguishes us from animals.

It is unnecessary and misleading to suppose that Wittgenstein's use of *Lebensform* in the *Philosophical Investigations* implicitly connotes or refers to basic human differences. This is shown partly by an examination of the passages of the text where the term is used, partly by the close connection of forms of life with natural history, and partly by the general thrust of Wittgenstein's work. In particular the identification of forms of life with language-games or activities is ruled out by the text on page 174, and would in any case be a wasteful duplication of terminology. The identification of forms of life with life-styles or cultures has no basis whatever in the text, and is particularly antithetical to Wittgenstein's thought.

These conclusions, although decisive as far as they go, remain fragmentary. Certain readings of the text have been rejected; but this is not to say that no alternative readings will work, nor that the reading given of these passages can be easily extended to other texts. Nor has the concept of 'form of life' been defined; definition would no doubt prove as problematic here as in the case of 'game' or 'language'. The points made about the concept of 'form of life'—that the traditional implications of 'form' should not be neglected, that forms of life are given as part of natural history, and that something's form of life is determined by and/or seen in its distinctive and characteristic activities—are vague, and together are insufficient to constitute a clear explanation. I am quite content with Black's conclusion that Wittgenstein's use of the term is deliberately and inextricably vague; for the present purposes the vagueness is an asset rather than a liability. Nor does it matter if forms of behavior are sometimes called 'forms of life', as would be consistent with the gloss given early in the paper, congenial to the standard view, and plausible for the passages cited from *PI* p. 226, *C&E*, and *RPP*. It does not even matter if—contrary to Malcolm, and in line with the quip from Nestroy—the idea of "form of life" is more to be scorned than cherished. The principal point is that, whatever exactly a "form of life" may be, and acknowledging that alternative forms of life may be imagined, a good reading of the texts results from the assumption that there is, as a very general fact of natural history, a single form of life common to all humankind.

16
Naturalism and the Transcendental

Belief in the causal nexus is superstition.

—*TLP* 5.1361

We had the experience but missed the meaning, and approach to the meaning restores the experience in a different form.

—T. S. Eliot

1. Problematic Terminology

Wittgenstein could not have written on this topic. The two words in the title of this chapter purport to represent philosophical doctrines, not anything in the natural world and not anything distinct or coherent enough for Wittgenstein to talk about. Wittgenstein seldom referred to such doctrines, and then generally to the effect that the supposed doctrines and the words that mean to refer to them are hopelessly confused. Both words, in their common application, are so tightly bound with epistemological assumptions that it is difficult to separate out their specifically metaphysical import, as must be done to appreciate Wittgenstein's challenge to epistemology. I make the effort as part of my interest, evident throughout this work, in spelling out (as he himself rarely did) Wittgenstein's relevance to aspects of contemporary philosophy.

Albert Schweitzer's call for a return from dogmatic to naturalistic philosophy, cited at the head of chapter fourteen, dates from another era. Naturalism has for at least half a century been nearly indistinguishable from scientism. To the metaphysical idea that everything real is part of the natural world, and that there is therefore no nonnatural or supernatural reality, has been added the epistemological doctrine that every question about life or the world, or even about their meaning, is amenable to scientific inquiry if it is meaningful at all, and that any meaningful statement must in principle be scientifically certifiable. Very often the epistemological dimension is primary, in conformity with the casual assumption of our three centuries of Cartesian philosophy that epistemology is always primary in philosophy. Consider, for example, Stampe and Fodor:

> Representation is an altogether 'natural' relation; there is nothing essentially conventional about it. There is nothing essentially mentalistic about it, it *may* be a wholly physical relation. Neither is there anything essentially *semantic* about it, in the narrower (proper) sense of the term. (Stampe 1979, 87)
>
> I want a *naturalized* theory of meaning; a theory that articulates, in nonsemantic and nonintentional terms, sufficient conditions for one bit of the world to *be about* (to express, represent, or be true of) another bit. (Fodor 1987, 98)

The demand for "sufficient conditions" is an epistemological demand, the epistemological demand that any *meaningful* statement be subject to scientific scrutiny. Stampe's demand for representation to be a "natural" relation, even while recognizing that representation will then not be "semantic" in the "proper" sense of the term, is a broader and more basic demand for a *causal* (scientific) account of denotative meaning. The requirements put on any acceptable definition of 'synonymy' by Quine (1953) in "Two Dogmas of Empiricism" could be taken as another specialized manifestation of a broad and all-inclusive scientistic naturalism, as the later writings of Quine make evident.

What Keil (1993, 23–33) calls "American Naturalism of the 40's" is already blatantly scientistic, affording little opportunity for even thinking of naturalism without an epistemological commitment to the unlimited application of scientific method. Thus, for example, Dewey, Nagel, Edel, and Hook (all cited from Keil):

> [Naturalism demands] the application of scientific methods of inquiry in the field of human social subject matter. (Dewey 1944, 3)
>
> [Naturalism] professes to accept the methods employed by the various empirical sciences for obtaining knowledge about the world. (Nagel 1944, 211)
>
> Reliance on scientific method, together with an appreciation of the primacy of matter and the pervasiveness of change, I take to be the

central points of naturalism as a philosophic outlook. . . . present-day naturalism is bound to emphasize the need for extending empirical or scientific method to the treatment of values. (Edel 1944, 65)

Despite the variety of specific doctrines which naturalists have professed from Democritus to Dewey, what unites them all is the whole-hearted acceptance of scientific method as the only reliable way of reaching truth about the world of nature, society, and man. The least common denominator of all historic naturalisms, therefore, is not so much a set of specific doctrines as the method of scientific or rational empiricism. (Hook 1944, 45)

Naturalism cannot be identified with scientism, as is commonly done, if Wittgenstein is to be seen as working out a new version of naturalism. Fortunately it need not be identified with scientism. In his 1983 Woodbridge Lectures (Strawson 1985), Peter Strawson complained of this all-too-common identification and proposed to distinguish "liberal or catholic" naturalism from "strict or reductive" naturalism (37ff.), the latter being the scientistic version. Strawson adopts the softer version, citing the precedent of Hume and Wittgenstein, partly on Hume's grounds that sceptical arguments are "powerless against the forces of nature" (13). Keil (1993) has also given persuasive grounds for reconsidering naturalism, though more through a critique of doctrines and paradoxes than through a critique of the concept itself. In the remainder of this chapter I shall use the term 'naturalism' to refer to the metaphysical doctrine that nothing is ultimately real other than that which is found in the natural world. If Wittgenstein shared that thought, as I think he did, he conceived the crux as a matter of either "grammar" or "natural history" rather than of science, and hence perhaps not a doctrine at all. In any case, what is given as grammar or natural history is and must be exempt from the scrutiny of science, and just as exempt from scientific support (confirmation) as from scientific scepticism.

The idea of the transcendental is as difficult as that of naturalism or natural history. The underlying perennial problem is how to accommodate the phenomena of meaning and understanding, a problem central to the work of both Kant and Wittgenstein and discussed brilliantly by Hubert Schwyzer in *The Unity of Understanding,* to which I have referred in chapter three. The force of the dualities in the very different (although historically related) dualisms of Kant and Frege meant to Wittgenstein, from the beginning to the end of his philosophical career, that there must be more than one dimension in any reality he recognized. There is, for him, no metaphysical reality other than the natural world (characterized as the "totality of facts" in the *Tractatus*), but we can and do consider and respond to the facts in different ways. Scientism cannot allow these further dimensions, for they involve cognitive methods other than the scientific. From the point of view of scientistic naturalism Wittgenstein is an enigma. His philosophy is both naturalistic and not naturalistic—which means that it is neither naturalistic nor not naturalistic. That is to say, the conception of scientistic naturalism prevents us from even seeing what Wittgenstein is up to. It will continue to serve as philosophical blinders unless and until we split apart the metaphysical from the epistemological ideas that are so comfortably and uncritically amalgamated in the common idea of naturalism. Human action is part of the natural world but transcends the scientific world, and something other than scientific methodology is necessary to describe the variety of human language-games.

It is the powerful dualities inherited from Kant, Schopenhauer, and Frege, particularly the need to recognize both meaning (false propositions) and truth as well as both necessity and contingency, that require some sort of cognition that transcends that of empirical science. The distinction between natural history and natural science, discussed in chapter nine, is indispensable to this line of thought. Since his naturalism derives from natural history rather than from natural science, there is immediately a sense in which the naturalism contains an element of the transcendental: it transcends knowledge, or natural science. Just as Kant restricted knowledge to make room for belief, so Wittgenstein restricts science to make room for natural history and grammar. This, to be sure, is not what Kant meant by 'transcendental', but it is a useful result within the larger project; I will have more to say about the sense of the expression later. The important thing to see at the outset is that a "soft" conception of naturalism, taking its lead from natural history rather than from scientific method, leaves room for something "transcendental" that is in no way "nonnatural" or supernatural.

There is, therefore, something transcendental in Wittgenstein's later philosophy, as in the *Tractatus,* in a sense derived from the sense in which Kant believed space, time, and causality to be objects of transcendental rather than empirical cognition. Let me review briefly points made in previous chapters. Critical Philosophy aims not simply at criticizing other philosophies, for *every* philosophy does that. It mainly aims at overcoming the usual philosophical controversies by renouncing criteria of significance that have not been shown to be justified. This aim raises a genuine and profound problem, the problem of how, if at all, such a criterion can be justified. For it seems that *something* must be taken for granted, or accepted as *given,* to get started at all; and if a critical criterion is not (with admitted dogmatism) to be taken for granted, then it would seem that its significance could only be certified by itself, with the obvious threat of vicious circularity. That is indeed the strategy—and it turns out to be more robust than the futile bootstrap operation its simplified description seems to imply. The idea is to take for granted something wholly nonphilosophical but distinctively human (factual judgments, moral judgments, everyday language, and so on), and then derive one's critical criterion from a description of how *these* things are possible. Wittgenstein's *Tractatus* was a failed attempt at reviving Critical Philosophy. It was an attempt because its criterion of significance was drawn from the account of how sentences are possible, that is to say, from the description of what a sentence (*Satz*) is. It was a failed attempt because it was, by its own lights, nonsense. Wittgenstein's later philosophy, on the other hand, successfully revives Critical Philosophy. What Wittgenstein takes for granted in the *Philosophical Investigations* is different from what is taken for granted by Kant or in the *Tractatus.* He takes for granted that we humans speak languages, that speaking a language means having mastered innumerable language-games, that grammar is the description (*not* explanation) of languages in terms of the rules which make them possible (constitutive rules), and that making grammatical remarks (e.g., while instructing children) is one of the language-games that is *universal,* albeit not primitive.

On the basis of these considerations it is not unreasonable to take grammar and the knowledge of grammar—especially that part of grammar which is invariant for different languages, as well as recognition of our complicated form of life—as being at the same time (1) a fact of natural history, (2) the principal characteristic which distinguishes the human form of life, and (3) the source of the critical criterion from which arises Wittgenstein's brand of Critical Philosophy. All these points are part of what I assume for present purposes, having argued for them in previous chapters.

The problems left to consider are whether, and in what sense, Wittgenstein's reliance on natural phenomena and natural history constitutes a form of naturalism, and to what extent this grammar and such a *Lebensform,* or our cognition of them, can or should be considered as something transcendental. These problems do not arise capriciously, but on the one hand from the mystery and awe which often surrounds discussions of grammar and *Lebensform,* combined with the inescapable fact that they are phenomena of our natural world; and on the other from a natural query about the parallel with Kant's Critical Philosophy, which had (and arguably had to have) a transcendental element.

If we assume, as is commonly done, that there is a necessary opposition between what is natural and what is transcendent or transcendental, then the questions posed can be answered in the negative without going further. What is "natural" in the Wittgenstein-ian *Weltanschauung* is everything encountered in the natural world rather than everything amenable to science; this corresponds well enough to common usage as well as to that of philosophers such as Aristotle and Schweitzer. What is "transcendental" is not the supernat-ural but what lies within nature and outside the reach of science; that is to say, natural phenomena not amenable to experiential knowledge, scientific proof, experimental refutation, empirical justification, and so on. The idea is that we recognize features of the natural world as elements or categories that enter our language and our activities as primitives, not questioned and not to be questioned, and that provide the basis or the framework for subsequent empirical investigations.

The idea that what is to be transcended is empirical knowledge and scientific methodology is similar to Kant's idea that he was restricting knowledge (*das Wissen*) to make room for belief (*das Glauben*). As Beck has pointed out (1965, 16ff.), he did not restrict or deny *reason.* Wittgenstein's wider category is facts of nature rather than reason, and therefore Wittgenstein's philosophy is of the sort that Schweitzer called for, whereas Kant's is not; but the category he denies or restricts is also *knowledge.* Clear evidence for this is seen in *PI* 246: "It can't be said of me at all that I *know* that I am in pain. . . ." It is, of course, not that I *don't* know it. On the contrary, it cannot be said of me *either* that I don't know that I am in pain (*PI* 408). The point is rather, as argued in chapter ten, that the *category* of knowledge does not apply here. The clearest evidence of the parallel between Wittgenstein's denial and Kant's denial of *Wissen* to make room for *Glauben* is the remark " 'Knowledge' and 'certainty' belong to different *categories*" (*OC* 308).

It has often been doubted (recently, for example, by Walker and by Bencivenga) whether any sense can possibly be made of Kant's Critical Philosophy if one excludes its transcendental aspects. Perhaps this is a feature of Kant's version of Critical Philosophy, rather than of Critical

Philosophy in itself. Such a restriction, however, seems implausible, since it seems central to the aim and strategy that there be a sharp distinction between what is known or cognized apriori and what is known empirically. Since Critical Philosophy aims to explain the *possibility* of empirical fact, its apriori objects must then be forms or possibilities of some sort. Grammar (whose objects are the possible employments of language) and *Lebensformen* (which both inhere in the world as we find it and at the same time involve possibilities of *different* actual behavior) seem Wittgenstein's analog of Kant's objects of transcendental knowledge, such as space, time, and causality.

So there is good reason to consider whether facts of natural history might also be transcendental. The transcendence at issue is going beyond the empirical or the epistemic without going beyond the natural world, and the naturalism is purely metaphysical and purely descriptive (in contrast to, say, Quine's or Dewey's), being associated with natural history rather than natural science.

2.   Wittgenstein's Naturalism

A great deal has already been said about Wittgenstein's naturalism in previous chapters of this work. In chapter one I pointed out that the Kantian character of his central question, "How is language possible?" presupposes a commitment to the world of plain fact, both in the *Tractatus* and in his later work. In chapter four I showed the similarity of his description of different psychological phenomena with Aristotle's categories, and argued that through this analogy he shares Aristotle's naturalism. In chapters nine and fourteen I made extensive reference to Wittgenstein's use of the concept of natural history to express his commitment to the natural world we all encounter. Naturalism is so pervasive in Wittgenstein's work, particularly his later work, that it is astonishing that it can be denied—a feat that is only accomplished by means of the perverse identification of naturalism with scientism.

Grammar, language-games, and forms of life are facts of natural history. Perhaps that means, as Hunter (1968) and Malcolm (1986) have suggested, that they are something organic or biological. They are surely subject to neither justification nor doubt, and are among those very general facts to which Wittgenstein calls our attention at critical junctures in his thought.

Early in the *Investigations*, shortly after his discussion of the builders and other artificial language-games, he says the following:

> It is sometimes said that animals do not talk because they lack the mental capacity. And this means: "they do not think, and that is why they do not talk." But—they simply do not talk. Or to put it better: they do not use language—if we except the most primitive forms of language.— Commanding, questioning, recounting, chatting, are as much a part of our natural history as walking, eating, drinking, playing. (*PI* 25)

Wittgenstein is here distinguishing the human form of life from others. That humans use language in complicated ways, whereas animals do not, is part of "what has to be accepted, the given" (*PI* p. 226). There is no question of justifying this fact of natural history, nor of challenging it; and in this passage Wittgenstein rules out the only plausible explanatory account for it, namely, one which refers to mental capacity. It is a fact of natural history that there are many human languages, and also a fact of natural history that the mastery of any one of them gives a person the capacity to do the sort of things mentioned in *PI* 25. So it is not *which* language a person speaks that determines his form of life, but rather the mastery of the use of *some language or other* (*PI* p. 174). Or to put it in words which echo *TLP* 6.44: given the world as it actually is, what determines our form of life is not *how* we use words and sentences, but *that* we use them.

In his last book (1986) Malcolm endorses the central place he gave to 'form of life' in his review (1954) of the first edition of the *Investigations*. In the previous chapter I distanced myself from that high evaluation of the concept, preferring the more deflationary stance of Nestroy and Black. Here I want to turn again to Malcolm, this time to try to understand the relation between the natural and the transcendental in this "landmark" of Wittgenstein's later philosophy. Here, again, is what Malcolm says at the end of the book:

> Another landmark of the second philosophy is the notion of '*a form of life*'. This expression is found in natural history, where different species of animals are described in terms of posture, locomotion, habitat, feeding, breeding, social organization, the sounds they make, the way they play. Some animals walk on two feet, some on four; some have tails; some live in trees, some in water. Wittgenstein says that what he is providing are "really remarks on the natural history of human beings" (*PI* 415); that "Ordering, questioning, recounting, chatting, are as much a part of our natural history as walking, eating, drinking, playing."

(*PI* 25) Using language in many different ways (different "language-games") belongs to human natural history as much as living in trees belongs to the natural history of monkeys. A language-game is language interwoven with activity, action, *doing* (*PI* 7). "To imagine a language means to imagine a form of life." (*PI* 19) (1986, 237-238)

Malcolm goes on immediately to say, "In seeking to clarify the meaning of some bit of language, Wittgenstein persistently asks—with what actions is it joined? What role does it play in our lives?" So meaning does not require another domain of reality; describing characteristic activities that are aspects of a form of life is one way of responding to a query about the *meaning* of what is said or done. "Im Anfang war die Tat." Since the clarification is achieved by means of a *description* rather than a definition or analysis or justification, natural history is an important part of Wittgenstein's aim to "do away with all *explanation*" (*PI* 109).

Malcolm makes two very useful points about the role of natural history in providing answers to questions about what something means. One is that it "brings requests for explanations and justifications—for *reasons*—to a stop!" (238) This is correct. Reasons and justifications invite further probing. It is part of their grammar that one *can* always ask another "Why?" A statement of the form "That's the way it is" does not invite such further probing; we use this form of statement precisely to rule it out. It should be further noted that grammatical remarks play the same role of bringing requests of explanations and justifications to an end. This observation makes Wittgenstein's association of grammar with natural history less bizarre than it first appears. As Malcolm observes, "The logic of our language is based on many facts of nature, including human nature" (239). Such facts include ones that might occur in grammatical remarks, such as that we just do speak or calculate in this or that way:

> In certain circumstances, for example, we regard a calculation as sufficiently checked. What gives us the right to do so? Experience? May that not have deceived us? Somewhere we must be finished with justification, and then there remains the statement that *this* is how we calculate. (*OC* 212)

Since it is generally by means of grammatical remarks that we clarify meaning or explain meaning, and since these remarks report aspects of our natural history, there is a naturalistic way to describe and explain meaning, even if meanings themselves are not naturalistic phenomena.

The other point Malcolm makes is that it is *only* through such naturalistic accounts that we can come to understand words and sentences:

> The third landmark [of Wittgenstein's second philosophy] . . . is the conception that words and sentences can be understood only in terms of the circumstances, the contexts, the life-surroundings, in which they are spoken. (239)

What we see here is an alternative to understanding that proceeds in terms of analysis and definition, as well as to the Kantian conception of understanding that requires subsumption under conceptual categories. Analysis and definition are tools of a scientistic or epistemological naturalism, and the articulation of an alternative to scientism, begun in the *Tractatus,* was one of the most persistent and difficult of the tasks Wittgenstein undertook in his later philosophy. I pointed out in chapter five that it is one of his least appreciated achievements. As Malcolm adds after the passage just cited, "This is a teaching that has not, for the most part, been taken in by present-day philosophy."

By being based on natural history rather than natural science, Wittgenstein's naturalism is set in a broader and more liberal framework than that provided by epistemology, and is therefore free from the regress problem and the unanswerable scepticism that necessarily plague what Strawson calls "strict or reductive" naturalism. Like Strawson's, therefore, his naturalism naturally leads into what Strawson calls "descriptive metaphysics," Wittgenstein's version of which I have described in some detail in chapters four and fourteen. Wittgenstein's naturalism is, however, richer than Strawson's, because his natural history of humans comprises grammar, language-games, and our complicated form of life. These human activities involve norms. Some of the norms of language are arbitrary, a highly liberating insight that (as Harris [1988] makes wonderfully clear) Wittgenstein shares with Saussure even though the two worked it out independently. Other norms, however, are so tightly woven into the fabric of our form of life that they are both culturally invariant and seemingly indispensable—as, for example, that each normal human being masters the use of a language, thereby acquiring access to innumerable language-games, each of which is a distinctively human activity. This naturalism therefore contains the seeds of normativity and of a certain sort of transcendence of the merely empirical and merely factual.

3. Senses of Transcendence

That our form of life differs from that of animals, that there is a single human form of life, that this complicated form of life is determined by the mastery of the use of language and by the consequent capacity to enter into countless language-games, that forms of life and their distinguishing characteristics are given and just have to be accepted—these are not remarks that can be verified by either analysis or scientific inquiry. Nor are they in any way doubtful, although it would be rash to assert that they *could* not be doubted. They are therefore, at the least, certainties which we never doubt and which escape notice only because they are always right in front of our eyes. Wittgenstein resists or avoids the idea that there might be something transcendental in this "comfortable certainty":

> Now I would like to regard this certainty, not as something akin to hastiness or superficiality, but as a form of life. (That is very badly expressed and probably badly thought as well.)
>
> But that just means that I want to conceive it as something that lies beyond being justified or unjustified; as it were, as something animal. (*OC* 358–59)

Nonetheless it cannot be denied that these certainties resemble synthetic apriori truths—synthetic because they are about the world and are contingent (and hence clearly not analytic), and apriori because they are presupposed by science and are immune to its challenges. Just as Wittgenstein's grammar concerns matters which grammarians ignore, and is not easy (as we saw in chapter fourteen) to distinguish from traditional metaphysics, so also his natural history treats facts which naturalists ignore, and presents parallel similarities with traditional metaphysics. There are at least three senses in which these remarks about grammar and forms of life might be considered transcendental.

The first sense of the transcendental is inherent in various features of grammar and natural history. One such feature which the remarks about form of life and other grammatical remarks share is that they "lie beyond being justified or unjustified" (*OC* 359), and hence beyond scientific challenge. They are "what has to be accepted, the given" (*PI* p. 226). This fixity is connected with their not being subject to doubt. In a certain sense, I cannot imagine the opposite; that is, I cannot take seriously the idea of my not being human, nor there being humans who do not exhibit the common human behavior. That is to say, such remarks have a certainty comparable to the certainty of Moore's famous assertions, which Wittgenstein discusses in *On Certainty*. Because "'Knowledge' and 'certainty' belong to different *categories*" (*OC* 308), these statements have nothing to do with scientific statements about evolution, neither as confirmation nor as contradiction. One of the familiar senses in which something can be considered transcendental is that it lies, in just this manner, beyond being justified or refuted by experience.

Another feature of statements of grammar and of natural history, including those about form of life, is that they neither require nor admit of explanation. This is not easy to explain, because as soon as one proposes specific forms of words, it seems possible to think of a scientific project to seek an answer. For example, it seems at first that we can do nothing with a question like "Why does a dog behave like a dog?" or "Why do human beings use language?" This is in part because we cannot easily imagine the alternatives which an explanatory answer would be meant to rule out: how else would a dog behave, except as a dog? Yet, as Jonathan Bennett pointed out in an earlier discussion of this chapter, the words can easily be construed as shorthand for a series of scientific investigations; for example, about why dogs pant, why they point, why they bark, why they urinate on trees and shrubs, and so forth. And Chomsky and Fodor might be thought of as trying to answer some of the corresponding questions about humans and language. It would be absurd—even given all of Wittgenstein's well-known hostility to science—to suppose Wittgenstein to be ruling out such canine or linguistic research. The point is rather that any such research presupposes beliefs that neither require nor admit of justification, among which are beliefs which enable us to recognize and identify dogs, cats, dolphins, and humans as different kinds of animals, as enjoying different forms of life—and these latter statements are ones which scientists and others accept without scrutiny or explanation.

A third feature of these statements is that we do not accept the findings of scientific research as overruling them. A scientist's claim that dogs really have a feline rather than a canine form of life would remain as unacceptable as Eddington's claim (see Stebbing, passim) that cobblestones and oak planks are not really solid.

It is, as I pointed out in the previous chapter, because they belong to an entirely different language-game that the certainties of natural history, which figure in Wittgensteinian grammar and contribute to the framework of our thought, do not clash with the defeasible hypotheses of scientific theory. That is the first, and weakest, sense in which they are transcendental.

The second sense in which Wittgenstein's grammar and forms of life and Wittgensteinian natural history are transcendental is that they are requirements of our understanding anything at all. Both grammar (that is, established language-games, *uses* of language) and form of life are requirements for understanding linguistic signs. To imagine a language, one must imagine how it is employed—that means not only to imagine how speaking the language is integral to certain activities, but also how these activities are integral to the lives of the speakers. For this, in turn, one must imagine the *form* of life of the speakers, which will comprise all that is or might be or might have been possible for them. So "If a lion could talk, we could not understand him" (*PI* p. 223), since the form of life of a lion includes no characteristic activities in which words or sentences play a role at all.

Although vague, because they lack a precise criterion or definition, the characteristic activities of a species give substance to its form of life; and therefore, "The common behavior of mankind (*die gemeinsame menschliche Handlundsweise*) is the reference system by means of which we interpret an unknown language" (*PI* 206). These certainties, requirements of communicating and understanding at all, are among the hinges on which our ordinary thought swings back and forth: "If I want the door to turn, the hinges must stay put" (*OC* 343). That the hinges stay put is a transcendental requirement. Grammar and forms of life are similarly a transcendental requirement, even though they are found in the natural world.

It is worth noting that this second sense of the transcendental is connected not just with what we see or what we are "given" but with what we *do;* that is, with meaning and with characteristic human activities. The natural world by itself consists of a totality of contingent facts—Spinoza's world without the necessity, one might say. Our ordinary human experience, on the other hand, is filled with modalities —with meanings and possibilities and necessities that go beyond the contingent facts and cannot possibly be inferred from them. It is not that these features belong to an entirely different reality. It is rather that they emerge from our *acting* in and on the world around us rather than merely observing it. There is undoubtedly an affinity with pragmatism, as Rorty (1979) emphasized, in this feature of Wittgenstein's thinking, as well as a more Continental echo of Goethe's remark in *Faust,* "Im

Anfang war die Tat," and of the basic duality with which Kant begins between the receptive (passive) and spontaneous (active) dimensions of our cognition.

The third sense in which grammar and forms of life are transcendental is that they are reflexive, or self-referential in the sense of Bubner; that is, they constitute a requirement for understanding in general, which is at the same time also a requirement for themselves. Wittgenstein says in this connection "My *life* consists in my being content to accept many things" (*OC* 344), and he refers to this absence of doubt—not absence of dubitability, but simple absence of doubt—as *"comfortable* certainty" (*OC* 357). I suppose that two persons might have different lives in part by being content to accept divergent sets of things; which is, no doubt, contingently true for any two of us. On the other hand a person would have a different *form* of life from us only if never content to accept anything. There are not any such persons, any more than there are any of Wittgenstein's builders or weird woodsellers, and it is difficult to see how there could be any. Our comfortable certainty would then seem to be self-referential in the sense of Bubner, and therefore transcendentally necessary.

The reflexivity is perhaps easier to see if we consider that being "comfortable" about the language we are speaking is one familiar form of the certainty in question. Grammar is simply a general description of the language; but at the same time it provides a criterion for the sense of what is said, and it "tells what kind of object anything is" (*PI* 373). Among other things, grammar will tell us what grammar is, and making grammatical remarks is among the countless language-games that make up language. If being comfortable about the language means accepting its grammatical criteria, that seems obviously self-referential—and self-referential in a way (*pace* Russell) that avoids any hint of vicious circularity.

4.   Wittgenstein vs. Quine and Dewey

The transcendental side of forms of life is not easy to focus in a clear and comprehensive picture, given Wittgenstein's insistence that they are, "as it were, something animal" and are to be found in the natural world. It is clear, however, that this hesitant metaphysics reflects a deep and abiding concern, which Wittgenstein shared with Kant and others, to characterize the sort of lives and experiences which are typical for us. Here we can see a continuity in Wittgenstein's philosophical method, with only the terminology changed, from the *Tractatus* through to *Zettel*. The key is that his detailed examination focuses on particular cases, but his interest lies in the phenomenon in general:

> A particular mode of signifying may be unimportant but it is always important that it is a *possible* mode of signifying. And that is generally so in philosophy: again and again the individual case turns out to be unimportant, but the possibility of each individual case discloses something about the essence of the world. (*TLP* 3.3421)
>
> How could human behavior be described? Surely only by sketching the actions of a variety of humans, as they are all mixed up together. What determines our judgment, our concepts and reactions, is not what *one* man is doing *now*, an individual action, but the whole hurly-burly of human actions, the background against which we see any action. (*Z* 567)

In the latter passage the issue is introduced with a question about how to describe human behavior. He obviously means human behavior in general, not just particular bits of it (although in the final analysis that is all one will be able to do). That is to say, it is a question about how to describe *die gemeinsame menschliche Handlundsweise*—and so, presumably, about how to describe our form of life. In neither this passage nor the one from the *Tractatus* does Wittgenstein offer even the slightest glimmer of a way to describe the general phenomenon (human behavior, the essence of the world) *directly,* by references to its common features or defining characteristics. And *a fortiori* neither our "complicated form of life" nor any of the other objects of the natural world can be introduced and explained by means of an analytic definition; the famous attack on essences in the *Philosophical Investigations* is indeed primarily an attack on just such definitions, rather than on common features or forms of life. The general phenomenon is rather to be described *indirectly,* by describing individual instances—not because of the indispensability of *these* instances nor their intrinsic importance, for other instances would serve as well; but to indicate, to characterize ostensively, the range of cases that count as instances of the general phenomenon.

Wittgenstein's discussions of language-games, of meaning, of hopes and fears, of science and mathematics, of religion, of knowledge and certainty, and so forth, all focus on what is distinctively human. He describes it indirectly, by characterizing particular human activities. He is constantly alert to differences, and loath to generalize. The differences which he mainly discusses, however, are not differences among individuals nor among human groups. They are differences among human activities and uses of language. *These* differences do not divide humanity, but are common to its diverse linguistic and cultural groups. They do not signify diverse forms of life, but rather they constitute an important aspect of "this complicated form of life" which is common to us all and which distinguishes us from animals. This transcendentality is only part of what has traditionally been thought of as transcendence; or it is perhaps more radically different from the tradition because of its unequivocal dissociation from epistemology. It is equivalent to not being able to prove or explain everything that must be accepted as fact. Anything ultimately "given" is thus bound to be transcendental.

Wittgenstein's natural history is indissolubly connected with the transcendence that is intrinsic to his philosophy. The transcendence is intrinsic because of Wittgenstein's "semantical Kantianism," to which Hintikka (1981) called attention. It is not just the texts that Hintikka cites that assure that meaning is transcendental but the very approach to philosophy that distinguishes Wittgenstein's work from beginning to end. Central to his work—central to what he draws from Frege as well as to his revision of Kant's version of critical philosophy—is the conviction that 'meaning' requires an entirely different basis, and must be pursued and explicated by an entirely different language-game from 'knowledge' (whose paradigm is scientific understanding). When we begin with natural history, with recognition of the facts that we fail to notice only because they are always in front of our eyes, his distinctive and persistent conviction on this point requires that there *must* be more than one way to deal with, or come to terms with, or understand, those facts. Wittgenstein's insistence on the priority of natural history over natural science, of certainty over knowledge, of deeds over words, and of practices over rules all come to focus on the point of intersection of naturalism and the transcendental—that there is no reality other than that of the natural world, but there are significant certainties and other modal features about that world that are both presupposed by science and also exempt from its questioning or confirmation.

By means of natural history Wittgenstein identifies ideas or propositions that are exempt from science, from theoretical explanation, from analytic definition, and from epistemic inquiry. This move distinguishes Wittgenstein's later philosophy from his own earlier work, from analytic philosophy in general, from Kant, and from the standard forms of American naturalism represented by Dewey and Quine.

His discussion in *On Certainty* of certain specific propositions, those put forth by Moore in his two famous articles, marks a great change from the way, in the *Tractatus,* he earlier kept the basic primitives hidden and unspecified. If they are exempt from definition and explanation, it is no wonder that, like *Lebensform,* they remain somewhat mysterious. The mystery, however, is much reduced. For one thing, they are—although necessarily vague—identified and specified, which is already a great demystification from the unspecified (and probably unspecifiable) objects and states of affairs of the *Tractatus.* In addition they enjoy a certainty which stems from their always being before our eyes, and from their being a part of natural history. The mystery remains, to the extent that it still exists, encapsulated in the undeniable fact that 'grammar' and 'form of life' are not well-defined concepts. Indeed not. There's the rub. Definitions are analytic by their very nature, and the call for well-defined concepts is a distinctive rubric of analytic philosophy. Wittgenstein's later philosophy is resoundingly anti-analytic. We must learn to *do* things, we must be trained in various uses of language, before we can ask or offer definitions. It is only for philosophers who must begin with definitions that Wittgenstein's grammar and natural history remain an unfathomable mystery.

I have cited Dewey earlier in this chapter and Quine in chapter two. In casting them as the alternatives to Wittgenstein's naturalism I do not mean to refer to any specific passages or arguments in their work. The point could be made by referring to various other philosophers, and I have named these two because they are great landmarks in the American philosophical scene. Each advocates naturalism and is recognized to be a naturalistic philosopher. Their naturalism, like the others cited at the beginning of the chapter, is thoroughly scientistic. Neither allows any fundamental division in the kinds or uses of sentences, both conceive the kind or type of a sentence to be connected with the way we know it, both allow no method other than scientific method for knowing anything, and neither allows for any propositions worth believing that are immune to scientific scrutiny. In these respects their naturalism conforms to the definition given by Arthur Danto in his article "Naturalism" in the *Encyclopedia of Philosophy:*

> Naturalism, in recent usage, is a species of philosophical monism according to which whatever exists or happens is *natural* in the sense of being susceptible to explanation through methods which, although paradigmatically exemplified in the natural sciences, are continuous from domain to domain of objects and events. (5.448)

It is just at this point that Wittgenstein might invoke the line he liked to quote from *King Lear:* "I'll teach you differences!" The central thrust of the *Philosophical Investigations* is or depends on the point with which the book begins, that there are very many different kinds of sentences, different kinds of use of language or language-games. The monism of scientistic naturalism is a monism on precisely this point, an insistence that every meaningful use of language is a scientific one. It is, as Strawson (1985) put it, reductionist where Wittgenstein is liberal. There is no room in this conception for a distinction between natural history and natural science, nor between knowledge and certainty. Nor is there any escape from the paradoxes of knowledge explained by Wolgast (1977) and in chapter ten. Wittgenstein's insistence on these differences makes eminently good sense. That language, uses of language, grammar, forms of life, language-games, and distinctly human behavior all exist in the world as we find it—these are not scientific pronouncements. That meaning changes sounds and signs from something physical and subject to science to something of a different sort, partly through phenomena of Gestalt and partly through arbitrary syntax and semantics, seems also an inescapable fact—a "transfiguration of the commonplace," to use Danto's wonderful phrase, that is as liberating as it is inescapable. Wittgenstein's treatment of grammar and form of life as natural phenomena, as facts of natural history, seems a genuine but nonreductive form of naturalism. Because it is nonreductive, elements of our world transcend science and are presupposed by science. By proposing a naturalism that incorporates elements of the transcendental, Wittgenstein challenges the conceptions we have inherited.

Wittgenstein also proposes limits to science and scientific explanation, and does so dramatically and emphatically. I have no reason to doubt that Wittgenstein worked alone to reach this conclusion, but it conforms neatly with the major achievements of twentieth-century science, and I doubt that he worked in ignorance or disdain of those achievements. I have in mind the achievements of Einstein, Planck, Heisenberg, and Gödel, each of whom demonstrated scientifically certain *limits* of scientific explanation, or of scientific theory, or of the generalization of scientific principles. Their work provides a decisive rebuttal to the Enlightenment vision of an overall Newtonian synthesis, that is, of an explanatory theory which will account for everything factual and within which natural history is replaced by natural science. Within the subdiscipline known as "philosophy of science" this rebuttal remains a simple negative, an absence of something. Scientistic naturalism is fighting a rear guard action against recognition of these limits. By resurrecting natural history as distinct from natural science, and certainty as distinct from knowledge, Wittgenstein makes a place for this absence in the larger landscape he sketches. And since he describes natural history and nonepistemic certainty as presuppositions of inquiry, that place is unquestionably "transcendental" in one of the traditional senses.

REFERENCES

Ackrill, J. L. 1963. *Aristotle's 'Categories' and 'De Interpretatione'*. Oxford: Clarendon Press.

Albritton, Rogers. 1959. On Wittgenstein's Use of the Term 'Criterion'. *Journal of Philosophy* 56:845–56.

Anscombe, G. E. M. 1959. *An Introduction to Wittgenstein's "Tractatus."* London: Hutchinson University Library.

Apel, Karl-Otto. 1973. *Die Transformation der Philosophie*. Frankfurt a.M.: Suhrkamp.

Austin, J. L. 1961. *Philosophical Papers*. Ed. J. O. Urmson and G. J. Warnock. Oxford: Clarendon Press.

———. 1963. Performative-Constative. In Charles E. Caton, ed., *Philosophy and Ordinary Language*. Urbana, Ill.: University of Illinois Press, 22–54.

———. [1962] 1975. *How to Do Things with Words*. Ed. J. O. Urmson and Marina Sbisá. 2d ed. Cambridge, Mass.: Harvard University Press.

Ayer, A. J. 1954. Can There Be a Private Language? *Proceedings of the Aristotelian Society*, supplementary volume 28: 63–76.

———. 1982. The Elementary Propositions of the *Tractatus*, in W. Leinfellner et al., eds. 1982: 419–28, referenced elsewhere.

Baker, G. P., and P. M. S. Hacker. 1984. *Scepticism, Rules and Language*. Oxford: Basil Blackwell.

Baker, Lynne Rudder. 1984. On the Very Idea of a Form of Life. *Inquiry* 27:277–89.

Beck, Lewis White. 1960. *A Commentary on Kant's "Critique of Practical Reason."* Chicago: University of Chicago Press.

————. 1965. *Studies in the Philosphy of Kant*. Indianapolis/New York: Bobbs-Merrill.

Bell, David. 1979. *Frege's Theory of Judgment*. Oxford: Clarendon Press.

Bencivenga, Ermanno. 1987. *Kant's Copernican Revolution*. New York/Oxford: Oxford University Press.

Bennett, J. F. 1966. *Kant's Analytic*. Cambridge/London: Cambridge University Press.

Benveniste, Emile. 1971. *Problems in General Linguistics*. Coral Gables, Fla.: University of Florida Press.

Beth, E. W. 1953/54. Kants Einteilung der Urteile in analytische und synthetische. *Alg. Ned. Tijds. voor Wijsbeg. en Psych.* 46:253–64.

Black, Max. 1964. *A Companion to Wittgenstein's "Tractatus."* Ithaca, N.Y.: Cornell University Press.

————. 1978. *Lebensform and Sprachspiel* in Wittgenstein's Later Work. In E. Leinfellner, et al., eds. 1978: 325–331, referenced elsewhere.

————. 1979. Wittgenstein's Language-games. *Dialectica* 33:337–53.

Block, Irving, ed. 1981. *Perspectives on the Philosophy of Wittgenstein*. Cambridge, Mass.: MIT Press.

Bradley, Raymond. 1992. *The Nature of All Being: A Study of Wittgenstein's Modal Atomism*. Oxford: Oxford University Press.

Bubner, Rüdiger. 1974. Zur Struktur eines transzendentalen Arguments. *Kantstudien* 65:15–27. This Sonderheft is the same as Funke, G., ed. 1974. *Akten des 4. Internationalen Kant-Kongresses*. Berlin/New York: de Gruyter.

————. 1975. Kant, Transcendental Arguments, and the Problem of Deduction. *Review of Metaphysics* 28:453–67.

Budd, Malcolm. 1989. *Wittgenstein's Philosophy*. London/New York: Routledge.

Caird, Edward. 1889. *The Critical Philosophy of Kant*. Glasgow: J. Maclehose.

Canfield, John V. 1981. *Wittgenstein, Language, and the World*. Amherst, Mass.: University of Massachusetts Press.

Cassirer, H. W. 1954. *Kant's First Critique*. London: Allen & Unwin.

Cavell, Stanley. 1979. *The Claim of Reason*. Oxford/New York: Oxford University Press.

Chomsky, Noam, and M. Halle. 1968. *Sound Pattern of English*. New York: Harper and Row.

Copi, I. M., and R. W. Beard, eds. 1966. *Essays on Wittgenstein's "Tractatus."* New York: Macmillan.

Corcoran, J., ed. 1974. *Ancient Logic*. Dordrecht, Netherlands: Reidel.

Curley, Edwin. 1969. *Spinoza's Metaphysics*. Cambridge, Mass.: Harvard University Press.

Danford, J. W. 1978. *Wittgenstein and Political Philosophy*. Chicago: University of Chicago Press.

Dummett, M. 1976. Frege as a Realist. *Inquiry* 19:455–68.

Engel, S. Morris. 1971. *Wittgenstein's Doctrine of the Tyranny of Language*. The Hague: Martinus Nijhoff.

Engelmann, Paul. 1967. *Letters from Wittgenstein, with a Memoir*. Trans. L. Furtmüller. Oxford: Basil Blackwell.

Finch, Henry Leroy. 1977. *Wittgenstein—The Later Philosophy: An Exposition of the* Philosophical Investigations. Atlantic Highlands, N.J.: Humanities Press.

Fischer, H. R. 1982. Wahrheit, grammatischer Satz und Lebensform: Der epistemologische Aspekt in Wittgensteins Privatsprachenargumentation. In W. Leinfellner, et al., eds. 1982: 479–82, referenced elsewhere.

———. 1987. *Sprache und Lebensform: Wittgenstein über Freud und die Geisteskrankheit*. Frankfurt am Main: Athenäum.

Fodor, Jerry. 1987. *Psychosemantics: The Problem of Meaning in the Philosophy of Mind*. Cambridge, Mass.: MIT Press.

Frege, G. 1950. *Foundations of Arithmetic*. Trans. J. L. Austin. Oxford: Basil Blackwell.

———. 1952. *Translations from the Philosophical Writings of Gottlob Frege*. Ed. and trans. Peter Geach and Max Black. Oxford: Basil Blackwell.

———. 1964. *Basic Laws of Arithmetic*. Trans. M. Furth. Berkeley, Calif.: University of California Press.

Furth, Montgomery. 1964. Introduction to Frege 1964, referenced above.

Garver, Newton, and Seung Chong Lee. 1994. *Derrida and Wittgenstein*. Philadelphia: Temple University Press.

Grene, Marjorie. 1976. *Philosophy In and Out of Europe*. Berkeley: University of California Press.

Grice, Paul, and Peter F. Strawson. [1956] 1989. In Defense of a Dogma. *Philosophical Review* 66:141–58. Reprinted in Grice, Paul, 1989: *Studies in the Ways of Words*. Cambridge, Mass.: Harvard University Press.

Griffin, James. 1964. *Wittgenstein's Logical Atomism*. Oxford: Clarendon Press.

Grossman, R. 1969. *Reflections on Frege's Philosophy*. Evanston, Ill.: Northwestern University Press.

Guyer, Paul. 1987. *Kant and the Claims of Knowledge*. London/New York: Cambridge University Press.

Hacker, Peter M. S. 1972. *Insight and Illusion: Wittgenstein on Philosophy and the Metaphysics of Experience.* Oxford: Clarendon Press.

———. 1986. *Insight and Illusion: Themes in the Philosophy of Wittgenstein.* Rev. ed. of Hacker 1972, referenced above. Oxford: Clarendon Press.

Haller, Rudolf. 1988. *Questions on Wittgenstein.* Lincoln, Nebr.: University of Nebraska Press.

Haller, R., and J. Brandl, eds. 1990. *Wittgenstein: Towards a Reevaluation: Proceedings of the 14th International Wittgenstein Symposium.* 3 vols. Vienna: Hölder-Pichler-Tempsky.

Hallett, G. 1977. *A Companion to Wittgenstein's "Philosophical Investigations."* Ithaca, N.Y.: Cornell University Press.

Harris, Roy. 1988. *Language, Saussure and Wittgenstein: How to Play Games with Words.* London: Routledge.

Hawkins, David. 1964. *The Language of Nature: An Essay in the Philosophy of Science.* San Francisco: W. H. Freeman.

Hilmy, S. Stephen. 1987. *The Later Wittgenstein: The Emergence of a New Philosophical Method.* Oxford: Basil Blackwell.

Hintikka, Jaakko. 1965. Are Logical Truths Analytic? *Philosophical Review* 74:178–203.

———. 1981. Wittgenstein's Semantical Kantianism. In *Ethics: Foundations, Problems, and Applications. Proceedings of the Fifth International Wittgenstein Symposium,* ed. E. Morscher and R. Stranzinger. Vienna: Hölder-Pichler-Tempsky, 375–90.

Hintikka, Merrill B., and Jaakko Hintikka. 1986. *Investigating Wittgenstein.* Oxford/New York: Basil Blackwell.

Hodges, Michael P. 1990. *Transcendence and Wittgenstein's "Tractatus."* Philadelphia: Temple University Press.

Householder, Fred W. 1971. *Linguistic Speculations.* London: Cambridge University Press.

Hunter, John F. M. 1968. 'Forms of Life' in Wittgenstein's *Philosophical Investigations. American Philosophical Quarterly* 5:233–43.

Ihde, Don, and R. M. Zaner, eds. 1975. *Dialogues in Phenomenology.* The Hague: Martinus Nijhoff.

Ishiguro, Hidè. 1969. The Use and Mention of Names. In Winch, ed. 1969: 20–50, referenced elsewhere.

———. 1989. Die Beziehung zwischen Welt und Sprache: Bemerkungen im Ausgang von Wittgensteins *Tractatus.* In McGuinness and Haller, eds. 1989: 49–68, referenced elsewhere.

———. 1990. Can the World Impose Logical Structure on Language? In Haller and Brandl, eds. 1990 I:21–34, referenced elsewhere.

Jakobson, R., C. G. M. Fant, and M. Halle. 1952. *Preliminaries to Speech Analysis.* Cambridge, Mass.: MIT Press.

Janik, Allen, and Stephen E. Toulmin. 1973. *Wittgenstein's Vienna.* New York: Simon and Schuster.

Kant, Immanuel. 1804. *Preisschrift über die Fortschritte der Metaphysik.* Berlin. Reprinted in the 1942 Academy edition of *Kants gesammelte Schriften* 20:253–332. Berlin: G. Reimer. Reprinted in *Weischedel,* volume 3.

———. 1954–64. (*Weischedel*) *Werke in sechs Banden.* Ed. Wilhelm Weischedel. Wiesbaden: Insel Verlag.

———. 1958. (*KdrV*) *Critique of Pure Reason.* Trans. N. Kemp Smith. New York: Modern Library.

Katz, J. J. 1966. *Philosophy of Language.* New York: Harper and Row.

Keil, Geert. 1993. *Kritik des Naturalismus.* Berlin/New York: de Gruyter.

Kemp Smith, N. 1962. *Commentary to Kant's "Critique of Pure Reason."* 2d ed. New York: Humanities Press. Originally published 1918.

Kenny, Anthony. 1973. *Wittgenstein.* Cambridge, Mass.: Harvard University Press.

———. 1984. *The Legacy of Wittgenstein.* Oxford: Basil Blackwell.

Klemke, E. D., ed. 1968. *Essays on Frege.* Urbana, Ill.: University of Illinois Press.

Kripke, Saul A. 1982. *Wittgenstein on Rules and Private Language.* Oxford: Basil Blackwell.

Kross, Matthias. 1993. *Klarheit als Selbstzweck: Wittgenstein über Philosophie, Religion, Ethik und Gewissheit.* Berlin: Akademie Verlag.

Leibniz, Gottfried Wilhelm. *Gerhardt.* In *Philosophische Schriften.* 7 vols. Hrsg. C. J. Gerhardt. Leipzig: Lorentz, 1879–1937.

Leinfellner, Elisabeth, Werner Leinfellner, Hal Berghel, and Adolf Hübner, eds. 1978. *Wittgenstein and His Impact on Contemporary Thought. Proceedings of the Second International Wittgenstein Symposium.* Vienna: Hölder-Pichler-Tempsky.

Leinfellner, Werner, Eric Krämer, and Jeffrey Schank, eds. 1982. *Language and Ontology: Proceedings of the Sixth International Wittgenstein Symposium.* Vienna: Hölder-Pichler-Tempsky.

Lewis, C. I. 1929. *Mind and the World Order.* New York: Dover.

———. 1946. *An Analysis of Knowledge and Valuation.* La Salle, Ill.: The Open Court Publishing Company.

Malcolm, Norman. 1966. Wittgenstein's *Philosophical Investigations.* In Pitcher, ed., 1966: 65–103, referenced elsewhere. Originally published 1954, *Philosophical Review* 63: 530–59.

————. 1958. Knowledge of Other Minds. *Journal of Philosophy* 55: 969–78.

————. 1959. *Dreaming.* London: Routledge & Kegan Paul.

————. 1982. Wittgenstein: The Relation of Language to Primitive Behavior. *Philosophical Investigations* 5:3–22.

————. 1986. *Nothing Is Hidden.* Ithaca, N.Y.: Cornell University Press.

Malinowski, Bronislaw. 1947. The Problem of Meaning in Primitive Languages. Appendix to Charles K. Ogden and Ivor A. Richards. *The Meaning of Meaning.* 8th ed. London: Routledge & Kegan Paul, 296–336.

Marc-Wogau, K. 1951. Kants Lehre vom analytischen Urteil. *Theoria* 17:140–54.

Mason, H. E. 1978. On the Multiplicity of Language Games. In E. Leinfellner, et al. 1978: 332–35, referenced elsewhere.

McGuinness, Brian. 1981. The So-called Realism of Wittgenstein's *Tractatus.* In Block, ed. 1981: 60–73, referenced elsewhere.

————. 1985. Language and Reality in the *Tractatus. Teoria* 5/2: 135–44.

————. 1988. *Wittgenstein: A Life. Young Ludwig 1889–1921.* Berkeley, Calif.: University of California Press.

————. 1989. Die 'Logische-Philosophische Abhandlung': Rezeption und Missverstandnisse. Unpublished lecture contributed to the Wittgenstein Congress in Vienna in April.

McGuinness, Brian, and Rudolf Haller, eds. 1989. *Wittgenstein in Focus.* Amsterdam/Atlanta: Rodopi.

Mill, J. S. 1865. *A System of Logic, Ratiocinative and Inductive, Being a Connected View of the Principles of Evidence and the Methods of Scientific Investigation.* London: Longmans, Green, and Co.

Moore, G. E. 1959. *Philosophical Papers.* London: Allen and Unwin.

Morick, Harold. 1978. Wittgenstein and Privileged Access. In E. Leinfellner, et al. 1978: 366–68, referenced elsewhere.

Morstein, Petra von. 1980. Kripke, Wittgenstein, and the Private Language Argument. *Grazer Philosophische Studien* 11:61–74.

Mosedale, Fred. 1978. Wittgenstein's Builders Revisited. In E. Leinfellner, et al. 1978: 340–43, referenced elsewhere.

Murdoch, Iris. 1992. *Metaphysics as a Guide to Morals.* New York: Allen Lane/The Penguin Press.

Nyiri, J. C. 1992. *Tradition and Individuality.* Dordrecht, Netherlands: Kluwer Academic Publishers.

Parkinson, G. H. R. 1960. Necessary Propositions and *a priori* Knowledge in Kant. *Mind* 69:391–97.

Paton, H. J. 1936. *Kant's Metaphysics of Experience.* New York: Macmillan.

Pears, David F. 1986. *Ludwig Wittgenstein*. Cambridge, Mass.: Harvard University Press.

———. 1987. *The False Prison*. 2 vols. Oxford: Clarendon Press.

Pike, Kenneth L. 1947. *Phonemics: A Technique for Reducing Language to Writing*. Ann Arbor: University of Michigan Press.

———. 1967. *Language in Relation to a Unified Theory of the Structure of Human Behavior*. The Hague: Mouton.

Pitcher, George. 1964. *The Philosophy of Wittgenstein*. Englewood Cliffs, N.J.: Prentice Hall.

Pitcher, George, ed. 1966. *Wittgenstein: The Philosophical Investigations*. Garden City, N.Y.: Anchor Books.

Proctor, G. L. 1959. Scientific Laws and Scientific Objects in the *Tractatus*. *British Journal for Philosophy of Science* 20:177–93.

Quine, W. V. O. [1951] 1953. Two Dogmas of Empiricism. In *From A Logical Point of View*. Cambridge, Mass.: Harvard University Press, 20–46. Originally published 1951, *Philosophical Review* 60:20–43.

Rawls, John. 1955. Two Concepts of Rules. *Philosophical Review* 64:1–32.

Rhees, Rush. 1954. Can There Be a Private Language? *Proceedings of the Aristotelian Society,* supplementary volume 28:77–94.

———. 1970. *Discussions of Wittgenstein*. New York: Schocken Books.

Robinson, Richard. 1958. Necessary Propositions. *Mind* 67:289–304.

Rorty, Richard. 1979. *Philosophy and the Mirror of Nature*. Princeton: Princeton University Press.

Rousseau, Jean-Jacques. 1968. *Essai sur l'origine des langues*. Ed. Charles Porset. Bordeaux: Ducros.

Russell, B. 1905. On Denoting. In Marsh, R. C., ed. *Logic and Knowledge*. New York: Simon and Schuster, 1956:. 39–56. Originally published in 1905, *Mind* 14:479–93.

———. 1918. The Philosophy of Logical Atomism. In Russell 1956: 175–281, cited below. Originally published in 1918–19, *Monist* 27:495–527, 29:32–63, 190–222, 345–80.

———. 1956. *Logic and Knowledge: Essays, 1901–1950*. London: George, Allen, and Unwin.

Ryle, Gilbert. 1949. *The Concept of Mind*. London: Hutchinson's.

———. 1971. *Collected Papers*. 2 vols. London: Hutchinson.

Saussure, Ferdinand de. 1959. *Course in General Linguistics*. Trans. Wade Baskin. New York: Philosophical Library.

Savigny, Eike von. 1991. "Common Behavior of Many a Kind: *Philosophical Investigations* section 206," in Robert L. Arrington and Hans-Johann Glock, eds., *Wittgenstein's Philosophical Investigations*. London/New York: Routledge.

Schirn, M. 1976. *Studien zu Frege*. Vol. 3. Stuttgart-Bad Cannstatt: Frommann-Holzboog.

Schulte, Joachim. 1989. *Wittgenstein: Eine Einführung*. Stuttgart: Reclam.

Schwyzer, Hubert. 1986. Thought and Reality: The Metaphysics of Kant and Wittgenstein. In Shanker, ed. 1986; 2:150–62, referenced elsewhere.

————. 1990. *The Unity of Understanding, A Study of Kantian Problems*. London/New York: Oxford University Press.

Scriven, Michael. 1959. The Logic of Criteria. *Journal of Philosophy* 56:861–68.

Searle, John. 1969. *Speech Acts*. Cambridge: Cambridge University Press.

Shanker, Stuart, ed. 1986. *Wittgenstein: Critical Assessments*. 5 vols. London: Croom Helm.

Shwayder, David. 1969. Wittgenstein on Mathematics. In Winch, ed. 1969: 66–116, referenced elsewhere.

————. 1976. In Schirn, ed. 1976, referenced elsewhere.

Sluga, H. D. 1977. Frege's Alleged Realism. *Inquiry* 20:227–42.

Spinoza, Baruch. 1985. *The Collected Works of Spinoza*. Ed. and trans. Edwin Curley. Princeton, N.J.: Princeton University Press. References are to the Gebhardt pagination, given marginally by Curley.

Spranger, Edouard. 1922. *Lebensformen*. Halle, Germany: Niemeyer.

Stampe, Dennis. 1979. Towards a Causal Theory of Linguistic Representation. In Peter French, ed., *Contemporary Perspectives in Philosophy of Language*. Minneapolis, Minn.: University of Minnesota Press.

Stebbing, L. Susan. 1937. *Philosophy and the Physicists*. London: Methuen and Company.

Stenius, Erik. 1960. *Wittgenstein's "Tractatus."* Ithaca, N.Y.: Cornell University Press.

————. 1965. Are True Numerical Statements Analytic or Synthetic? *Philosophical Review* 74:357–72.

Stern, David G. 1991. Heraclitus' and Wittgenstein's River Images: Stepping Twice into the Same River. *Monist* 74: 579–604.

Strawson, Peter F. 1966. *Bounds of Sense*. London: Methuen and Company.

————. 1985. *Scepticism and Naturalism: Some Varieties. The Woodbridge Lectures at Columbia University*. New York: Columbia University Press.

Stroud, Barry. 1966. Wittgenstein and Logical Necessity. In Pitcher 1966: 477–96, referenced elsewhere. Originally published 1965, *Philosophical Review* 64:504–18.

Thiele, Susanne. 1983. *Die Verwicklung im Denken Wittgensteins*. Freiburg/München: Alber.

Trigg, R. 1973. *Reason and Commitment*. London: Cambridge University Press.

Waismann, F. 1930. Logische Analyse der Wahrscheinlichkreitsbegriff. *Erkenntnis* 1: 228–48.

Walker, Ralph C. S. 1978. *Kant*. London/Boston: Routledge & Kegan Paul.

Warnock, Geoffrey. 1949. Concepts and Schematism. *Analysis* 9 (April):77–82.

White, Morton G. 1950. The Analytic and the Synthetic: An Untenable Dualism. In Hook, Sidney, ed. 1950. *John Dewey: Philosopher of Science and Freedom*, 316–30. New York: Dial Press. Reprinted in Linsky, L., ed. 1952. *Semantics and the Philosophy of Language*. Urbana, Ill.: University of Illinois Press.

Whittaker, J. H. 1978. Language-games and Forms of Life Unconfused. *Philosophical Investigations* 1:44–45.

Winch, Peter. 1958. *The Idea of Social Science and its Relation to Philosophy*. London: Routledge & Paul.

———. 1987. *Trying to Make Sense*. Oxford: Blackwell.

Winch, Peter, ed. 1969. *Studies in the Philosophy of Wittgenstein*. London/New York: Routledge & Kegan Paul/Humanities Press.

Wittgenstein, Ludwig. 1958. *(BB) The Blue and Brown Books*. New York: Harper.

———. [1976] 1993. *(C&E)* Cause and Effect: Intuitive Awareness. *Philosophia* 6:409–25. Reprinted in Wittgenstein 1993, referenced elsewhere.

———. 1982. *(LW) Last Writings on the Philosophy of Psychology*. Volume 1. Ed. G. H. von Wright and Heikki Nyman. Trans. C. G. Luckhardt and Maximillian A. E. Aue. Oxford: Blackwell.

———. 1974. *(Letters) Letters to Russell, Keynes and Moore*. Ed. G. H. von Wright. Ithaca, N.Y.: Cornell University Press.

———. 1959. *(M)* Wittgenstein's Lectures in 1930–33. In Moore 1959: 252–324, referenced elsewhere. Reprinted in Wittgenstein 1993, referenced elsewhere.

———. 1979. *(NB) Notebooks 1914–16*. 2d. ed. Oxford: Blackwell.

———. 1969. *(OC) On Certainty*. Oxford: Blackwell. References are to numbered sections.

———. 1974. *(PG) Philosophical Grammar*. Ed. R. Rhees. Trans. Anthony Kenny. Berkeley: University of California Press. References are to page numbers.

———. 1958. *(PI) Philosophical Investigations*. Trans. G. E. M. Anscombe. 2d ed. Oxford: Blackwell. References are to numbered sections in part I and to page numbers in part II.

———. 1993. *Philosophical Occasions*. Ed. James Klagge and Alfred Nordmann. Indianapolis/Cambridge: Hackett.

————. 1975. (*PR*) *Philosophical Remarks*. Ed. R. Rhees. Trans. R. Hargreaves and R. White. Oxford: Blackwell; New York: Barnes and Noble.

————. 1977. (*RC*) *Remarks on Color*. Berkeley, Calif.: University of California Press.

————. 1979. (*RF*) *Remarks on Frazer's "Golden Bough."* Ed. Rush Rhees; trans. A.C. Miles. Atlantic Highlands, N.J.: Humanities Press. Reprinted in Wittgenstein 1993, referenced elsewhere.

————. 1978. (*RFM*) *Remarks on the Foundations of Mathematics*. Ed. G. H. von Wright, R. Rhees, and G. E. M. Anscombe; trans. G. E. M. Anscombe. 2d ed. Oxford/Cambridge, Mass.: Basil Blackwell/MIT Press. Roman numerals refer to parts, and Arabic numerals refer to numbered sections within the specified part.

————. 1980. (*RPP*) *Remarks on the Philosophy of Psychology*. 2 vols. Oxford: Blackwell.

————. 1967. *Schriften*. 8 vols. Frankfurt am Main: Suhrkamp.

————. 1961. (*TLP*) *Tractatus Logico-Philosophicus*. Trans. David F. Pears and Brian McGuinness. London: Routledge & Kegan Paul.

————. 1979. (*WVC*) *Wittgenstein and the Vienna Circle*. Ed. B. F. McGuinness. Trans. B. F. McGuinness and J. Schulte. Oxford: Blackwell.

————. 1967. (*Z*) *Zettel*. Ed. G. E. M. Anscombe and G. H. von Wright; trans. G. E. M. Anscombe. Oxford: Basil Blackwell.

Wolgast, Elizabeth. 1977. *Paradoxes of Knowledge*. Ithaca, N.Y.: Cornell University Press.

Wolniewicz, B. 1990. The Essence of Logical Atomism. In Haller and Brandl, eds. 1990 1:106–11, referenced elsewhere.

Ziff, Paul. 1960. *Semantic Analysis*. Ithaca, N.Y.: Cornell University Press.

INDEX OF CITATIONS

NAME INDEX

SUBJECT INDEX